SAN ANTONIO AT BAT

SAN ANTONIO AT BAT

*Professional Baseball
in the Alamo City*

DAVID KING

Texas A&M University Press • College Station

The paper used in this book meets the minimum requirements

of the American National Standard for Permanence

of Paper for Printed Library Materials, z39.48-1984.

Binding materials have been chosen for durability.

Library of Congress Cataloging-in-Publication Data

King, David, 1958–

    San Antonio at bat : professional baseball in the Alamo city /
David King.—1st ed.

      p. cm.

    Includes bibliographical references and index.

    ISBN 1-58544-345-x (cloth : alk. paper)—

    ISBN 1-58544-376-x (pbk. : alk. paper)

    1. Baseball—Texas—San Antonio—History. 2. Baseball—
Texas—San Antonio—Anecdotes. I. Title.

GV863.T42S365 2004

796.357'09764'351—dc22   2003022757

Contents

Acknowledgments

No work of history can be written without the help of diligent historians. In San Antonio I was lucky enough to have several. Scott Hanzelka and Chris Foltz are passionate about recording the history of local baseball teams—and passionate about making sure their records are correct, to the point of editing each other's meticulous reports. Their assistance and attention to detail throughout the years has been invaluable.

The Texas League also is lucky to have Tom Kayser as its president, and San Antonio is lucky to have his office here. Since 1992 he has built an amazing collection of photographs and memorabilia from the league's history, and his search continues unabated. Kayser also has compiled day-by-day historical highlights for the league, the source of much of the detail in this book. And he very generously provided a copy of the hard-to-find *History of the Texas League,* written in 1951 by league historian and statistician William Ruggles.

The San Antonio Missions, including Pres. Burl Yarbrough and former media relations director Jody Hinkel, were generous with their time and resources, even taking photos off their office walls for use in the book. Missions owner Dave Elmore deserves some credit for getting the idea of a history of the club going, thanks to a chance meeting at Game Seven of the 2002 League Championship Series, as does former *San Antonio Express-News* book editor Gregg Barrios, who directed me to the superb people at the Texas A&M University Press.

Dozens of former and current ballplayers graciously agreed to be interviewed for the book, which grew out of a series of stories I wrote for the *San Antonio Express-News* in the summer of 2000. Many friends encouraged me along the way, especially when it looked like the book was never going to be finished.

Finally, more thanks than I can ever express must go to my family, including my wife, Patricia Yznaga, and sons Patrick King and Alex King. Patty kept prompting me along, then got to the point where she did not want to hear "just one more chapter" anymore. They all put up with me holing up in our little garage office for hours on end, hunched over the laptop, mumbling and shuffling through reams of paper. The boys deserve some credit for letting me drag them to ballgames, from Nuevo Laredo to Arizona to the former Enron Field. Baseball is not always the most appealing sport to teenagers, but my sons went along with good spirits and good cheer. Thanks and love.

SAN ANTONIO AT BAT

Introduction

IN BASEBALL, above all else, players are supposed to follow the signs. When the third-base coach throws up his hands to stop a runner, the runner is supposed to stop. When a catcher gives the pitcher the sign for a fastball, the pitcher is supposed to throw a fastball. When the manager signals to the bullpen to bring in the hard-throwing right-handed relief pitcher, he wants the right-hander.

San Antonio got a sign about professional baseball the first week of its existence in the city, in 1888. An unidentified reporter for the *Daily Express* newspaper, dispatched to the Government Hill diamond to cover the Texas Base Ball League game between teams from San Antonio and Dallas, had a little mishap on the trolley conveying him back to the newspaper's downtown office. The deed was reported in the game story the next morning: "The Express regrets that some miscreant stole the full score from the reporter while coming to town on a street car." Oh, the times that San Antonio baseball fans wish that miscreant had discouraged the city from following baseball at all.

In the last 115 years, the local nine—be they nicknamed Bullets or Bears, Aces or Indians, Missions or Mustangs—have broken a million hearts. San Antonio has had more than its share of truly awful ballgames, hapless last-place clubs, mediocre players, and inept owners. San Antonio has finished with the worst record in the Texas League fourteen times and been on the wrong end of no-hitters twenty times.

Sometimes the near misses were just as painful. The club nearly was purchased by baseball legend Ty Cobb in 1928. Instead, controlling interest was sold to the team's secretary-treasurer, who had the double misfortune of buying the team just before the stock market crash and at a time when it was truly awful.

Thirty-one years later, a long-armed power-hitting kid from Alabama named Billy Williams showed up with the club from spring training. Williams got off to a fast start, but on a trip through some of Texas' less-enlightened locales, he became disenchanted with the travel and the racism and left the team. Officials of the parent club, the Chicago Cubs, finally talked him into rejoining the Missions. He played four more games with San Antonio, then was promoted to Triple A, where he hit .670 the first week. Baseball immortals Carl Warwick (a .248 hitter in the majors), Howie Bedell (.193 in the big leagues), and Al Nagel (who never made the majors) dominated the Texas League's statistics instead, and San Antonio finished 10½ games out of first place. Williams went on to the Baseball Hall of Fame.

Still, San Antonio embraced its team for years. In the early days, opening day was a cause for parades to the ballpark—for both white and black teams. (Those black teams, by the way, were for a time more successful than their white counterparts, and one of them produced another Hall of Famer, pitcher "Smokey" Joe Williams.) The newspapers were splashed with opening-day photos of the players and filled with opening-day-related advertising.

For decades—especially before the advent of football, both professional and college—baseball was the dominant sports theme in the papers. Winter, spring, summer, or fall, there rarely was a day in the years before World War II when there was not some kind of baseball story in the *Express,* the *News,* or the *Light.*

Of course, those papers were fighting a pitched battle for circulation, especially the afternoon papers, the *Light* and the *News* (the *News* had been started by the Express Publishing Company to compete head-to-head with the *Light*). As baseball reporting became more sophisticated through the 1930s, the sports pages grew. From just running the line scores of local games, to carrying detailed box scores, to eventually carrying results from every Texas League and Major League game, the newspapers evolved along with—and because of—baseball.

Minor-league baseball boomed briefly in the years after World War II, with attendance soaring as the teams returned from their self-imposed wartime hibernation and players returned from the war. The integration of baseball also helped the boom, with thousands of African American fans flowing into ballparks to see the likes of Jackie Robinson and Don Newcombe.

The Texas League was slower to integrate—it took five years after Robinson's debut in 1947 for a club to sign the first black player—but some of the teams, including San Antonio, integrated with gusto. After years of struggling, the Missions would take anybody who could play. The first two black players in San Antonio were welcomed by the city in 1953, and both were showered with gifts on their "nights," sponsored by the African American chamber of commerce and radio station.

Still, baseball could not overcome three factors that sent the game into a rapid decline in the 1950s—air conditioning, television, and football. Air conditioning in the home meant fans did not have to go out to the ballparks, which had been built to catch the prevailing evening breezes. Television meant they did not have to go to the ballpark to see a game anymore. And finally football caught sports fans' fancy, evolving into a juggernaut in Texas that supplanted baseball for year-round coverage and overwhelmed it in the media. San Antonio's fan base dwindled as interest in baseball sank nationwide. One of the best teams in local baseball history, the 1964 Bullets, finished last in the league in attendance, prompting the ownership to move the franchise to Amarillo.

The ownership? The parent club, the Houston Colt .45s, which became the Astros in 1965. When the Texas League left town following the 1964 season, it marked the end of a long era of big-league teams owning the local franchise.

The perennially inept St. Louis Browns owned the team from the 1930s to the 1950s, with mixed results. The Browns seemed to be able to find good players—San Antonio made the playoffs in seven of the first nine seasons of the affiliation—but the Browns always seemed to trade away potential stars (for example, Bob Turley, who won the Cy Young Award in 1959 while pitching for the New York Yankees, came up through the Browns' farm system, including San Antonio). When

the Browns became the Baltimore Orioles for the 1954 season, the relationship began to sour. The new owners of the Orioles wanted out
of the business of running minor-league teams, but when they could
not find a buyer, they threatened to fold the Missions entirely. San
Antonians bought the franchise and fielded an unaffiliated team (at
least officially unaffiliated—the American League forced the Orioles
into sending some players to the Missions) in 1958, then signed on
with the Cubs.

There have been years when being unaffiliated with a big-league
team might not have been a bad idea, though. In 1973 the parent Cleveland Indians told management to use an untested rookie instead of a
proven veteran in the deciding game of the Texas League Championship Series. San Antonio lost. In 1980 the Dodgers promoted Fernando
Valenzuela to the majors amid the championship series. San Antonio
lost that series too.

But being a Dodgers affiliate did boost San Antonio in a number of
ways. After racing through four affiliates in nine years, the local ownership and the Dodgers formed a long-term bond, one that lasted from
1977 to 2000. Some of the greatest Dodgers players of the era came
through San Antonio, including Valenzuela, Steve Sax, Orel Hershiser,
Eric Karros, and Mike Piazza. For much of the period, the Dodgers
were considered one of the elite organizations in all of baseball, and
the big-league club made nine playoff appearances while affiliated with
San Antonio.

Fan interest in San Antonio—and throughout the minor leagues—
also began to pick up during this time. In the late 1980s a series of
nostalgic movies about the game (including *Field of Dreams* and *The
Natural*) sparked fans' interest. In addition, a new set of requirements
for stadiums and facilities came down from the National Association
(the governing body of the minors), setting off a stadium-building
boom that resulted in dozens of new ballparks around the country,
including one in San Antonio.

Community leaders had used some clever dealing and a consider-
able amount of scrounging to bring baseball back to the city in 1968.
With Astros owner Roy Hofheinz refusing to let anyone use Mission
Stadium (which had sat idle since he moved the team following the

1964 season), San Antonians worked out a deal to expand a small stadium on the campus of St. Mary's University. Collecting bits and pieces
from several ballparks around the state, they soon turned V. J. Keefe
Field into a cozy, fan-friendly park that served as the minor-league
team's home from 1968 to 1993.

Politics and business always have been part of the game in San Antonio. Mayors perennially threw out first pitches, as did more than one
governor. Local business leaders stepped up to buy the team at critical
times through the years. Morris Block purchased the franchise in 1905,
the last year it was in the South Texas League. Harry J. Benson took
over from Block in 1915 and ran the team out of his downtown to-
bacco shop, fighting an uphill battle against the Fort Worth dynasty of
the postwar era. In 1958 a group led by Dan Sullivan took over the
team and kept it in San Antonio. Another group of businessmen, led
by attorney Henry Christopher and including Nelson Wolff, brought
baseball back in 1968. Convenience store magnate Tom Turner bought
the team in the late 1970s and brought cheerleaders (the Dodger Dollies) and barbeque grills to Keefe Field.

But Keefe Field was outdated by the late 1980s, leading to an ultimatum from the National Association—get a new stadium or lose the
team. City Councilman—and subsequently mayor—Nelson Wolff used
much of his considerable business and political skill and will to get a
stadium built and keep the team. Between his efforts and the ownership of minor-league-sports entrepreneur Dave Elmore, the city got
its new ballpark in 1994—and immediately set the Texas League record
for single-season attendance. San Antonio's new stadium, which was
named for Wolff in 1995, got the city into the minor-league baseball
boom.

But there was still one thing missing—a championship. San Antonio had come close three times since the Bullets' pennant in 1964, but
it took a collection of young prospects, players on the way back up,
and an ambitious young manager to break a thirty-two-year drought.
Just one player from the 1997 Missions went on to be an all-star in the
major leagues (catcher Paul LoDuca), but with good timing, solid pitching, and the stable leadership of manager Ron Roenicke, San Antonio
got its pennant in 1997. And while it was not celebrated like some in

the past—by this time the NBA's Spurs were the city's favorite franchise—the pennant did serve as a fitting finale for the Dodgers era.

The latest affiliation for the Missions, with the Seattle Mariners, has produced three of the most successful seasons in local baseball history. San Antonio lost in the final game of the Western Division playoffs in 2001, then won the pennant in 2002 with a team that finished last in the first half of the season. In 2003 the Missions recorded their best first-half record ever, won both halves of the season, and clinched a spot in the postseason for the third year in a row—just the fourth time in franchise history the team has made it three consecutive years or more. They then topped off the season by beating Frisco four games to one in the Texas League Championship Series, marking the first time San Antonio has won back-to-back titles.

Baseball has come a long way from those early days of 1888, indeed. Perhaps it is a good thing that San Antonio did not heed that initial sign after all.

Welcoming the
National Pastime, 1888–1900

IN HIS SIXTY YEARS in baseball, John McCloskey was never the best player in any league. He manned a variety of positions, none with any distinction. He holds just one record of note, that for the worst career winning percentage for anyone who managed three hundred or more games in the majors (.312, 197 wins and 434 losses, for St. Louis and pre-1900 Louisville).[1] His clubs usually finished closer to the bottom than to the top of the standings. But "Honest John," as he was called, had a passion for baseball unmatched in the game's early history, and even though his name is largely forgotten, he is one of the key figures in the history of minor-league baseball.

Born in Louisville, Kentucky, in 1862, McCloskey got his first job in baseball in 1876, as a bat boy for the local team. By 1882 he was on the Louisville roster. Two years later McCloskey came to Texas for the first time, as one of the "imported" catchers in a semi-pro league that included Houston, Galveston, San Antonio, Waco, Fort Worth, and Dallas.[2] His batterymate was pitcher Red Ehret, who went on to pitch in the major leagues for eleven seasons before the turn of the twentieth century.

In the fall of 1887, McCloskey came back to Texas, barnstorming his way to the West Coast with a team of all-stars he had put together from the Western League. His Joplin (Missouri) Independents played games against local teams in Fort Worth and Waco before coming across their biggest challenge in Austin. There a couple of local businessmen—lumberman Sam French and contractor Ed Byrne—had put together a team to knock off the Independents. "A friendly clerk in the hotel tipped me off to the fact that the Austin folk had gotten together the star players of the Southern League," McCloskey told Texas League historian William Ruggles in 1931.[3] Instead, McCloskey's team won.

French and Byrne, sensing that baseball might just turn into a side business, then arranged an even bigger challenge. They lined up a three-game series for the Independents against the New York Giants, who were touring Texas at the same time. "The Giants demanded a thousand dollars guarantee, with the winner to take 65 percent," McCloskey told Ruggles. "Byrne wired back that the offer was accepted but the winner would have to take 85 percent. I was not especially confident, but we did have a good team."[4] Good enough, it turned out, to beat the Giants in the first two games of the series in front of big crowds attracted to Austin by the opening of the new capitol building. The Giants refused to play the final game and slunk out of town, but McCloskey stayed long enough to drum up support from leaders around the state.

Austin was "wild with enthusiasm" about the idea of professional baseball, so in December, 1887, French and Byrne gathered businessmen from Austin, Houston, Dallas, and New Orleans, and they set up a plan for a professional baseball league to begin play in April, 1888. A subsequent meeting in January led to more structure—New Orleans had bolted to the Southern League, but Galveston, Fort Worth, and San Antonio were granted teams in the newly minted Texas League of Base Ball Clubs.[5]

McCloskey took no leadership role with the league, instead bringing almost his entire roster of Joplin Independents to Texas to become the Austin team. He played center field on opening day, April 8, when Austin took on San Antonio at the "base ball park on Government hill," as the Sunday *Daily Express* described it. His Austin team featured five players who would go on to play in the major leagues, while San Antonio's team barely had five players who could be considered professionals. But Honest John, who always seemed to be thinking of the league instead of his own team, tried to keep things relatively close: "San Antonio's strong battery, Sig Smith and Hofferd, have not yet arrived from Philadelphia," the *Express* reported on April 8. "In order to make the contest closer, Austin has weakened its team by substitution of the reserve battery for the strong one, thus establishing an evenness of strength of the two nines."[6] Even so, Austin won the first Texas League game ever played in San Antonio, 9-3.

"Base ball, the national game, is the rage now in San Antonio," the *Express* reported. "The town has been a little slow to getting excited, but has finally caught on, as the vulgar people in Dallas and Fort Worth say." A crowd estimated at 1,100—"including many ladies," the *Light* pointed out—turned out for opening day, and there was hope on the way in the form of the a couple of ringers from St. Louis. "Austin came over with the crack team of the League and mopped the diamond field up with San Antonio to the very bitter anguish and embarrassment of everybody but the visitors," the *Express* reported. "Then people began to talk and conjecture. They said San Antonio, of course, couldn't play base ball, never could and never would and that most any aggregation of chumps, even from Seguin or Castroville, could come here and win. But the Express cautioned them that they were wrong, and begged them not to be too fast."[7]

San Antonio's first Texas League victory came in its fourth game, a 5-3 win over Dallas. That attracted a crowd of between seventeen hundred and eighteen hundred to the next game, on a Saturday afternoon. They went home disappointed, a common occurrence, even after the arrival of pitcher Hofferd and catcher Sixsmith (not, as previously reported, Sig Smith).[8] The team lost two in a row to Dallas, then two more to Fort Worth.

"San Antonio people appear to have wearied and grown heart sore at going out to the base ball park to see their team beaten by every team that comes along," the *Express* reported. "Everybody acquainted with the situation expected nothing better than defeat for the home team Monday for the reason of the assignment of positions by Manager [John] Cavanaugh against the advice of all who arrogated to themselves the right to make certain suggestions to him for what they conceived to be the best interests of the club, the management of which has been entrusted to him." In other words, Cavanaugh was not listening to the owners, the directors of the baseball association. So to cut down on expenses for the team's first road trip, they fired him, "though Mr. Cavanaugh will accompany the team as temporary manager without salary," the *Express* reported.[9] The team staggered through the road trip, losing soundly in Galveston, Houston, and Fort Worth.

During the next homestand, McCloskey tried to come to the team's aid, trading hard-hitting third baseman James "Mikado" Flynn to San Antonio for shortstop George Bright. Flynn, who earned his nickname because of his long Asian-style mustache, was one of the original Joplin Independents, and he played a big part in San Antonio's 10-2 win over Austin the day of the trade, May 7.[10]

That week San Antonio also named second baseman Robert Rose as its new manager, with instructions from the board to "see to it that his men from this on exert themselves to their utmost, failing to do which he is to release them without any exhibition of favoritism and replace them with the best players available in the country," the *Express* said.[11]

He had little success. "It is the same old story, and the excuses are becoming so well worn and some charitable and witty person should be employed at a good salary by the directors to furnish new excuses for the nine's lucklessness," the *Light* said after a 4-3 loss to Fort Worth. "The Light does not wish to compete for this very trying position, but if a little suggestion to Manager Rose is timely, would simply say that the beer and whisky ration of some of the players might be cut off to about the size of the club's success . . . Then too, the boys might just as well be tucked in their little beds something earlier than 3 A.M. and it should be seen that they sleep at home occasionally. A man can not be a sport and a professional base ball player at the same time."[12] The next day, May 24, the team's record fell to 6-28 with a 6-5 loss to Fort Worth. The board, no doubt tired of taking abuse from the newspapers and the fans, folded the team, even though crowds were still fairly good.

San Antonio was not the only team that struggled financially, though. Fort Worth's club lasted just another month, and Austin was ready to give up on McCloskey's team by late June. That is when Honest John came up with a plan: His Austin club went on a road trip over the Fourth of July weekend and never came home. The story from a July 4 game in Houston identified the team as being from San Antonio, mentioning a couple of players from Austin's team—including future big-leaguer Farmer Weaver—who now claimed to represent San Antonio. It marked one of only two times in Texas League history where a city was represented by two completely different teams in the same season.[13] And, in what would become a trend for San Antonio, the new team lost, 6-3, on July 4 to the oddly named Houston Babies.

But they won enough in the ensuing days to stir up interest in San Antonio. When the team returned on July 14 to take on Houston, a "much larger crowd of spectators occupied the grand stand than was anticipated."[14] Fully four hundred fans packed into Muth's Park to see San Antonio's 4-2 victory. The team played in front of home crowds as big as fifteen hundred in July. But many in the big crowds were getting in for free—including all the women on the frequent ladies' days— and the gate receipts were not nearly enough to cover expenses, not when even paying customers were charged no more than fifty cents a head.

On July 30 McCloskey told a meeting of team supporters the bad news—he had not been able to pay his players in a month, and unless someone could come up with $600 a month to cover expenses, he was going to have to move the team to Fort Worth. "After a few enthusiastic speeches were made nearly every man and boy in the room stepped up to the secretary's desk and signed his name for a monthly subscription until the expiration of the league season," the *Express* reported. Led by a $100 promise by Col. A. Belknap—who promptly was elected president of the city's baseball association—the meeting netted pledges of $340 a month, and a committee was appointed to canvass the city for the balance.[15]

It worked—McCloskey's team finished the season in San Antonio, playing through the end of August and posting a record of 14-11. McCloskey combined that record with the 24-18 the team put up in Austin and claimed the first league championship. Of course, Dallas had an argument since its team finished 55-27, and the record book tends to lean toward the team with the best record, not the one with a pioneer as its manager. McCloskey moved his club to Houston and won two pennants in the league's next three seasons. San Antonio did not have another team until 1892.

Honest John went on to a distinguished career in baseball, helping establish leagues—including the predecessor to the Pacific Coast League—all over the country. He frequently took on the weakest franchises as president, manager, or both, which explains both his mediocre record as a manager and his poor financial condition as he advanced in age. McCloskey was still helping build leagues at the age of seventy-two, getting the Midwest's Kitty League going again in 1934, but he died poor and somewhat embittered in 1940 in his hometown of Louisville.[16]

In a rambling letter to Texas League president Alvin Gardner in 1938, he talked about how he was owed upward of four thousand dollars in salary from owners around the country. "But let me owe one dollar, and I am put down as a crook," he noted. After his death, his image was restored. The city of Louisville erected a monument in his honor at its ballpark in the 1940s, and McCloskey was named to the Texas Sports Hall of Fame in 1962. Perhaps most noteworthy, historian Ruggles called him "the father of the Texas League."[17]

For a guy who was an average ballplayer and a mediocre manager, it was the highest form of praise.

Like most of the minor leagues of the earliest days, the Texas League was an unstable organization. The league played the 1889 and 1890 seasons without San Antonio, then did not play at all in 1891. In 1892, when teams from Dallas and Fort Worth dropped out in early July, San Antonio was readmitted to the four-team league, along with Waco. The San Antonio squad went 11-20.

The league reformed in 1895, but four teams—including San Antonio—did not finish the season. But one historical note did emerge, for the local club was called the Missionaries (a nickname that had been used by local amateur clubs in the past), shortened by the newspapers to just Missions.[18] The following year the team—now nicknamed the Bronchos—actually finished the season, which was divided into three

1888 AUSTIN–SAN ANTONIO ROSTER

The nucleus of the Austin–San Antonio team in the Texas League's inaugural season of 1888:

John McCloskey. One of the organizers of the league, he served as president of the team, its field manager, and its center fielder.

Red Ehret. McCloskey's batterymate in the 1884 precursor to the Texas League, he went on to pitch in the major leagues for eleven seasons, from the end of the 1888 season to 1898.

Farmer Weaver. A catcher and an outfielder, Weaver finished the 1888 season with Louisville, which was in the major leagues at the time, and wound up hitting .278 in seven big-league seasons.

Harry Raymond. A third baseman, he played parts of five seasons in the major leagues. Raymond is one of the players thought to be responsible for the term "Texas leaguer" as a way to describe a shallow fly ball that falls for a base hit.

"Scrappy" Bill Joyce. An infielder in the Texas League, he went on to hit .294 in eight big-league seasons—the last three for John McGraw's New York Giants, the team the Joplin Independents shocked in 1887 to spur the development of the Texas League. Joyce also managed the Giants in 1896–98, the first Texas Leaguer to lead a big-league team.

James "Mikado" Flynn. The infielder was traded from Austin to the first San Antonio team early in the season. But when the first San Antonio nine folded, McCloskey picked him up, and he wound up playing for both San Antonio teams.

Sherry Sherringhausen. He went on to play five more seasons in the Texas League and was considered one of the league's best players of the 1890s.

Frank Hoffman. The team's number-two pitcher had some pretty good numbers—231 strikeouts and an earned-run average of 0.70.

Emmett Rodgers. He did not start the season with McCloskey's team but joined soon after the season began. Rodgers went on to play four more years in the Texas League, including twelve games in 1906, and also managed three teams in the league.

John Tobias. He was one of McCloskey's original players and one of the league's top players for four seasons.

parts, the last with just four teams and lasting just a month. San Antonio won none of them, but just finishing was an accomplishment in itself.

In 1897 San Antonio had its best team to date, running away with the first half of the season by going 46-24. Manager "Big Mike" O'Connor, in the middle of a career that saw him play thirteen Texas League seasons, manage eight different teams, and wind up as an umpire, had taken over the Bronchos at the end of the 1896 season and led them to a 12-8 record.

But the fans were not coming. The team needed a gimmick, something to get San Antonians out to San Pedro Park. That gimmick was electricity. The newspapers were full of ads for the new and mysterious commodity: "Mutual Electric Light Company, with the latest improved machinery and lamps, can guarantee the best service," one proclaimed in the *Daily Express*. "San Antonio Gas Company sells Gas Stoves, Gas Heaters and Fixtures, and Electric Lights, any Kind and Power," said another. "San Antonio Electric Co., 207 to 215 Losoya St., LIGHT, HEAT AND POWER. Telephone 426," read yet another in the *Daily Light*.

Electricity was still a luxury for many people in the 1890s, and it certainly was not the safest way to light up a house, not with a maze of marginally insulated wires running up and down the walls. But people were fascinated by electricity and its potential uses—including the possibility of baseball under lights.

Someone hatched the idea of stringing electric bulbs around San Pedro Park and playing two exhibition games. O'Connor and pitcher/outfielder Charles Weber, who were running the team after the investors bailed out early in the season, agreed. After all, a crowd of more than one thousand had paid the princely sum of fifty cents each to see Galveston play Houston under lights in 1892, and the proceeds from that exhibition game had allowed the two teams to finish the season.[19] So night games were scheduled for June 30 and July 1, 1897.

To help boost ticket sales, the team announced that a part of the proceeds would benefit the Belknap Rifles, a popular precision-marching unit based in San Antonio. The spit-polished group in all-white uniforms competed statewide and performed across the country at

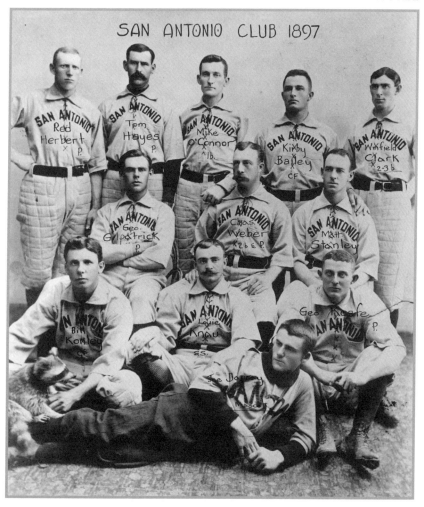

The 1897 team, the first to be nicknamed the Missions, claimed a portion of the league title that year. Courtesy San Antonio Missions

events like the Manhattan Centennial, and its share of the take was to be applied to new uniforms and travel expenses. In addition, its founder, Col. A. Belknap, had been one of the investors in the city's first Texas League team back in 1888. Members of the unit sold tickets, and the team placed ads in the local papers touting the game: "See the Grand Illuminated Ball Game and Exhibition by the Famous Belknaps. Admission 25 cents."

Temporary posts were placed in the ground at San Pedro Park, and "twenty-five arc lights will be placed around the park so as to make the expanse as bright as day," the *Daily Express* reported. By game time, 8:30 P.M., the modest grandstands at the field were packed with fifteen hundred curious fans, drawn by the wonder of electricity and the fact that the sewer lines were finally repaired in the vicinity of the park, allowing streetcars to run there from downtown again.[20]

By all reports, the exhibition was a success, even though Houston beat San Antonio 3-2. "Cheap balls were used to prevent any lively hitting, and the balls were mostly kept on the ground," the *Daily Light* reported, perhaps giving in to the notion that the lights did not exactly turn the expanse as bright as day. The Belknap Rifles, originally scheduled to appear after the game "under the command of Captain McAdoo," instead took to the field between the fourth and fifth innings and stayed on the field for "over half an hour, and on a constant move," the *Daily Light* reported.[21]

Apparently, everyone who was interested in night baseball—including the umpires—showed up the first night. "The second and last of the electric light ball games was played last night before a very small crowd," the *Daily Express* reported July 2. "Lack of auditors [the umpires] and absence of enthusiasm had a somewhat dampening effect on the ardor of the players, but they played innings that were full of funny antics and ludicrous errors." The score, the best the paper could estimate, was about 14-3, Galveston. O'Connor designated himself as the starting pitcher for the Bronchos. He lasted two innings in what was probably his only pitching appearance and gave up all of the Sand Crabs' runs. Captain McAdoo reserved his unit's performance for the end of the game.[22]

Baseball under the lights did not return to San Antonio until May 3, 1930. That night the Negro Leagues' Kansas City Monarchs, who traveled with a portable set of lights, played the San Antonio Black Indians at League Park. On July 24 of that year, the Texas League's San Antonio Indians played their first night game at League Park, which was the fourth stadium in that league to install lights. That event stirred the poet in *Express* sports editor Fred Mosebach: "The soft glow from the milk-colored Mazda lights that are strung in clusters 60 feet overhead, nestling in giant reflectors bearing a resemblance to porcelain bath tubs, lends an entrancing effect, and the scene becomes an animated picture pleasing to the eye and restful to the mind as the players dart hither and yon on the greensward like so many tots in a romp." Tots in a romp, yes; precision military marching units, no.[23]

The take from the publicity stunt kept O'Connor's lads going until August, 1897. Austin, citing financial woes, dropped out of the league on August 4. Two days later, over loud protests from O'Connor and Weber, the rest of the league's directors voted to drop San Antonio to give the league an even number of teams. Houston was awarded the first-half title. A week later it took in a whopping twenty dollars at the gate for an afternoon game, and the team walked out, ending the Bayou City club's season.[24]

After several weeks of confusion, including a playoff series between Fort Worth and Dallas (which had finished sixth and seventh respectively) for the first-half title, the league's executives decided to award San Antonio a first-half pennant and Galveston one for the second half.

The 1898 campaign lasted barely longer than the 1897 controversy. Because of the Spanish-American War, the season ran from April 9 to May 13, somehow working in two halves. San Antonio, with O'Connor and most of his stars long gone, finished last in both.

With the war over, the league was revived in 1899—at least until July 5, when all the teams agreed to disband. Galveston was the only team to finish above .500; San Antonio went 35-40. The early end to the 1899 season almost was the undoing of the Texas League. The league disappeared for the next two years, and San Antonio would not have professional baseball again until 1903.

But what a comeback the game would make.

Soaring, Sinking, and Soaring Again,
1903–1908

PROFESSIONAL BASEBALL was still a less-than-stable industry in the first decade of the twentieth century. Leagues were coming and going on a regular basis, and sometimes regional interests seemed to outweigh common sense.

Such was the case with the Texas League, which reorganized in 1902 but did not enlist old standbys like Houston, Galveston, or San Antonio. Not surprisingly, the season ended early because of poor attendance (the fact that Corsicana went 58-9 in the first half and 30-14 in the second might have dampened the rest of the league's enthusiasm too).[1]

That led leaders in those cities to get together with entrepreneurs from Beaumont and form the South Texas League in the winter of 1902–1903. Among those leaders was a twenty-four-year-old catcher named Wade Hampton Moore, who had managed Paris in the Texas League the year before. Moore came to San Antonio and—in a tradition established by the newly founded American League—joined the rest of the South Texas League owners in raiding the Texas League of its best players.

Moore was the owner, president, field manager, and catcher for his team, so he basically made all of the important decisions. From

Corsicana he signed pitcher Bill "Lucky" Wright and shortstop Walter Morris. Outfielder/pitcher Eddie Switzer came with Moore from Paris, and left-handed pitcher Eddie Taylor was lured away from that franchise after the season had started.[2]

But Moore did more than spend money to build a team. To stir interest in the community, he got the *Daily Light* to sponsor a "name the team" contest in April, leading up to opening day. The suggestions flowed in: Hottentotts, Dusters, Pilgrims, Comanches, Davy Crocketts, Tigers, Stars, Moros, Champions, Invincibles, Red Stocking Sluggers, Defenders, and Athletics. "Ladies are taking great interest in the contest and several suggestions are from the fair ones," the *Light* reported. The final choice was a matter of alliteration: Moore's Mustangs. The winner received a season ticket. "The mustang is a fiery horse abounding on the plains of West Texas, and the name is considered a very appropriate one in that it suggests life and ginger, two great essentials for a ball team, and will no doubt be used by other teams later on as was the case with the name Bronchos, which since it was given to the San Antonio team in 1896 has been applied to the team of Montreal, Canada, in the Eastern League and was last year used for the Cleveland team of the American League," the *Light* said.[3]

A crowd of thirteen hundred turned out at San Pedro Park on opening day, April 25, as *Light* publisher T. B. Johnson "shot a beautiful drop curve straight over the base" to Moore for the team's ceremonial first pitch. Moore's Mustangs beat the Beaumont Oil Gushers 9-4 that day.

San Antonio's lineup was filled with the future stars of the Texas League, both on and off the field:

- Morris, who turned out to be the star shortstop, would go on to run three different Texas League teams and serve as the league's president. He was briefly even an umpire in the league during a twenty-six-year career.
- First baseman Pat Newnam stayed active during his twenty seasons in the South Texas/Texas League as a player and manager.
- Third baseman Paul LaGrave, as the business manager, later

    would build the Fort Worth Cats dynasty of the 1910s and
    1920s.

- Outfielder Max Gibbs would go on to run teams in Sherman
  for a number of years.[4]

But in 1903 such men were simply part of a good team. Led by pitching brothers Orth "Odd Tom" Thomas and "Sir" Richard Thomas and powered by Moore's hitting (he was at .338 when he broke a finger in mid-June), the Mustangs quickly took a big lead in the pennant race. Even when Moore went out, the Mustangs kept winning. They were 32-19—the only team of the four in the league above .500—when the first half of the season ended on June 19.

Injuries to Wright and Richard Thomas slowed the Mustangs during the second half, and Gene Burns threw a no-hitter against them on August 7 in Houston. The team stayed around .500 for most of the second half, hanging on for a postseason battle for the Mistrot Medal, which had been donated by a Galveston businessman to honor the league's champion.

Moore continued to juggle his multiple duties as well. One day in August a foul-up with the train schedules almost kept the team from making it from Beaumont to a 4:30 P.M. game in Houston and earning its guaranteed payment from the Houston management. "Moore is so smooth that his shadow glistens, and he made the requisite play," the *Houston Chronicle* reported. "The railroad came properly across and the men were bundled into a special that looked a whole lot like a cattle train." Houston manager Claud Rielly, who was eating lunch at the depot in Houston, looked out the window just in time to hear "a bump in the train shed and the sound of pattering feet just as if a whole line of ball players was trying to steal second at once. Rielly turned around in time to see the phalanx with Wade Moore at its head dodging rain drops in a dash for a street car." The game was rained out, but the Mustangs got their guarantee the next day with a doubleheader.[5]

Galveston ran away with the second-half title, and the best-of-thirteen championship series was scheduled to begin September 1, with the first six games in San Antonio. Just before the regular season ended, though, Moore added three more players from Corsicana, which did not make the Texas League playoffs. Among them was Ike Pendleton, who would go on to play eight more years in the league, most of them in San Antonio, and become a fixture at Texas League ballparks in the city into the 1960s.[6] Eddie Taylor beat the Sand Crabs 3-2 in Game One, and new Mustang C. E. Robb won Game Two 7-2. Lucky Wright took the third game, 3-1, and Orth Thomas won Game Four 3-2.

The fifth game produced one of the odder twists in the history of the league. Wilson Matthews, who had played briefly for both San Antonio and Galveston during the season, had umpired the first four games. But he resigned his post before Game Five—and became Galveston's second baseman and captain, with a promise to be the club's manager in 1904. Matthews's presence did not help the Sand Crabs: Eddie Taylor threw a no-hitter for San Antonio, allowing just one runner to reach third base in the 3-0 decision.[7]

The Mustangs, who by this time were being called the Tamales by the newspapers because they were so hot, lost the first game in Galveston. But the next day—playing against Orth Thomas, who had been sold to the Sand Crabs for the day for $175—San Antonio clinched the series with a 6-3 victory. Fittingly, Moore hit a home run to drive in the first two runs for his Mustangs.

The season was a success on a number of levels. "While there may have been considerable [opportunity] to criticize in the conduct of the organization—mistakes naturally due to inexperience—there has been much to commend, and on the whole it is safe to say that every lover of national game has had his or her fill of good baseball, sandwiched at times with erratic contests," the *Light* said. "The low salary limit precluded the engagement of high-calibre players and proved the means of bringing to the front a lot of bright, hustling youngsters who had reputations to make. The good behavior, on and off the field, of these quiet, well-dressed young men—some of them college graduates—has been very marked." Attendance, the same report noted, was "unusually large" throughout the league.[8]

But the final proof of Moore's success came early the next season. On May 17 he sold the team for one thousand dollars to Charles Blackburn. It was, according to league historian William Ruggles, "the

The 1903 Bronchos, led by owner-manager-player Wade Moore, won the South Texas League pennant. Courtesy Texas League

first time a franchise in the Alamo City had ever had a negotiable value." Moore went on to play for Houston and Beaumont in 1904, and in 1905 he managed the Houston Buffaloes—dubbed "Moore's Marvels"— to victories in both halves of the pennant race, going 44-18 the first half and 39-24 the second.[9]

San Antonio, meanwhile, finished last in both halves in the 1904 South Texas League race. The year was significant, though, for one reason. It marked the first time a major-league team conducted spring training in San Antonio, as the Cleveland Indians spent part of March working out before hitting the road north.[10]

Early in the 1905 season, Blackburn gave up on the club—which had been renamed the Warriors—and sold it to cigar-store owner Morris Block for a $250 loss. Block, who had a keen sense of salesmanship, used one business to market the other, though the results did not show up right away. The team finished second to Houston in both halves, then a year later went 57-70 in the final season for the South

Texas League. The highlight of that year was a pitching duel between Fred Winchell Cook (he played in the league under both last names, though not at the same time) and Houston's Prince Gaskill. The two battled to a sixteen-inning 0-0 tie, and both were credited with complete games.[11]

The 1907 season brought back the consolidated Texas League, including Dallas, Houston, Fort Worth, Galveston, Waco, and Temple. It also marked the return of the budding rivalry between San Antonio and Austin, two cities that have never had to work hard to build a healthy dislike for each other. San Antonio was around when Austin was still a wide spot in the road called Waterloo. Austin one-upped San Antonio when it was made the capital of the republic and then the state. San Antonio has its quaint downtown, with winding streets and the San Antonio River snaking through it. Austin's streets were laid out on a strict north-south, east-west grid, and the Colorado River was then just a flood-prone nuisance. But it took baseball—in fact, the most one-sided game in Texas League history—to work up a real rivalry.

Dallas, San Antonio, and Austin were first, second, and third, fighting for the pennant on July 23, 1907. The Bronchos and Senators were scheduled for a doubleheader at Austin's Riverside Park. The Bronchos were led by first-year manager Sam La Rocque, and they also had two future San Antonio managers on the club—first baseman Pat Newnam and outfielder George "Cap" Leidy—as well as Ike Pendleton, who would go on to manage several clubs around the state, at shortstop. But their reputation in 1907 was not for on-field leadership; it was for rowdiness. San Antonio led the league in umpire-baiting in 1907, and it caught up with them in Austin that day.

The Bronchos were leading 5-4 with one out in the bottom of the eighth inning of the first game when the Senators' Eddie Cermack overslid third base and was tagged by Frank Everhardt a full three feet off the bag. Jack Shuster—who in the common practice of the day was the only umpire on the field—called Cermack safe. "Umpire Schuster [his name was commonly misspelled] seemed to have an off day, and several decisions looked a bit off," the *Light*'s correspondent in Austin reported.[12]

The Bronchos, who not surprisingly had been working on the umpire all day anyway, complained loudly but eventually returned to their positions. Then La Rocque came in from the outfield to argue the point with Shuster. Their conversation "was not audible in the grandstands," both papers reported, but something offensive must have been said, for La Rocque was "ordered from the field." Then Newnam took in after Shuster. He also was "ordered from the field," but an Austin policeman had to escort him away.

At that point the Bronchos had had enough, and they all walked off the field. Shuster ordered them back, then took out his watch. They refused to budge, despite howls of protest from the Austin fans. The umpire turned to the official scorer and declared a forfeit for Austin. "The crowd then went wild," the *Light* reported. "It was evident that it sided with the visitors on that third-base decision, but it looked raw to have them act as they did. The policemen had their hands full keeping order between games."[13]

The San Antonio players, meanwhile, were cooking up a surprise. Knowing that another forfeit would cost the franchise a considerable fine, money that would probably come out of their paychecks, they decided to play on, in a way. Art Griggs, an infielder, started the game on the mound and allowed twelve runs in the first inning, as the Bronchos simply let ground balls roll past them or fly balls drop uncaught in the outfield. Pendleton relicved Griggs, then Leidy came on, with no more success. "Home runs were the rule, and a three-ring circus might have got pointers at the game," the *Light* reported. "All the comedy acts known to the circus ring went on in the second game," the *Express* commented. "Home runs were common and such ridiculous plays were made that the game was enjoyable."[14]

It certainly was enjoyable for the Senators, who were credited with forty-four runs and thirty-three hits. Those hits included two doubles, three triples, and six home runs. Austin also stole twenty-three bases, which still stands as a league record. The Bronchos were charged with nine errors. "In the second game, the Bronchos batted whenever they felt like it, batting out of order," the *Express* reported. "It is impossible to give a correct box score of this game. The change of pitchers made it impossible to give bases on balls and strike-outs, except for Austin." Robert Gould, covering his first ballgame for the *Austin Statesman*, attempted to keep a box score, though he admitted to Ruggles that it was not entirely accurate.[15]

Not everyone was amused. "A petition was started to send to [Texas League] President [William] Robbie, complaining of the conduct of the San Antonio players," according to the *Light*. "Many signed their names thereto." The fallout started sooner, though. Newnam was arrested after the game for "reported bad language to the umpire," the *Light* reported. "The case would have fallen through had not Shortstop [H. B.] McCulley of Austin [been] subpoenaed to appear against Newnam and swear to the charge. It cost the latter a snug sum to square himself. He did not have time to get counsel." Robbie received the petition from the Austin fans four days later and declared he was going to "strike at the root of the problem. The 44 to 0 score at Austin alone would not have earned more than a passing amusement had it not been brought about by conduct reprehensible from any viewpoint," he said in a statement to the *Light*. "The complaint of the Austin fans is just, but in my action I will not in any manner be swayed by it."[16]

As far as can be determined, though, no one was ever fined over the 44-0 game. But on July 30 the *Express* reported that La Rocque was resigning to take care of "business interests most vital." La Rocque blamed shortstop George Markley for all the club's recent problems, though Markley was not even in the lineup on July 23. Robbie denied that he had fined La Rocque, noting that the manager had helped build Electric Park, the best diamond in the state, and had put together a pennant contender in San Antonio. But others said the farce in Austin was the reason he was going first to Montreal and then home to Birmingham, Alabama, where he was expected to accept "one of several offers he has received to coach college teams." Bronchos president Morris Block named Newnam as manager.[17]

That same day the *Light* reported that San Antonians were putting together "an additional and very powerful incentive" for the club—a pot that they hoped would wind up totaling fifteen hundred dollars to be divided among the players if they won the pennant. Block and Louis Lindheim, another club official, started it off with fifty dollars each, and local banker Fred Groos kicked in ten dollars more.[18]

Box Score from Austin's 44-0 Victory over San Antonio
At Riverside Park, July 23, 1907

SAN ANTONIO					AUSTIN				
Player	*AB*	*R*	*H*	*E*	*Player*	*AB*	*R*	*H*	*E*
McMurry, p, c, ss,	4	0	0	0	Short, lf	9	7	5	0
Collins, lf	3	0	2	0	McCully, ss	7	5	4	0
Leidy, cf, ss, p	4	0	0	3	Gardner, 2b	8	7	6	0
Griggs, p, c, 2b	4	0	0	0	Gordon, c	5	3	4	0
Stovall, rf, 1b	2	0	0	1	Alexander, c	3	1	1	0
Colgrove, rf	2	0	0	1	Bradley, rf	5	4	2	0
Robb, 2b	3	0	0	1	Firestine, 3b	5	5	3	0
Pendleton, ss, p, c	3	0	1	1	Adams, 1b	7	3	2	0
Everhardt, 3b, ss	3	0	1	3	Cermack, cf	6	4	2	0
					McGill, p	8	5	3	0
Totals	28	0	4	9		63	44	32	0

San Antonio   000 000 000 — 0
Austin   (12)20 (11)13 (10)5 — 44

    2B—Short, Eberhardt. 3B—Short, Firestine, McGill. HR—McCully, Gardner, Gordon, Adams, Cermack, McGill. SB—Short 4, McCully, Gardner 3, Gordon 4, Bradley 2, Firestine 2, Adams, Cermack 2, McGill 2, Collins 2. Sacrifice—McCully.

SAN ANTONIO

Pitcher	*BB*	*SO*
Griggs	2	0
Pendleton	3	1
Leidy	3	0

AUSTIN

Pitcher	*BB*	*SO*
McGill	1	3

    Umpire—Shuster. Time—1:45.

The Bronchos and Senators went back and forth between first and second the entire month. Buck Harris's no-hitter against Dallas on August 11 kept the race close, and on the twenty-fifth Austin was a game up going into a doubleheader at Electric Park. In the crowd that day were "fifteen hundred condescending Capital City rooters plastered with two-thirds that many white badges raking up old personalities and rubbing it in," the *Light* reported. The badges worn by the Austin fans that day bore no words, just "44-0." San Antonio won the first game of the doubleheader in the bottom of the ninth, when Harris drove in Leidy with a sharp single. The Bronchos won the second game 5-3 to move into first place. An unidentified member of the team ceremoniously buried one of the ribbons in the dirt behind home plate.[19] The Bronchos beat the Senators again the next day for a two-game advantage but then were swept by Austin on Tuesday and went into a spin thereafter. A week later the Senators wrapped up their second pennant in three years (including a South Texas League title) by beating the Bronchos 9-2 in Austin.

Even then the controversy would not die. Newnam had played in Austin despite numerous threatening letters from people there, apparently over a spiking incident. San Antonio filed a protest with the league over the presence of T. R. Vinson in the Austin lineup, supposedly playing without a valid contract. (Oddly enough, if Austin had been forced to forfeit the games, Dallas would have won the pennant— "As against Austin, most of the local fans would prefer Dallas," the *Light* noted.) The appeal—which was supported by Houston and Galveston—was turned down, and the Senators had their pennant. By the next spring, though, Austin had hit the skids, well on the way to a last-place finish, bankruptcy, and a two-year absence from the league.[20]

The big talk in the spring of 1908 was about the San Antonio Bronchos. After hiring and firing managers at a George Steinbrenner– like pace in the two-plus seasons he had owned the team—a total of eight men had run the club since the start of the 1905 season—Block had given the job to minor-league veteran George "Cap" Leidy.

Leidy had been a player of note before the turn of the century, but it was his eye for talent that made him a great choice to manage. He was credited with finding, among others, "Wee" Willie Keeler, who went on to make the Baseball Hall of Fame, and Eddie Cicotte, whose brilliant career was cut short by the Black Sox scandal of 1919. Leidy also was credited with turning around the career of Ty Cobb when the talented young player was in the low minors in Georgia. The new skipper had played in the outfield in 1907 for the Bronchos, who went 81-58 and finished third.[21]

But the city's other Bronchos were coming off what they considered a championship season. The San Antonio Black Bronchos—owned and operated by East Side businessman Charlie Bellinger—had beaten the Birmingham (Alabama) Greater Giants in a best-of-seven series for the "Negro Baseball Championship of the South" in Austin the summer before. The team played in the same ballpark as their white counterparts, Electric Park, when the Texas League club was on the road. And they drew crowds as large as or larger than those attracted by the Bronchos, integrated crowds that often, as the *Light* reported, had as many white faces as black ones.[22]

From the few records available of the games, the Black Bronchos were 13-4 in 1907, playing series with teams like the Houston Black Mud Cats, the Waco Yellow Jackets, and the Fort Worth Black Panthers as well as Birmingham. They were led by players with colorful nicknames, monikers that sometimes were the only way they were identified—for example, "Black Cat," "Baby" Webb, and Dick "The Austin Demon" Walker. But none were greater than the pitcher often identified in newspaper reports simply as "Cyclone Joe."

Joe Williams was six feet, five inches tall; long-armed; and long-legged, with a deceptively slow windup that hid a powerful fastball. He had piercing eyes and a hawk nose, inherited from his mother, supposedly a full-blooded Cherokee. He was from Seguin, forty miles up the road from San Antonio, and was twenty-two years old when the Black Bronchos opened their 1908 season in Waco on Sunday, April 19.[23]

The day before, the Texas League season had opened with great fanfare in San Antonio. Both the Bronchos and the Dallas Giants were carried by a parade of carriages from the team's offices to Electric Park, led by a marching band. San Antonio mayor Bryan Callaghan made a brief speech and threw out the ceremonial first pitch, with Texas League president William Robbie serving as the ceremonial umpire; "Whether it was a ball or a strike has not yet been decided," the *Daily Express* observed. An overflow crowd of more than one thousand turned out to the little stadium, which was adjacent to the Electric Park Amusement Park, just north of the main part of the city. The amusement park, which also opened for the season on April 18, was a major attraction, with its Ferris wheel, roller coaster, merry-go-round, and boat rides, not to mention its shooting gallery, pool hall, and assortment of restaurants, all illuminated for nighttime visitors.[24]

Dallas, which would battle San Antonio for the league lead the entire season, won 2-1 on opening day, beating Fred Winchell Cook, a submarine-style curveball pitcher in his third year with the Bronchos. The next day, Cyclone Joe gave up three hits in ten innings as the Black Bronchos beat Waco 1-0, and the team went on to compile a 9-1-1 record in its first eleven games, all on the road.[25]

When the white Bronchos finally left town—after fifteen games— the Black Bronchos had their own version of opening day on May 10. "Then there was a full-fledged orchestra that emitted sounds every time one of the Black Bronchos did something," the *Light* reported, "and the best of all was the Black Bronchos Glorifying Glee Club, 73 voices, count 'em 73." In addition to the band and the glee club, the estimated crowd of five hundred was treated to a show by "Umpire Earl," who "furnished some new stunts that could well be placed in the vaudeville," according to the *Light*. "Every decision was rendered in a voice that was audible to the free spectators on surrounding house tops," the paper said of the umpire. On the field the Black Bronchos whipped the Fort Worth Black Wonders 9-1, with Cyclone Joe striking out seven and allowing seven hits, five in the last three innings.[26]

That same afternoon, the white Bronchos scored five runs in the seventh inning to beat Shreveport 5-3, one day after scoring five in the ninth for an 8-6 victory. They were beginning to get on a roll, one that would carry them to a 12-5 record on their first road trip of the season and into first place.

By now San Antonio was beginning to warm up to both sets of Bronchos. The Black Bronchos Rooters Association had built its membership up to 107 by the time the Waco Yellow Jackets came to town for a game on May 17. A week later the white Rooters Club of San Antonio was announced, with plans to give the Bronchos players a banquet at the Menger Hotel at the end of the season and put together excursions to out-of-town games.[27]

The Bronchos went 22-6 in May, topped by a 1-0 victory in Galveston on May 30. San Antonio pitcher Buck Harris threw a three-hitter, and veteran shortstop George Markley won the game with a home run in the eighth inning.

Both San Antonio teams kept on winning as the summer wore on, though both had to overcome a series of injuries to their catchers— Leidy had to recruit a local amateur, A. Knaupp, early in the season when Bill "Kid" Alexander was hurt, then he signed former Southern League catcher John Coveney in late May. The Black Bronchos did not have that luxury—their main pitchers, Williams and Webb, took turns catching after starter Sam Lampkin broke a finger in June.

But the teams relied more and more on pitching for their victories. Harris threw another three-hit shutout against Waco on June 20, getting three runs of support in the bottom of the first inning in a 5-0 win. "With Buck on the strip, the three engraved tallies on the board looked like a thousand," the *Light* reported. The next day Winchell was even better. He did not allow the Navigators a hit through the first 11⅔ innings and did not allow a run through 12. But the Bronchos could not deliver a key hit—they left eleven on base, including four runners at third—and Waco finally caught up with Winchell, scoring twice in the thirteenth inning for a 2-0 victory. It was the first time a San Antonio pitcher had taken a no-hitter past 9 innings; and to this day it remains a San Antonio record for the longest string of no-hit innings in a single game.[28]

The loss slipped San Antonio a ½ game behind Dallas in the standings and got Leidy back to work looking for players. On July 1 he traded pitcher William Burns, who was 8-2, and third baseman/outfielder Ike Pendleton, a local boy popular with the fans, to Fort Worth for Alex Dupree, one of the top pitchers in the league and at the time the only man to have thrown two no-hitters in one season. The team responded by winning seven of its first nine games in July, including a double-header sweep on July 4 in front of an overflow crowd that was still coming into the park in the third inning. Roy Mitchell gave up five hits in beating Houston in the morning game, and Winchell won the afternoon game against Galveston 8-3.

But Leidy was not done. Outfielder Sam Stovall came down with typhoid fever while on a road trip, forcing the manager to use a pitcher, Winchell, and a catcher, Coveney, in right field and leading to talks to bring back Pendleton from Fort Worth. And in the second week of July, apparently unhappy with the play of George Ebright, whom he had signed to play third base when Pendleton was traded, Leidy signed George Wisterzil, who two months earlier had graduated from San Antonio High School. "It is not exactly an easy job Wisterzil is now holding," the *Light* observed. "Aside from the actual work in the game, there are other things that will make his fight no cinch. It would take a major league player in that position to satisfy some of the fans who are still mourning the departure of Ike, and any slip, no matter how slight, will be magnified by such to considerable proportions." Leidy also made a deal for one of the most famous names in San Antonio baseball history, getting left-handed pitcher Harry Ables in a trade with Dallas. In 1910 Ables set a Texas League record for strikeouts (310) that still stands, and he was the president of the club during the 1920s.[29]

Meanwhile, the Black Bronchos were taking on the Dallas Black Giants in a best-of-five series for the state championship. Williams struck out sixteen in the deciding game, a thirteen-inning victory on July 15 decided on a home run by outfielder Johnnie White. The next week the Birmingham Greater Giants came to town for the start of a series for the southern black baseball championship. They beat Williams 2-0 in the first game, scoring both runs in a nightmare of a seventh inning that saw the Black Bronchos commit four errors, two by Williams. He gave up three hits and struck out eight. San Antonio won the middle game, but then Williams lost to the Greater Giants 1-0, despite ten strikeouts and just five hits. Johnnie "Steel Arm" Taylor held the Black Bronchos to two hits. "The game was the best seen on the local lot this season," the *Daily Express* reported. "At no time was [the] game lacking in ginger, and this alone helped to pull off many plays that seemed almost impossible." Birmingham scored its only run in the seventh, on a single, a close-call stolen base, and a double.[30]

EVERYDAY LINEUP FOR THE 1908 BRONCHOS

First base. Pat Newnam, who wound up playing parts of twenty seasons in the Texas League, led the league in home runs in 1908 with eighteen. He also played parts of two seasons with the St. Louis Browns.

Second base. Arthur Griggs went on to play parts of seven seasons in the major leagues, then was the president of the league's Tulsa team from 1933 to 1938.

Shortstop. George Markley, who led the league's shortstops in fielding percentage in 1908, wound up playing on four pennant-winning teams in the league in eight seasons.

Third base. Ike Pendleton, who started the season at third, played ten seasons in the Texas League and wound up living in San Antonio for the rest of his life. George Wisterzil played in the Federal League, an alternative major league, for two seasons and was a career .290 hitter in 540 games in the Texas League.

Left field. Ed Collins led the league in runs scored in 1908 and also stole sixty-eight bases.

Center field. George "Cap" Leidy managed San Antonio until July 20, 1912, then came back to run the team again in 1915 and part of 1916.

Right field. Sam Stovall survived typhoid fever during the season and went on to play two more seasons in the Texas League.

Catcher. Bill Alexander, who was a thirteen-year veteran of the Texas League in 1908, has the longest period between his league debut and his final game in league history; his last Texas League game was in 1929.

Pitchers. Fred Winchell (Cook), who alternated between Winchell and Cook as his last name, was 22-11 in 1908 and led the league in strikeouts the next year. Buck Harris was 22-9 in 1908 and wound up with a Texas League career record of 69-55. Harry Ables, who was 15-6 with an earned-run average of 2.04, went on to play briefly in the major leagues and then came back to San Antonio to operate a successful lumber yard. Roy Mitchell went on to pitch in the major leagues for parts of three seasons and won 120 games in the Texas League.

The other Bronchos were slowly beginning to pull away from Dallas, thanks to more outstanding pitching. Dupree and Ables led a doubleheader sweep at Austin on July 25—a game marred by a near riot that required a police escort for the umpire to his hotel. On July 30 Winchell took a no-hitter into the seventh inning and wound up with a two-hitter win against Dallas in the first game of a doubleheader. Mitchell won the second game, shortened to five innings because of a tight train schedule, and San Antonio moved into first place to stay.

On August 10, backers of the team announced they were following the lead of other cities in the state and putting together a purse to be given to the players if they won the Texas League pennant. "The knowledge that the fans at home are appreciating their efforts will not hurt their game at all," the *Light* reported. "They ought to have a chance at something that is offered the [Dallas] Giants or the [Houston] Buffaloes in case of victory." Perhaps coincidentally, the Bronchos rallied from a 4-0 deficit that day to beat Dallas 5-4, then came back from 2-1 down with a three-run seventh inning the next afternoon.[31]

"In contemplation of the Bronchos' present elevated position, one thing must not be overlooked," the *Light* noted on August 15. "George Leidy has been hammered everywhere, but he has picked a winner, or something that at present looks like a pretty good imitation. Very few false moves he has made when all is considered, and the winning of the pennant will carry a big weight of credit to lay at Uncle George's door. Together with the owners, he has stood pat where it has developed to be the best policy, and he has made changes that have been in almost all cases justified. He has his enemies, but he has delivered a big bale of goods to the San Antonio fans."

The pennant talk—and the talk about the perfect manager-owner team—was almost premature. In the span of a week, both catchers, Coveney and Alexander, broke fingers and had to leave the team. Their backup, infielder Dolly Stark, was hit in the head by a foul ball and had to sit out. Second baseman Arthur Griggs gave catching a try and allowed four stolen bases and a passed ball in a 4-1 loss on August 16 in Fort Worth.

Leidy was ejected that day for arguing a close call during the Panthers' three-run eighth inning, and something else apparently happened over the weekend as well. The August 19 *Light* reported that he had resigned as manager of the team, with first baseman Pat Newnam taking over. Leidy agreed to stay and play center field. "No reason is given in the telegram for this action being taken by Manager Leidy, who at first wanted to leave the team," the paper said.[32]

Four days later, though, Leidy was back. "It is reported that [owner] Morris Block and Newnam had a talk with Leidy and persuaded the veteran warrior to take charge again," the *Light* reported. "He finally consented to do so, and everyone is again satisfied in every way. Leidy has placed the team where it now is, and the winning of the pennant will carry no little credit to his management of the club. Newnam is about the gladdest man in the act over the change, and says that his time is pretty well filled at first base."[33]

No official explanations were ever reported about Leidy's brief resignation. Even with the injuries, the team was playing well. He had the power to make virtually all the personnel moves (though as the *Light* observed, not without some griping by local fans). And he was playing every day. There might have been some friction with Block, whose out-front style was fairly unusual for owners of the time. His caricature —pursued by a gang of loyal fans—appeared in the local newspaper, and his cigar-store business had boomed since he took over ownership of the baseball team (in fact, he had to hire an extra phone operator on game days to answer calls to the store for scores). Block also traveled with the team regularly, which may have been a little irksome to a veteran like Leidy.

The turmoil seemed to make little difference on the field, as Harris and Dupree led a doubleheader sweep in Houston the day Leidy came back, and the Bronchos proceeded to go on a seventeen-game winning streak, a team record that lasted until 2003.

The Black Bronchos were headed for a title at the same time, taking on Birmingham in a continuation of the teams' series for the black baseball championship. The Greater Giants shelled Williams in the first game, winning 10-6 on a muddy field that contributed to eight errors, four by each team. But San Antonio came back in the second contest 3-1, thanks to some typical "blackball" plays. Black Cat scored San Antonio's first run on a double, a wild pitch, and a throwing error in the first, then scored the winning run in the seventh on a walk, stolen base, passed ball, and an error. Baby Webb shut out the Greater Giants 3-0 the next afternoon, tying the series at 3-3. "One-hand stops and catches were too common to be mentioned one by one," the *Light* reported. "And when the game had a tendency to slow down, a hit or two always set both parties once more on edge."[34]

The deciding game came down to the teams' two best pitchers—Williams and Taylor, and Williams delivered. "The Black Broncs are the negro champions of Dixie," the *Light* reported. "In the supreme test of the playoff yesterday afternoon at the local ball yard, they blanked the Birmingham Giants 2 to 0. Cyclone Joe Williams came near being the whole game. Joe had not been showing a great deal of late, but he was all on deck yesterday. Six innings went the visitors without a hit, and one in the seventh was all they could annex. And it was Joe's homer in the fifth that hoisted the colored pennant of the south on the Black Broncho staff."[35]

Williams struck out nine, walked two, and hit three. "Twice did Cyclone get out of a pit of his own digging," the *Light* reported. "Once in the first inning, when his wild heave to first put a man on third with no one out, and again in the seventh when he neglected to throw to third for the force. Both times the Giants died there on the last two corners." Because not all of the games were completely reported, it is impossible to determine Williams's record for the season. Historians have pieced together a 35-8 record for the 1908 Black Bronchos, including one last victory over Houston after the Birmingham series.[36]

On the day of Cyclone's last victory, August 22, the white Bronchos beat Houston 3-2. They did not lose again until September 7, a seventeen-game winning streak that included the official pennant-clincher on September 4 against defending champion Austin. Included in the run were a fifteen-strikeout game from Ables, a 5-for-5 day for Wisterzil, and a benefit. All of the home team's gate proceeds from San Antonio's doubleheader with Austin on September 6 went into the pennant purse, swelling it to $795.15. Among the names listed as donors in the *Light* were Block ($100), team secretary Louis Lindheim ($100), the Two Brothers Bar ($5), and local banker Frank Groos ($5).[37]

THE 1908 BRONCHOS' SEVENTEEN-GAME WINNING STREAK

Aug. 21: San Antonio 3, @ Houston 2.

Aug. 22: San Antonio 5-3, @ Houston 0-2 (doubleheader). Buck Harris pitched a two-hitter for the Bronchos in the first game.

Aug. 23: San Antonio 4, @ Houston 1.

Aug. 24: San Antonio 9, Galveston 6. The series was moved from Galveston because of poor attendance.

Aug. 25: San Antonio 5, Galveston 3.

Aug. 26: San Antonio 9, Galveston 1. Roy Mitchell allowed three hits.

Aug. 27: San Antonio 5, Galveston 1.

Aug. 28: San Antonio 8, Galveston 0. Harry Ables pitched a three-hitter and struck out fifteen.

Aug. 29: San Antonio 9, Galveston 8.

Aug. 30: San Antonio 14, Houston 1. George Wisterzil went 5 for 5 with a home run.

Aug. 31: San Antonio 7, Houston 6.

Sept. 1: San Antonio 14, Houston 1.

Sept. 2: San Antonio 10, Austin 3. Wisterzil hit two home runs and a double.

Sept. 3: San Antonio 4, Austin 3. The Senators rallied from a 3-1 deficit in the ninth, but the Bronchos scored the winning run in the bottom of the ninth to clinch the pennant.

Sept. 4: San Antonio 5, Austin 4.

Sept. 5: San Antonio 11-4, Austin 2-5 (doubleheader). Utility infielder George Markley was the starting pitcher in the first game and second baseman Arthur Griggs started the second. Shortstop Monroe "Dolly" Stark also pitched in the second game, which ended the winning streak after eighteen games.

It turns out, though, that the team did not get its banquet at the Menger Hotel. Instead the players were taken to 410 Matamoros Street, one of the largest and fanciest houses in the city's red-light district. They were escorted to a fine dining room and toasted by local business leaders as well as the formally dressed young women of the home. Wisterzil, who was sixteen and wearing his high school graduation suit, received promises from the older players that they would "protect" him.

Leidy received a large engraved trophy, and the players were told to look under their plates. Each found a crisp $100 bill—a considerable amount of money in a time when the finest suit at a local haberdashery cost $45. (That was in addition to their shares of the pennant purse.) There are no further records of the night's activities.[38]

Leidy was busy soon afterward, for winning a championship usually meant that your players were good enough to move up to the next level of the minors—which many did. "A winning team is all that goes from now on, and if Leidy cannot get one together over the winter there is none to be had anywhere," the *Light* reported. "Fortunately, he has already taken steps to fill the impending vacancies, and no time will be wasted in getting the balance of the men needed."[39]

But the manager could not deliver another pennant. He lost his entire starting infield and every outfielder but himself in 1909, and the main highlight of the season was the emergence of left-handed pitcher Willie Mitchell. On June 26 Mitchell threw a no-hitter against Shreveport. On August 21 he struck out twenty Galveston hitters in a nine-inning game, setting a record that would stand until 1978. San Antonio finished third in each of the next three seasons.[40]

Meanwhile, Joe Williams reportedly went 32-8 for the Black Bronchos in 1909. In 1910 he joined the Chicago Giants, starting his career in the top levels of the Negro Leagues, and he pitched for the New York Lincoln Giants from 1911 to 1923 and the Homestead Grays from 1925 to 1932. On August 7, 1930, he struck out twenty-seven members of the Kansas City Monarchs in a twelve-inning game, and during his time in the Negro Leagues, he defeated five members of the Baseball Hall of Fame in exhibition games—Grover Cleveland Alexander, Chief Bender, Waite Hoyt, Walter Johnson, and Rube Marquard.

A poll conducted in 1952 by the African American *Pittsburgh Courier* newspaper named Joe Williams—and not the legendary Satchel Paige—as the greatest pitcher in Negro Leagues history.[41] He was elected to the Baseball Hall of Fame in 1999, the only pitcher with a professional connection to San Antonio to join the Hall.

But there were some great pitchers coming after him, and within just one year after Williams's departure, as a matter of fact.

Hometown Heroes,

1910–23

SOME OF THE BEST players in baseball history never made it to the major leagues. Of course, no African American players were in the big leagues from 1884 to 1946 due to an unwritten agreement among team owners. But even among white players, the opportunities were limited. Scouting, especially before 1940, was a hit-or-miss proposition, hindered by small budgets and difficult travel. Many prospects simply never were seen by big-league scouts. And while there were hundreds of minor-league teams, there were no real affiliation agreements between those teams and their major-league brothers, so there was no real way to develop young players. The true "farm" system did not come along until the St. Louis Cardinals started buying up teams and using them to develop athletes during the late 1920s.

Minor-league coaching staffs were small, so young players often were left to learn skills on their own. Also, until 1962 there were just sixteen teams in the major leagues, limiting the opportunities for players even further. But there were players who simply chose to stay in the minors since salaries at the higher levels were not all that much smaller than those in the majors (especially true in the case of the Pacific Coast League, which for a while was considered to be on par with the American and National Leagues).[1]

Of course, some young players did make it to the majors. It rarely was easy, though, with many failures along the way. Such was the case for Ross Youngs, a San Antonio boy who played one game for his home-town team at the age of sixteen and a handful for the worst team in Texas League history the next. He eventually played ten seasons in the majors and was named to the Baseball Hall of Fame in 1972. Some-times, players never could find a place to play in the field, which was the case for Ike Boone, who had a record-setting year at the plate in 1923. Others did not perform well in brief tryouts with major-league clubs, as was the case with pitcher Harry Ables, who had one of the greatest seasons in San Antonio history in 1910.

Harry Ables was, quite simply, a freak of nature. At six feet, four inches tall, he was a giant among the men of 1910. His fingers were so long that he could wrap them completely around a baseball. As a pitcher, he was capable of going on streaks where he was all but unhittable. And for ten years he struck out men by the score, including 310 in 1910 for the San Antonio Bronchos—the oldest single-season record in Texas League history.[2]

Ables was a farm boy, born in 1884 and raised near the small North Texas town of Terrell (which, incidentally, also was his middle name). The Texas League's Corsicana Oilers recruited him off the campus of Southwestern University for the 1904 playoffs, but he did not get his real start in the league until 1905.

He was a left-handed strikeout pitcher, plain and simple. In his first full year of professional baseball, he struck out 180 batters in 292 in-nings for Dallas and the American League's St. Louis Browns. In 1908 he struck out 151. In 1909 he fanned 283, including 24 in thirty innings for Cleveland in the American League.[3] But 1910 was his biggest sea-son, for he and teammate Harry Billiard kept the Bronchos in the pen-nant race into the final weeks.

Ables's first big performance came on April 27, 1910, when he struck out fifteen in a 1-0 win over Oklahoma City. "He had a drop ball work-ing that almost broke the batter's back when he attempted to connect with it, and twirled in mid-season form," the *Daily Light and Gazette* reported. He struck out the first seven hitters and allowed just four hits. The final out was Indians manager Jay Andrews, who inserted himself into the game as a pinch hitter. "Manager Andrews went to bat for [John] Walsh in the ninth—merely to show how easy Ables really was," the *Daily Express* reported. "He hit into two fouls, and then allowed one of Big Hal's elusive drops to slip squarely across the pan."[4]

On June 13 Ables was even better. Pitching against league-leading Dallas, he did not allow a hit through the first ten innings, while his hapless teammates were getting picked off base four times, botching a squeeze play and leaving a man at third in each of the first three innings. "In the meantime, Dallas was helpless," the *Light* reported. "However, the fans had seen Ables pitch so many wonderful games, only to lose by a fluke, that they were scared blind half the time."

Giants shortstop Jewel Ens broke up the no-hitter in the eleventh but was thrown out trying to steal to end the inning. In the top of the fourteenth, former San Antonio star Tony Thebo singled (for Dallas's second and last hit) and stole second and third. But he was left on base when Jack Onslow grounded out. In the bottom of the inning, Otto McIver led off with a walk. George Stinson got the sign for a hit-and-run but fouled off the first pitch. Then he got the sign for a bunt, but it rolled just foul. With the count full, Stinson was allowed to swing away— and did he, hitting the next pitch completely out of Electric Park and onto nearby Flores Street. McIver topped off his trot around the bases with a flip. Stinson, in the scoring rules of the day, only got credit for a triple. Ables struck out nineteen in pitching all fourteen innings.[5]

On July 5 the Bronchos had a doubleheader scheduled with the Waco Navigators, with Ables starting the first seven-inning game against Arthur Loudell. Waco scored a run in the first. San Antonio scored one in the sixth. Then they played, and played, and played some more. By the time umpire Gus Weyhing called the game because of darkness, the game had lasted twenty-three innings. Ables gave up sixteen hits and struck out seventeen in pitching all twenty-three; Loudell allowed fifteen hits and struck out eleven, also going the distance. "Scintillating with brilliant plays, featured by the classiest kind of pitching and abounding in snappy, sharp fielding, the contest was the greatest that has ever been played not only in San Antonio but anywhere else in the state or the country," the *Light* reported on its front page. "Contrary to the usual run of extra inning contests there was never an idle moment during the long, hard struggle and the fans were kept at a fever pitch all the time." San Antonio left sixteen runners on base—many of them, apparently, by manager–center fielder George "Cap" Leidy, who was 0 for 10. "The leader of the Broncs had several chances to push a runner across the plate with a wallop into unoccupied territory, but 'Cap' failed to deliver," the *Light* reported.[6]

The game still stands as the longest tie in Texas League history and was the longest of any kind by time (four hours, fifteen minutes) until 1960. Ables still holds the record (probably never to be challenged) of twenty-two consecutive shutout innings in one game.

But he still was not done. Just over a month later, on August 8, he struck out the first ten batters in a game at Dallas, also a league record that still stands. "They were lucky to get a foul off his delivery at any time," the *Express* reported of the sixteen-strikeout performance, which was the key to San Antonio's 4-2 win. Ables allowed four hits, and his outfield handled just one fly ball the entire afternoon. Among the victims in the ten-strikeout run were some of the of the league's top players: Hank Gowdy, who won the batting title and led the league in doubles and total bases; Harry Storch, who tied with Gowdy and the Bronchos' Stinson for the league lead in home runs; and George Jackson, who led the league in stolen bases.[7]

And then in his last start of the season, Ables was part of perhaps the greatest pitching tandem in league history. On September 4 Ables threw a no-hitter in the first game of a doubleheader against Waco, then watched as teammate Fred Blanding gave up just one hit—an infield dribbler—in the second game. Both games were 1-0 contests, and both finished in exactly sixty minutes. "One dispectic [*sic*] hit— an infield poke that was beaten out in a hot sprint—was the total of Waco's hickory smiting yesterday afternoon in a double-header of seven-inning games," the *Express* reported. San Antonio scored its only run for Ables on a close play at the plate in the first inning. McIver, who had walked and gone to second on a wild pickoff play, slid just under the tag following a single by Stinson. San Antonio had faded from the pennant race by September, but the sweep did assure the team of a third-place finish.[8]

Ables finished the season 19-12. It was not even the best record on the team, for Blanding was 20-9. But two of his records probably never will be touched—the twenty-two shutout innings and the 310 strikeouts. No one is ever going to throw twenty-two innings in a game again. The second-highest single-season total for strikeouts is 277, and no one has topped 200 since the San Antonio Dodgers' Sid Fernandez struck out 209 in 1983.[9]

Ables went on to pitch briefly for the New York Yankees in 1911 but was 0-1 in three appearances and finished the season with Oakland in the Pacific Coast League. He led that league in wins (twenty-five), strikeouts (303), and walks (134) in 1912 but never again made it to the majors. After retiring, he led a group that bought the San Antonio Bears in 1925 and was president of the club from 1925 to 1928. As a publicity stunt, he pitched in a game for the Bears in 1925 at the age of forty, giving up five hits and three runs in five innings and getting the loss. He did it again in 1926 but got a win with four innings of one-hit ball. The stunts did not hurt his minor-league numbers much: in 344 games, he was 158-129, struck out 1,901 men in 2,669 innings, and had an earned-run average of 2.26.[10]

San Antonio still fielded strong teams in 1911 and 1912 without Ables, but once again faded down the stretch, finishing third in 1911 and second in 1912. The greatest excitement of the 1912 season might have come at the league meetings, though. Dallas owner Joe Gardner jumped into a swimming pool and saved San Antonio owner Morris Block from drowning.

The Bronchos had lots of promise heading into the 1913 season, though. Block had brought in a new manager, George Stinson, and predicted the club would be competitive with anyone in the league. He also built a new ballpark—which he modestly named for himself— south of downtown. And to keep fans comfortable at Block Stadium, the owner rented seat cushions before the games, which he paid local kids to collect afterward. A few of the luckier boys even got jobs shagging balls for the team during batting practice before games.

Ross Youngs was sixteen that summer, a small kid three years away from finishing high school. He hardly looked sixteen—he always had been the smallest boy in his class—and even when fully grown he barely reached five feet, eight inches. But he was passionate about baseball, coming by it honestly and early. His father, Stonewall Jackson (Jack to his friends) Youngs had been the successful manager of the club in Shiner, a small town ninety miles east of San Antonio, in 1903 and 1904. But when his leg was crushed in an accident on the job—he worked for the San Antonio and Aransas Pass Railway—he and wife Henrie opened a small trackside hotel in Shiner, a full-time seven-day-a-week job.[11]

But even in a town like Shiner, which was on the main line of a busy railroad that ran north to south through the heart of the state, a small hotel was not much of a moneymaker. So family—including Ross and his brothers Arthur and Jack Jr.—moved to San Antonio in 1907. Jack Sr. ran a few head of cattle south of town, and Henrie operated a downtown boarding house. When Jack disappeared sometime around 1910— with all the money he made from selling the herd—Arthur went out and got a job delivering the *San Antonio Daily Express.* Ross went to work at the ballpark.

During the summer of 1913, Ross was around Block Stadium a lot. He got to know the Bronchos players—an undistinguished group that would finish the year 74-78—and Stinson, who it turned out was in his first and only season as the team's manager. Both players and manager knew Youngs had talent. At a grammar school track meet, he had won the 50-yard dash, the 100, the 220, and the broad jump and had finished second in the pole vault.[12] In the spring of 1913, he had played on the San Antonio High School baseball team, which won a loosely defined state championship. Given a few chances at swings during batting practice, he could spray the field with line drives. With the season fading and interest in the Bronchos lagging, Ross got his first break in pro baseball.

Eligibility rules were a lot less stringent in the early days of the minors. Teams—especially mediocre ones like the Bronchos—would sometimes use dozens of different players during a season, trying to find the right combination if things were not going well or if players were hurt. No big-league teams were providing young prospects to the minors, at least not in the Texas League. Brief "tryouts" were common. Even so, a sixteen-year-old in a Texas League game was an unusual sight.

Stinson did not reveal his plans to anyone beforehand, but on the afternoon of August 26, 1913, the San Antonio Bronchos sent Ross Youngs out to play second base. The *San Antonio Express* made note of the moment, four paragraphs into a story on the Bronchos' 2-0 loss to the Galveston Pirates. (It also marked a career-long problem with people dropping the "s" off the end of his name):

YOUNGSTER DOES WELL

Ross Young, a San Antonio High youngster, who has been chasing flies for the batters all season, was given a uniform and tried out at second base. He is but 16 years of age, and, of course, very unsettled as of yet. But he showed promise of a future. The manner in which he goes after the chances looks very good. At bat he fanned twice, but once only after he had hit a long one to left just a foot foul by reason of the high wind, and that, too, with a man on base.

Young is not yet of Texas League caliber, for all his cleverness in the field. But he is so good a prospect that he is likely to be right there in uniform in the spring with a fine chance to stick. If he listens to reason and stays down to earth when given a lengthy trial, he is expected to be a sure enough pastimer within a couple of years.[13]

Elsewhere in the story it was noted that he made a good stop but a wild throw to first base in the fourth inning—the inning in which Galveston scored both of its runs. Youngs also apparently made two stellar plays in the field, throwing out a runner from the seat of his pants and going deep into the hole to stop a grounder.

The "tryout" ended that day, and Youngs went back to school in the fall. The next season he got a thirteen-game tryout with the Austin Senators, who were even more desperate for players than the Bronchos. The 1914 Senators were the worst team in Texas League history, finishing 31-114, an incredible 67½ games behind co-champs Houston and Waco. The Senators also posted a league-record thirty-one-game losing streak.[14] Youngs hit just .103.

He never played for his hometown team again, but by 1915 Youngs was playing regularly in the minors, and the next year he was spotted by a scout for the New York Giants. By the end of the 1917 season, he was in the major leagues with the Giants and was one of the main reasons the team went to the World Series four straight times in the 1920s.

While Austin was posting the worst record in league history in 1914, San Antonio was doing little better. The Bronchos went 46-103, 54½ games out. The only highlight of the season was a no-hitter by George Crable against Dallas, secured only by a San Antonio run in the bottom of the ninth.

The club zoomed back to second place in 1915, thanks in part to the return of Manager Cap Leidy, but then sank to seventh the next year, getting off to a 35-40 start that cost Leidy his job again. The Bronchos had pretty good pitching in 1916—Harry Stewart and Slim Harding both threw no-hitters. Stewart was "rewarded" with the manager's job on July 31, finishing out the 66-79 season.

In 1917 new owner Harry Benson hired former big-league shortstop Charley O'Leary to manage the team. O'Leary, aware of the team's recent struggles, decided he would try some old-fashioned Irish luck on the team. He ordered uniforms with green pinstripes, green socks, and green caps and nicknamed them the Shamrocks. But Charley forgot to recruit enough good players, and after a 27-39 start, he too was fired. The Shamrocks/Bronchos finished fifth.

The next season, baseball was unsure of its status as the nation became more and more involved with the war in Europe. On May 23 the federal government issued its "work or fight" order, which classified jobs as essential or nonessential to the war effort. Baseball was determined nonessential, and leagues began shutting down. The Texas League season ended July 7, and the World Series was played in September for the first and only time. The war ended just two months later.

World War I changed the United States in a number of ways, including forcing it to take a more global view of events. But unlike World War II, which helped spark social change from coast to coast, the "war to end all wars" left the country as divided as ever. Blacks and whites lived separate worlds in 1919, even in places far from the Deep South like San Antonio. They drank from separate water fountains, used separate restrooms, went to separate schools, worked at separate businesses, and lived in separate neighborhoods. Segregation was simply a way of life, and groups like the Ku Klux Klan—which turned up with regularity in the news—wanted to keep it that way.

But something went strangely awry in San Antonio in September of that year. On Friday, September 12, the *San Antonio Evening News* featured a full-page-wide photo of twelve African American men looking very serious but at the same time very proud. "A Dozen Black Aces Sure Make Winning Hand," the headline above the photo proclaimed. Scratched on the original image was the legend "S.A. Black Aces, Season 1919." They were, for at least a month in 1919, San Antonio's team.[15]

The city's franchise in the all-white Texas League was suffering through a particularly woeful year. The Aces were well on their way to finishing last, 31½ games behind the first of seven straight pennant-winning teams from Fort Worth. San Antonio had not won a pennant since 1908 and had failed to finish in the first division in four years.

But the Black Aces were entirely different. The team actually began the loosely organized Texas Colored League as the Waco Black Navigators, owned by a white restaurant owner named Franks. But when April and May produced abundant rains—and little baseball—Franks began looking to get out of a money-losing enterprise. He sold his players to San Antonio businessman L. W. Moore, whose club played at League Park whenever the white Aces were out of town.[16]

News reports through the season were spotty, but the Black Aces supposedly went 16-2 after Moore added the players from Waco. The team played a big series with the Dallas Black Marines during the Fourth of July holiday, splitting a doubleheader on the fourth in front of three thousand fans and then taking a single game on the fifth. San Antonio's winning pitcher on the fourth was George Washington Jefferson Davis, a left-hander better known as "Steel Arm." On the fifth John Paul Jones beat the Black Marines with a one-hitter.[17] Their catcher both days was the one player from the team who has come the closest to baseball immortality.

His name was Raleigh Mackey. He had grown up in nearby Luling, the first of a long line of top-flight athletes from his family to come from the oilfield town. He was probably the best athlete on the Black

Aces, since he could catch, pitch, and play shortstop. And though there was no mention of it at the time, he probably already was on his way to earning the nickname that would stick with him through a baseball career that would last into the 1940s—"Biz." One legend says he earned the name because he always would call for the business section—the "Biz"—when someone brought a newspaper into the clubhouse. A more likely source was the fact that he was well known for a constant stream of chatter on the field, directed at his teammates as well as opponents. He was giving them "the business," the "biz" for short. "Did you ever hear a magpie chattering and jabbering?" the *Evening News* noted in a story that accompanied the photo of the Black Aces. "Well, Riley [sic] Mackey (no, he is not Irish), is the epitome of 'jaberation.' There is not a second when he is behind the bat that he is not chattering and jabbering, exhorting his teammates to show 'a little pepah out dere.'"[18]

Mackey went on to play in the Negro Leagues, earning a reputation as the best defensive catcher in the game. He had an arm so powerful he could throw out runners without coming out of his crouch, and he earned lavish praise from every pitcher he ever caught. Hilton Smith, who was elected to the Baseball Hall of Fame in 2001, recalled one game he pitched in 1944 with an aging Mackey behind the plate. "Oooh my goodness, I didn't know he was such a catcher! I think I struck out fifteen of those guys. That guy was such a marvelous catcher!" But Mackey's greatest achievement probably was his tutoring of Roy Campanella with the Baltimore Elite Giants in the years before World War II. "Biz wasn't satisfied for me to do just one or two things good. He wanted me to do everything good. And the onliest way I was going to improve myself was by working at the game, working . . . working . . . working. Not just playing at catching, but working the position! There were times when Biz Mackey made me cry with his constant dogging. But nobody ever had a better teacher."[19]

After the July series with Dallas, the Black Aces did not appear in San Antonio sports pages again until the day after Labor Day. Mackey pitched the first game of a doubleheader sweep of the Austin Black Senators, throwing a shutout. The teams played to a 3-3 tie the next day. A week later, on September 9, the *Evening News* reported that the

Black Aces, who were 45-10 and first in the Texas Colored League, would take on second-place Dallas in a best-of-five series for the state title at League Park. "San Antonio will not be deprived of a championship baseball series," the paper reported. "Although the White Aces are down near the bottom of the percentage column, the Black Aces have come to the fore and now top the Texas Colored League with an average of .818. Baseball fans who have watched the Black Aces in action declare that the dark-skinned ball tossers put up a great exhibition and to say that the series between the league leaders will be hotly contested is superfluous. That goes without saying, and as a further incentive a side bet of $1,000 has been put up for the winning team." Later that week the eight-column-wide photo of the team appeared in the *Evening News*, along with a full-length story with details about the series and the players.[20]

Moore had outdone himself. Sam C. Bell, the mayor of San Antonio, was going to lead a parade in the team's honor from downtown to the ballpark. The rest of the city commissioners, as well as the fire chief and police chief, also were going to take part in the procession of both teams, which was going to be welcomed to the park by a Dixieland band.

The *Evening News* extolled the talents of the team, paying particular attention to first baseman Bob "Highpockets" Hudspeth, who stood six feet, four inches and played the position with, apparently, a great deal of flair. "He really is the 'Hermann' of baseball when it comes to sleight-of-hand stunts with the horsehide. He can stretch a dozen yards and no throw is too hard for him to stop." The same article noted that Steel Arm Davis had pitched in twenty-eight games and lost just two, with nineteen shutouts, and Mackey had thrown four shutouts in four pitching appearances. "Manager [*sic*] L. W. Moore, a baseball man and a regular fellow, leaves tonight for Dallas to make the final arrangements for the series," the item added. "Moore is also the manager of the club and he is right in there fighting all the time for his team to win. Besides watching the proceeds of the gate, he directs his team in action and many fans refer to him as the Black Connie Mack."[21]

When the big day arrived, the *Evening News* noted that "fans from Dallas are coming in here by the hundreds. The black teams have a big following of white fans and many of the latter declare they would rather see the dark ball tossers in action than go to the Texas League pennant series. They declare they get more real action for their money." For some reason, none of the San Antonio papers covered the first game of the series, which San Antonio won 3-0 on a Friday afternoon at League Park. Dallas won 2-1 the next day, with Steel Arm Davis taking the loss against Dallas ace Nacadoces Ross. Ross was "as tickled as a Bolsheveek over a new consignment of TNT" with the victory, the paper reported. San Antonio's only run came when Hudspeth singled in Namon Washington in the fifth; the Black Aces missed a chance to tie it in the sixth when Crush Holloway tripled but was thrown out trying to score on a short fly ball to right.

San Antonio's Bob McClure allowed the Black Marines just four hits in Game Three, which the Black Aces won 8-1 to take a 2-1 lead going into a doubleheader. Dallas beat San Antonio 2-1 in the first game, setting up a decisive Game Five.

"To say there was blood in the eyes of the Black Aces is putting it mildly," the *Evening News* reported. "Their heart's desire was in the balance and down went their dobbers and spirits, when the Black Marines stacked up a five-run leading before the Aces started to do anything with Ross' delivery." Davis gave up two runs in the first inning and got just one out, so Mackey went to the mound. He gave up a single run in the third and two more in the fifth. But San Antonio scored five times in the bottom of the fifth. McClure's bases-loaded single scored two runs, and Holloway followed with a two-run double. Mackey then tied it by scoring Holloway with a single.

The game remained at 5-5 until the bottom of the eighth. San Antonio's Grant Don and Andrew Wilson reached base against Ross, bringing up Davis, who had moved from the mound to center field. "And then that moment which is dear to every ball player, whether he is white or black, came to him," the *Evening News* dramatized. Davis worked the count to 2-2, then ripped a pitch to the deepest part of the park for a two-run double. "Without a doubt it was one of the wildest celebrations ever witnessed on a local ball lot when the rangy negro cracked out the winning poke," the columnist reported. "Cushions, bottles, hats, coats and other bits of wearing apparel rained upon the diamond in such quantities that it was necessary to call the game to clean the field for play. . . . It has been many a year that we have got such a thrill from a ball game. We have been writing baseball for about 16 years in the big leagues, the AA outfits and the bushes, but it has seldom been our privilege to see maniacal fans go absolutely nutty as they did yesterday."

Mackey retired the side in the ninth, and San Antonio had its championship.[22]

That day a small item appeared in the *Daily Express,* the morning newspaper: "Negro League Likely To Be Formed Next Year." It noted that the white Aces' manager, Mike Finn, had predicted the formation of regional and national leagues of black players in a column earlier in the year. "By strengthening with Cuban stars and crack negro players from Chicago, St. Louis and New York, some strong clubs could be formed," the report said.[23]

In fact Texan Rube Walker founded the Negro National League the next season. And in July at least seven members of the Black Aces bolted for the league's Indianapolis ABCs, including Mackey, Hudspeth, and Holloway, recommended by San Antonio businessman Charlie Bellinger to ABCs owner C. I. Taylor.[24]

Of all the group, Mackey went on to the greatest success, between his playing career and his tutoring of young players. He led the Hilldale club to three straight pennants in the 1920s and hit .400 in 1930 and .371 in 1931. He also was part of highly successful but little-known barnstorming tours of Japan by Negro Leagues players in 1927, 1934, and 1935. In addition to Campanella, he managed future Baseball Hall of Fame members Monte Irvin and Larry Doby during the 1940s and even made an all-star appearance—he was walked—at the age of fifty in 1947.[25] When the Los Angeles Dodgers had Roy Campanella Day at the L.A. Coliseum in 1959, the catcher—who by then had been paralyzed in a car accident—made it a point to invite and recognize his mentor, who was working in Los Angeles at the time. Mackey has been mentioned a number of times as a Veterans Committee candidate for the Baseball Hall of Fame, but he has yet to be elected.

While Mackey and the Black Aces stayed and were successful at the start of the 1920 season, the white club—renamed, in a pun, the Bears

(San Antonio is the seat of Bexar—pronounced "bear"—County)—was mediocre again, finishing fifth behind the second of seven straight pennant-winners in Fort Worth. On August 25 the Bears were particularly testy after catcher Elmer Johnson and umpire Ed Doyle got into a fight at home plate. After police restored order, San Antonio players refused to return to the field, and Doyle forfeited the game to Beaumont.[26]

By 1922 Benson—and the rest of the league—was doing whatever he could to break the Fort Worth Panthers' grip on the league. Among the players he signed for the 1922 season was Kedzi Kirkham, a natural hitter who posted a franchise-record thirty-two-game hitting streak and led the league in walks with 114. The Bears had a big-hitting team that season, including a nine-run rally in the bottom of the ninth to beat Beaumont 18-16 on August 12.[27]

But the really big signing came in November. "Ike Boone, champion hitter of the Southern Association in 1921 and an outfield tryout with the New York Giants during the last season, will be a San Antonio Bear in 1923," the *Light* reported on the tenth. He had hit .389 for New Orleans in 1921, and had been with the Giants to start the 1922 season. When Casey Stengel started to hit the ball with authority for New York, Boone was sent to the minor-league team in Toledo, Ohio, and later moved on to Little Rock.[28]

Boone came to San Antonio with as much publicity as any player in team history, thanks to his impressive statistics. But the early history of professional baseball in San Antonio, from the very beginning, was littered with promise and usually filled with disappointment. As far back as 1888, the team had signed two "ringers" from Philadelphia who turned out to be little better than the players already in San Antonio.

Of course, managers could not just pick up the phone and call their big-league club for another player. Before the late 1920s that system did not exist—minor-league teams were not officially affiliated with any one big-league team, which meant there was no ready supply of up-and-coming talent sent down to the minors each spring. With no real national scouting below the major-league level, signing players was often a gamble, one that never quite paid off for San Antonio from 1900 to 1922. In that time the Bronchos, Aces, and Bears won just two

Ike Boone was the dominant hitter in the Texas League in 1923, and he still holds a number of San Antonio batting records. Courtesy National Baseball Hall of Fame Library, Cooperstown, New York

pennants and finished second three other times. And while Benson's gamble in 1923 did not pay off in a pennant, it did deliver one of the greatest single seasons in league history.

Boone, who was twenty-five in 1923, came out of the University of Alabama in 1920 and led the Georgia State League in hitting (.403), hits (117), runs scored (sixty-three), and home runs (ten). In 1921 he led the Southern Association in batting average (.389), doubles (forty-six), and triples (twenty-seven). New York Giants manager John McGraw reportedly spent ten thousand dollars to sign him in 1922, though Boone played in just two games with the team in 1922, instead hitting a combined .316 with Toledo in the American Association and Little Rock in the Southern Association.[29]

McGraw, who brought his teams to San Antonio for spring training on a regular basis, sent Boone to his old friend Benson with a prediction—that he would lead the league in hitting. The *Evening News* noted Boone's arrival at the Bears' training camp on March 6, 1923: "Boone is the hard-hitting fly chaser from the Southern League, on whom a good

Ike Boone's Career Statistics

YR	TEAM	LG	G	AB	R	H	2B	3B	HR	RBI	AVG
20	Cedartown	Ga. State	72	290	**63**	**117**	23	10	**10**	NA	**.403**
21	New Orleans	S. Assoc.	156	574	118	223	**46**	27	5	126	**.389**
22	New York	National	2	2	0	1	0	0	0	0	.500
	Toledo	Am. Assoc.	26	88	9	24	5	1	0	13	.273
	Little Rock	S. Assoc.	83	307	60	101	17	10	6	NA	.329
23	San Antonio	Texas	148	600	**134**	**241**	53	**26**	15	**135**	**.402**
	Boston	American	5	15	1	4	0	1	0	2	.267
24	Boston	American	127	481	70	160	29	3	13	95	.333
25	Boston	American	133	476	79	157	34	5	9	68	.330
26	Mission	Pac. Coast	172	626	140	238	55	3	32	137	.380
27	Chicago	American	29	53	10	12	4	0	1	11	.226
28	Portland /Mission	Pac. Coast	166	594	92	210	46	1	9	104	.354
29	Mission	Pac. Coast	198	794	195	**323**	49	8	**55**	218	**.407**
30	Mission	Pac. Coast	83	310	76	139	22	3	22	96	.448
	Brooklyn	National	40	101	13	30	9	1	3	13	.297
31	Brooklyn	National	6	5	0	1	0	0	0	0	.200
	Newark	International	124	469	82	167	33	9	18	92	**.356**
32	Brooklyn	National	13	21	2	3	1	0	0	2	.143
	Jersey City	International	135	491	102	157	29	4	16	95	.320
33	Toronto	International	157	558	100	199	36	7	11	103	.357
34	Toronto	International	136	500	87	186	32	9	6	108	**.372**
35	Toronto	International	130	437	82	153	23	8	9	85	.350
36	Toronto	International	71	169	22	43	8	2	3	22	.254
Major-league totals			355	1,154	175	368	77	10	26	191	.319
Minor-league totals			1,857	6,807	1,362	2,521	477	128	217	1,334	.370

Bold indicates led league.

share of San Antonio's 1923 pennant hopes are planned. He looked as fit as a fiddle in his first work-out and apparently is able to fulfill all the flattering things that have been said about him."

After an 0-for-4 day in the second game of the season, he went on a fifteen-game hitting streak that included a 4-for-5 day in a 19-9 rout of Beaumont on April 30. One day after that streak was broken, he started another, this one of fourteen games, including six straight with at least one extra-base hit. The fifth was on May 10, when he tripled in the bottom of the ninth and trotted home with the winning run on Moke Meyers's single. The sixth was the next day, when he tripled in the first inning, hit an inside-the-park homer in the fourth, doubled in the fifth, and singled in both the seventh and the eighth. His "cycle" topped off an amazing span that boosted his batting average to .449, with eight triples and ten doubles.

But Boone was helping San Antonio with more than just his bat. Twice in the first two months of the season, he made headlines in the local newspapers for defensive plays in left field, including a shoestring grab in the ninth inning of a 2-1 win over Galveston on June 10. He also was installed as one of the judges in an early "Kangaroo court" in the Bears' clubhouse. "The ball players themselves have taken it into their own hands to see that there is no loafing," the Evening News reported early in the season. "A man who does not run out a batted ball or loafs on the bases is subjected to a fine, which consists of a 'treat' for every member of the team. Phil Todt is the bimbo that suggested the idea and now even Phil runs out a foul ball. Bob Coleman, Bob Couchman, Ike Boone and Jim Galloway compose the 'judges' who decide whether a player is guilty of 'laying down on the job.'"

Boone had cooled off to just .387—still good for the league lead—in late June when he hit a home run off Fort Worth spitball pitcher Paul Wachtel (who still holds the league record for career wins) in a 7-3 loss in Fort Worth. That hit started a streak that was not beaten by a Texas League player for almost half a century and has yet to be matched by a San Antonio player—thirty-five straight games with at least one hit. During the streak, Boone hit .542, with eighteen doubles, three triples, and five home runs. In twenty-five of the games, he had two or more hits, including two 4-for-5 days. And as Boone's average soared, so did the Bears, going 22-13 and jumping from fifth place in the eight-team league to within a game of second place.[30]

As the streak lengthened, the newspapers began to notice. After twenty games a box in each morning's Express reported where the streak stood. On July 22, with the streak at twenty-nine, Boone was featured in a five-photo package in the Light, titled "The Mightiest Slugger of Them All." His average at that point was .407; the runner-up in the league was at .368. He tied the record of thirty-three—set in 1922 by

San Antonio's Kedzi Kirkham—in a loss at Fort Worth on July 25. The next day he broke the mark by going 3 for 6 in a 7-6 eleven-inning loss at Wichita Falls.

The streak finally ended on July 27 in the second match of a double-header at Wichita Falls, when Boone went 0 for 2 with a walk in a seven-inning game. "The boys are still talking about the tough luck Boone had in the second game of the doubleheader Friday, when [pitcher Floyd] Wheeler stopped his consecutive games hitting record," the *Express* reported on July 30. "Both of the times the slugger was charged with a time at bat he hit the ball over the fence and the high wind blew it back into the park, so that [outfielder Robert] Bescher could get under it. The second time Bescher had stopped, thinking it a sure homer."

Boone was hitting .419 at the end of the streak, but the inconsistent Bears were struggling to stay in the first division. Even as Boone continued to hit—he had a two-homer day July 31 at Shreveport—the Bears lost seven of ten games on a road trip to Shreveport, Beaumont, and Houston. But then they won eight of nine at home, and a three-game sweep of Dallas at the end of August moved the Bears back into third place.

Eight days later news came that Benson had sold Boone to the Boston Red Sox effective at the end of the Texas League season. On September 15 San Antonio moved into second place with a 7-0 win over Shreveport; Boone went 4 for 4. He was 0 for 4 the next day and left for Boston immediately after the game.

For the season Boone hit .402, making him the only player in the league's modern era (since 1900) to top the .400 mark. He broke league records for hits with 241, total bases with 391, runs with 134, and triples with twenty-six, and he tied the record for doubles with fifty-three. He also led the league with 135 runs batted in. It would be forty-six seasons before his thirty-five-game hitting streak was beaten.[31]

For all his success in the Texas League, though, Ike Boone never made it big in the major leagues. He hit .333 for the Red Sox in 1924 and .330 in 1925, but complaints about his lack of speed led to his release. He played in 29 games for the Chicago White Sox in 1927 and a total of 46 for the Brooklyn Dodgers in 1930–31. His greatest achievements came in the minors. In 1929, playing for the San Francisco–based Mission Reds of the Pacific Coast League, he hit a league-high .407, with 218 runs batted in and 323 hits in a 198-game schedule. He had 553 total bases that season, a record for every level of baseball that still stands today.

In 1934 Boone managed Toronto to the International League pennant while also winning the batting title and the most-valuable-player award. He finished his career with a .370 lifetime batting average in the minors.[32]

And while San Antonio did not win a pennant in 1923, the Bears came closer than they had in years, finishing second. Without Boone, the Bears slumped to fifth in 1924, and during the off-season, Benson died suddenly. His widow, Mabel, took over the club and even attended the annual meetings in Hartford, Connecticut, handling club business as Manager Bob Coleman looked for players. She also oversaw a project her husband had started the year before, moving the team from Block Stadium (which had been renamed League Park after Block sold the club to Benson) to a renovated facility that had served as home of the semipro All-Gold Coffee Giants. The former Broadway Athletic Field, with a variety of improvements, became League Park. Mabel Benson, the first and only woman to run a Texas League club, sold it to a group led by Harry Ables at midseason.[33]

The 1925 Bears had a couple of other noteworthy moments as well on the way to a fourth-place finish. On April 23 the team got a 7-for-7 day from its left fielders when Si Rosenthal hit two home runs and a triple in his first three Texas League at-bats, then yielded the position to Lymon Nason, who had two singles and two triples. Coincidentally, San Antonio won the game with Beaumont 21-1. On May 21, perhaps as incensed by their own team's ineptitude as that of the umpires, San Antonio fans stormed the field during the fifth inning of a game with Fort Worth. After the police restored order, the umpires refused to come back, perhaps also offended by the Bears' incompetence. The Panthers won the game 24-12 and outscored the Bears in a three-game series 72-28.

San Antonio actually finished ahead of Fort Worth in the standings in 1926, as the Panthers' string of seven-straight pennants ended. But

Dallas won the title, ending the season 3½ games ahead of the Bears; Fort Worth was third, 6½ back.

The runner-up finish was a high point for the Bears for seven years—San Antonio did not finish second in the regular-season standings again until 1934, then not again until 1938 and 1940. But that did not mean that the city did not see more than its share of baseball, including some of the greatest personalities in the history of the game.

Characters Coming and Going,

1927–40

BIG-LEAGUE BASEBALL was the nation's passion in the first half of the twentieth century. But since the major leagues were concentrated in the North (with the exception of St. Louis), most of its stars were known to fans only through the pages of the local newspapers.

A spring-training visit from a big-league club—or even an appearance by former big-leaguer in the minors—was enough to pack ballparks from coast to coast. Some of the biggest crowds in San Antonio baseball history came out for just such occasions, including two visits by Babe Ruth and the New York Yankees and an appearance by Dizzy Dean, trying to make it back to the majors with the Tulsa Oilers of the Texas League.

A few fans also were lucky enough to hear legendary stories of the big-leagues first-hand—if a player, manager, umpire, or scout lived in their town. That was the case with George "Cap" Leidy, who spent forty years in baseball, including many in San Antonio. San Antonians were lucky too because Leidy was widely acknowledged as one of the best baseball storytellers around. Leidy had tales to tell about his playing days, which began in 1887. He had stories about men he had managed from Georgia to Texas, from the nineteenth and the twentieth centuries. He could talk for hours about his days as an umpire, his days as a scout, or both.

So it was no wonder that on a cool, clear Saturday afternoon, December 3, 1927, the day of his funeral, virtually everyone connected with professional baseball in San Antonio—as well as some of the city's most powerful men—gathered at the Hagy-McCollum Funeral Chapel and Parlor to share stories about Cap Leidy.

Leidy had undergone surgery the week before at San Antonio's Physicians and Surgeons Hospital and seemed to be recovering. But he died suddenly at 4:00 A.M. on December 1 of heart failure. He was fifty-nine. Word spread quickly since the death occurred during the news cycles of the city's two biggest newspapers, the *Light* and the *Evening News*. The *Light* featured a large current photo of Leidy and a banner headline on its sports page; the *News* had an oval-shaped photo and a three-line headline as well.

The pallbearers were announced the next day. Four of them had played either with Leidy on the San Antonio Bronchos in 1907 or for him when he managed the club to an outright Texas League pennant—the city's only one to that point—in 1908:

- Pat Newnam, the veteran first baseman who was one of the Texas League's first true stars.
- George Wisterzil, who had gone from San Antonio High School in May to the Bronchos in July.
- Billie "Kid" Alexander, who had been in organized ball for twelve years before catching for the 1908 Bronchos.
- Ike Pendleton, who had been traded away from the Bronchos in 1908—to make room for Wisterzil—but always made his home in San Antonio.

The other two were Leidy's protégés, men who had learned about the game from him, pitchers Frank Browning and Clyde Goodwin. The thirty-nine honorary pallbearers included past, present, and future owners of the local Texas League club, the team's veteran groundskeeper, seven doctors, three sportswriters, the president of the Texas League, and one Tyrus R. Cobb, better known as Ty Cobb.[1]

In 1905 Cobb was playing for the Augusta (Georgia) Tourists of the Class-C South Atlantic League, a talented team that was just going through the motions under Manager Andy Roth. Roth was fired at midseason and replaced by Cap Leidy, who immediately earned the players' respect, thanks to eighteen years in the game. Late in one of Leidy's first games with the club, Cobb strolled out to his position in the outfield with a bag of popcorn in his hand. A fly ball came his way—ironically off the bat of his former manager, Roth, now playing for Savannah—and he managed to drop both the popcorn and the fly ball, allowing a run to score.

Leidy, who had recognized Cobb's skills early on, realized the young man needed a little prodding. "I think you can go down in the history books," Cobb later quoted his manager as saying that summer. "I honestly believe that you can go on and have every boy in America idolizing you. But not unless you stop fooling around and keep you eye on the ball every instant." Leidy began to work with Cobb on every aspect of his game, focusing on "place hitting"—putting the ball exactly where he wanted in every at-bat—and the art of bunting. By August Cobb was leading the league in hitting. By the end of the month, he was in the big leagues to stay.[2]

But it was not just the Ty Cobb story getting tossed around at Cap Leidy's funeral. Wisterzil, who had gone on to play in the Federal League—the short-lived third major league—in 1914–15, remembered an early experience under Leidy. "The first thing Cap did was send me to the outfield," the *Express* quoted him as saying. "I never played the outfield and I told him so, but he told me to do the best I can. I was playing alongside of [veteran outfielder and pitcher] Sam Stovall, and the first thing Sam did was to whisper to me, 'Say, kid, you'd better take all you can get today, for I ain't feeling any too good.'"

Once the laughs died down, Morris Block, the cigar-store magnate who owned the Bronchos from 1905–14 and hired Leidy as his manager in 1908, piped up with his story, at the expense of Browning. "Frank and Cap one time planned to go into vaudeville," Block was quoted in the *Express*. "They had rehearsed a number of songs, but the act never went through." A mental picture of Leidy and Browning doing a soft-shoe on some downtown stage probably stirred a few chuckles—they both were barely five feet, six inches tall; tanned to a leathery brown; and suited to little else but baseball.[3]

After he quit managing the Bronchos, Leidy served as an umpire in the East Texas, Western, and Texas Leagues, and he also scouted Texas for a number of big-league clubs—a profession he had perfected through years of on-the-job training.[4] *Light* sports editor Harold Scherwitz noted in one report that in addition to Cobb, Leidy also had discovered and helped develop a number of other big leaguers, including Nap Rucker, who pitched for ten seasons in the majors; Eddie Cicotte, whose brilliant fourteen-year career ended with the Black Sox scandal; and Wee Willie Keeler, perhaps the best place hitter in the game's history and a member of the Baseball Hall of Fame.

Leidy's last job was finding talent for Bears president Harry Ables, who had set the Texas League single-season strikeout record while pitching for Cap in 1910. Ables sent his ace scout on a trip to Florida in the spring of 1926 to look at players in the big-league camps—especially shortstops and third basemen. "But before Cap reached the scene, Ables with [Manager] Honus Mitze connected up with Ray Flaskamper and signed up Kal Segrist, and Cap was called back," the *Express* reported.

It was left up to Fred Mosebach, the *Express* sports editor and one of the honorary pallbearers, to sum up the day: "And so, Cap Leidy has passed from the scene. And while he is gone his spirit still lives, and those who remember him when he piloted the Bronchos to a championship will never forget him."[5]

After the funeral, Leidy's body was shipped back to his hometown of Easton, Pennsylvania, where he was buried in the family plot.

Perhaps the most popular player in early San Antonio baseball history was in the prime of his career in the 1920s. Leo Najo played for the Bears in parts of seven seasons from 1924 to 1932, and his exploits in center field always drew fans to League Park from the city's Hispanic-dominated West Side. And it was no wonder why. "He was really one of the first [Hispanics] to play professional baseball in the area," said Rene Torres, a baseball historian who lives in Brownsville. "It's a story like the Jim Crow laws. It was unheard of to have a minority playing pro ball. It was out of this world to these people."[6]

PALLBEARERS FOR GEORGE "CAP" LEIDY'S FUNERAL, 1927

Pallbearers

Pat Newnam, player, 1908

George Wisterzil, player, 1908

Bill Alexander, player, 1908

Ike Pendleton, player, 1908

Frank Browning, player, 1912–13, 1915, and part of 1916

Clyde Goodwin, player, 1911–13, part of 1914; manager, part of 1914

Honorary pallbearers

C. T. Abbey, rancher

Harry Ables, local franchise president and former pitcher for Leidy

Wilbur P. Allen, former president of Texas League and Austin franchise

W. S. Anderson, Thirty-Seventh District Court judge in San Antonio

Barclay Andrews, local oilman

John Armstrong, rancher

Morris Block, former owner and president of local franchise

Fagan Burch, former San Antonio player

John H. Burleson, chairman of the board, Bexar County Hospital District

W. H. Cade, physician

A. F. Clark, physician

Tyrus R. Cobb, former player under Leidy and future member of the Baseball Hall of Fame

Tom Conner, businessman

Samuel P. Cunningham, local physician

Dick Dunavan, longtime groundskeeper for San Antonio ballparks

Paul Ehlert, owner, X-ray laboratory

E. S. Fomby, owner, Fomby Clothing store

Girard Fraser, co-owner, Fraser Concrete Company

Marvill Gill, sports editor, *San Antonio News*

John W. Goode, physician and secretary-treasurer of the Bexar County Medical Library

PALLBEARERS, CONT.

Francis "Pug" Griffin, Texas League player

Homer H. Hammond, secretary of local franchise

Enoch Jones, merchant and longtime San Antonio resident

Carl Honus Mitze, manager of franchise in San Antonio

Fred Mosebach, sports editor, *San Antonio Express*

Dick Phelan, longtime San Antonio baseball supporter

Burt Ransom, president, Metropolitan Club

J. Doak Roberts, president of the Texas League

Claude Robertson, former player-manager in Dallas

Harold Scherwitz, sports editor, *San Antonio Light*

Otto Sens, former president of Houston franchise

Bernard F. Smith, physician

J. S. Steele, president of the Eye, Ear, Nose, and Throat Hospital

George B. Taliaferro, attorney, president of Commercial National
    Bank, Travis Building and Loan Association

Fred A. Tallmadge, owner of five local cafes and coffee houses

Dick O. Terrell, attorney

Thomas J. Walthall, physician and treasurer of the Eye, Ear, Nose,
    and Throat Hospital

Charles N. Wuest, local businessman

J. L. Yarborough, businessman

But Najo was popular with San Antonio fans for more than one reason. He also was a speedy, superb fielder and a daring baserunner, a leadoff hitter who could get on base and unnerve pitchers. In fact, he earned his nickname—his real surname was Alaniz—because of his quickness. "Najo" was a condensation of the Spanish word for rabbit, *conejo*. He is "Leo Najo" in virtually every newspaper report of the era as well as early Texas League record books.[7]

His speed and ability to cover ground in the outfield was legendary: Twice he stole second, third, and home in the same inning. And in a game in 1928, he recorded an amazing twelve putouts, believed to be a record at the time for center fielders.

Alaniz played 463 games for San Antonio in the Texas League and had a tryout with the Chicago White Sox in 1926. But he broke his leg that spring training and did not make the team. After retiring from professional ball, he played for and managed semipro teams for many more years in Mission, his adopted hometown. Among his former players was Tom Landry, who went on to coach the Dallas Cowboys. Alaniz was in the first group inducted into the Mexican Baseball Hall of Fame, and his memory is kept alive in the Rio Grande Valley by historians like Torres.[8]

In the spring of 1930, perhaps one man in the United States—Pres. Herbert Hoover—was more recognizable than George Herman Ruth. And, as the Babe himself observed, he was having a better year than Hoover anyway.

Weeks after signing a two-year contract for an astronomical eighty thousand dollars a season, Ruth made his second and last appearance in San Antonio. And like everywhere else, he was mobbed wherever he went, including the twenty feet between the curb and the lobby of the Menger Hotel just before 8:00 A.M., when the Yankees' traveling party arrived from the Southern Pacific depot.

Babe Ruth connects for a first-inning home run during his appearance at League Park in 1930. University of Texas at San Antonio Institute of Texan Cultures; illustration no. 0216-H

Box Score from Babe Ruth's Last Game in San Antonio
At League Park, March 31, 1930

NEW YORK					SAN ANTONIO				
Player	*AB*	*R*	*H*	*RBI*	*Player*	*AB*	*R*	*H*	*RBI*
Combs, cf	5	2	1	1	McCullough, 3b	3	1	2	1
Koenig, ss	6	1	2	1	Tate, 3b	1	1	0	0
Ruth, rf	3	4	3	3	Kott, ss	5	0	1	0
Gehrig, 1b	6	2	3	2	Dondero, 2b	4	0	2	2
Lazzeri, 2b	5	2	3	2	Farrell, 1b	4	0	1	1
Byrd, rf	4	0	1	2	Schinkel, lf	4	0	1	0
Chapman, 3b	4	0	1	1	Strain, cf	4	0	0	0
Dickey, c	5	1	3	2	Ballew, rf	2	0	0	0
Wells, p	2	0	0	0	Estell, p	2	0	1	0
Durst, ph	1	0	0	0	Lapan, c	1	0	0	0
Johnson, p	2	1	0	0	Meyers, c	2	1	1	0
Richardson, p	0	0	0	0					
					Collins, ph	1	0	0	0
					Malicky, p	0	0	0	0
					Tucker, ph, rf	3	1	1	0
Totals	**44**	**14**	**18**	**14**		**36**	**4**	**10**	**4**

New York   200 030 207 — 14
San Antonio   100 000 030 — 4

2B—Byrd 2, Gehrig, Ruth. HR—Ruth, McCullough. DP—New York (Lazzeri to Koenig to Gehrig). Sacrifice—Chapman, Ruth. LOB—New York 9, San Antonio 7.

NEW YORK

Pitcher	*IP*	*H*	*R*	*BB*	*SO*
Wells	5	3	1	1	2
Johnson	4	1	3	2	4

SAN ANTONIO

Pitcher	*IP*	*H*	*R*	*BB*	*SO*
Richardson	3	3	2	2	1
Malicky	3	6	3	0	2
Estell	3	9	9	1	1

Umpires—Couchman and Owens. Time—2:15. Attendance—10,000 (est.)

"Huge, immaculate in blue, burned coffee-colored by the sun, the home-run king of professional baseball, in San Antonio for an exhibition game Monday afternoon in which he plays for the New York Yankees against the San Antonio Indians of the Texas League, stood docile under the bombardment of question, greetings and mixed stares of curiosity and admiration," Harold Scherwitz wrote on the front page of the *Light* (in one of the few sports stories, aside from the World Series, that found its way to the front of the Hearst-owned afternoon paper).

"Sorta pester you a little wherever you go, don't they?" he was asked.

Babe's look of cheerful helplessness—maybe that look gave him the name "Babe"—changed for an instant to a broad grin.

"Yeah," he said. "But I like it."[9]

Ruth loved the limelight, and it loved him. There was a reason why he was the highest-paid player in the game, even at the age of thirty-five. He was a showman with a flair for the dramatic, something he displayed on March 31, 1930, in San Antonio.

The Yankees were in the middle of a circuitous series of exhibition games that started in St. Petersburg, Florida, and eventually wound up at Yankee Stadium. It was, as Ruth described it, a collection of one-day jumps—on Sunday they had played a game in Houston, and on Tuesday they were scheduled to play the University of Texas in Austin.

The news had been spreading for months that the Yankees were going to play the local club, which had been renamed the Indians in 1929, in San Antonio. Groups from as far away as Eagle Pass had bought blocks of tickets at League Park, which on a big day could cram in six thousand. But this was not just a big day. The gates opened at 1:00 P.M. for the 3:00 P.M. game, and by the time the Yankees came to bat in the first inning, all the foul ground beyond the bases was roped off for standing room—and filled. "The crowd was a little better than 10,000 paid admissions," the *Light* reported. "How many kids came over the fences can only be guessed. There were plenty. Not enough tickets were printed. The girl at the side gate checked in $57 too much. A lot of people just shoved a dollar at her and pushed on in."[10]

Ruth gave the crowd its money's worth in his first trip to the plate. He came up and asked Indians catcher Pete Lapan about a famous homer that the New York Giants' Mel Ott had hit there during spring training. Lapan pointed out where it had disappeared, just to the right of the scoreboard in the deepest part of the park. "Well, I'm going to crack it over the other side of the board," he was quoted as saying in the *Light*. He did just that.

But Ruth's monster homer to dead center field was not the most noteworthy of his hits that day. That one came in the ninth inning, with details recounted by Scherwitz nine years later in a column. The Indians' roster that season included Tom Estell, one of the few pitchers left in the game who could still throw a spitball legally (when the pitch was banned in the early 1920s, any pitcher using it regularly could register and was allowed to keep using it). Estell sat in the dugout most of the day, bragging about how he could fool the mighty Babe with the spitter. He finally got into the game in the ninth inning. Scherwitz recalled:

> Eventually, Ruth came to bat. Amid some kidding from the bench, Tom prepared to give Babe the works. He brought his glove up before the face, freely dampened the ball behind it, slowly wound up— and let fly.
>
> As he did, to the amazement of the huge throng, he whirled and, locking his hands behind his neck, ran for all his might toward center field.
>
> Ruth leaned into the pitch with all his might, sent a whistling drive straight back. The ball seemed to miss Tom's bowed and fleeing head by about a foot and then began to rise. . . .
>
> When the general hee-haw died down, Estell explained that he knew as soon as the ball left his hand that it wasn't properly delivered and that it wouldn't break. In other words, it was a batting practice pitch to the mightiest ball-buster in the game—and so Tom just got out of the way as fast as he could.

Ruth's line-drive shot never got high enough to leave the park, but it reportedly knocked out a fan standing along the outfield fence. Ruth took second on the ground-rule double, then jogged out to check on the fan.[11]

It was the culmination of a busy day on the field for the Bambino, who also walked twice and singled—and signed hundreds of autographs, many while the game was going on. "In between turns at bat, Ruth stood in left field and autographed baseballs, scorecards, gloves, bits of cardboard, linings of caps, schoolbooks—anything the kids who swirled around him out of the great overflow crowd passed up to him," the *Light* reported. "The Indian batters were considerate and didn't break up his informal outfield parties, only one fly ball coming his way." *Evening News* columnist Marville Gill reported one exception to his generosity.

> We have authoritative advice that the only time Ruth turned down a request for an autograph was the instance in which a small, freckled lad brought out a bank check to be signed.
>
> "That's one I had better not sign, sonny," Ruth stated.

Once the game was over, Ruth and the Yankees returned to the Menger Hotel. His teammates took the evening off, but the Babe had one more obligation—to speak to 2,500 kids, members of the Indians' Knothole Gang. The crowd was so big, the gathering was moved to the brand-new Municipal Auditorium, just blocks from the Menger. After signing hundreds more baseballs at the door, Ruth gave the group a brief talk. "Early to bed, no smoking and no profanity was his admonishment," Fred Maly reported in the *Evening News*. Ruth also encouraged the boys to mind their parents and do their schoolwork. "'In every walk of life, and especially in baseball, one must think fast with the rest of the people,' said Babe."

Ten years later another legend of the game came to San Antonio and played in front of an overflow crowd.

Dizzy Dean had started his baseball career in San Antonio, playing for teams at Fort Sam Houston while serving as, in his own words, "worst soldier in God's livin' world." He was well-known for sneaking off the fort to pitch for small-town teams in the San Antonio area—

that is until his sergeant, an old left-handed pitcher named Jimmy Brought, locked him up in the stockade on the weekends so he could be fresh enough to pitch for Brought's team.[12]

Supposedly, Brought also was the man who gave Jay Hanna Dean his nickname, catching him early one morning peeling potatoes and then throwing them across the basement of the kitchen—at fastball speed—into a pail. "Dean, you dizzy son of a bitch!" Brought yelled when he discovered what his prized pitcher—and buck private—was doing. The name, which fit the flaky kid from Arkansas, fit, and it stuck.[13]

Dean left the army in 1928 and had been spotted by a scout for the St. Louis Cardinals in 1929, when he was playing for the Public Service Utilities semipro team. He dominated the Texas League in 1931 while pitching for Houston, and by 1932 he was in the majors to stay. He had gone on to win twenty games in 1933, thirty in 1934, twenty-eight in 1935, and twenty-four in 1936. He also led the Cardinals' "Gas House Gang" to wins in the World Series in 1931 and 1934.

But at the 1937 All-Star Game in Washington, D.C., things changed forever. The last man he faced in the game, Cleveland outfielder Earl Averill, ripped a line drive right at Diz that hit him squarely on the big toe of his left foot. The ball bounced to Chicago Cubs second baseman Billy Herman, who threw out Averill to end the inning. Little was made of the play in reports on the game, but a check later in the day showed the toe was broken. The doctors told Dean to sit out for three weeks to let it heal. But the Cardinals began to slide in the standings without him, so he was rushed back into the lineup on July 21 at Boston. Unable to use his legs properly, he strained his arm and went just 1-3 the rest of the season, not even going on the team's season-ending road trip.

After a poor spring training in 1938, the Cardinals traded Dean to the Chicago Cubs. He struggled with a sore arm all season and threw nothing but junk balls—his blazing fastball was gone—but still went 7-1 with a 1.88 earned-run average as Chicago won the National League. He tied the New York Yankees in knots in Game Two of the World Series but faded down the stretch and lost 6-3. His arm was worse in 1939, as he went 6-3, and by 1940 there was talk of retirement. Instead he agreed at midseason to move closer to his Dallas home and pitch for the Cubs' affiliate in the Texas League, the Tulsa Oilers.[14]

Baseball and Dizzy Dean had helped the nation survive the Great Depression, and Dean had gained fans from coast to coast—fans who had only heard about him on the radio, read about him in the newspaper, or seen him on newsreels at the movie theaters. A chance to see a real-life legend was too good to pass up. A crowd of more than 7,500 showed up for his first start in Tulsa. In Dallas 5,631 turned out, about 4,631 more than usually showed up for the Rebels' games. In Houston it was 7,300 fans, and in Shreveport more than 8,000 went to the ballpark.

But the biggest of all was in San Antonio on August 2. The newspapers started the buzz early in the week as it became apparent that Dean would be making a start against San Antonio, which had changed its nickname to the Missions in 1933 and its home park to Tech Field in 1932. His opponent, Bob Muncrief, was looking for his twentieth win of the season. Muncrief and teammate Maury Newlin—who wound up winning a league-high twenty-three games that year—were the main reason San Antonio was headed for its fourth straight playoff appearance. And while having a good team was one way to draw fans, having Dizzy Dean on the mound was even better.

Still the showman, Dean posed for a photo with five-year-old Pinkey Whitney Jr. to run in the *Light* the day of the game, he and the little boy in identical positions, pitching from the stretch. "I'm taking pointers from him," Dean kidded. "Look at that form. A future big leaguer [for] sure."

Hundreds were waiting outside the gates when they opened at 5:00 P.M. By 6:00 P.M. hundreds were already in the seats. By 7:30 all the tickets were sold. There were 7,042 paid admissions, 4,804 women admitted for free (actually, they were charged the ticket tax on ladies' day), and 110 pass-holders for a total gate of 11,956—the biggest crowd to ever see a baseball game at Tech Field and the third-largest crowd to ever see a game in San Antonio. The total included "none of the concession employees, ground keepers, ushers, baseball writers, etc., and does not include the many that scooted over the fences behind the overflow crowd," the *Light* reported. There were so many people in the park, the start of the game was delayed by almost a half hour.

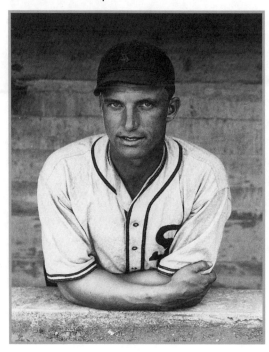

Bob Muncrief won twenty games in 1940 and was the Texas League Pitcher of the Year. But the biggest crowd of the season showed up on the night he pitched against Dizzy Dean. University of Texas at San Antonio Institute of Texan Cultures; illustration no. 0989

Fans sat in foul ground and were ten deep along the entire outfield fence—any ball hit into the crowd on the fly or the ground was ruled a ground-rule double. "I had never seen anything like it," said Missions catcher Sam Harshaney. "That was the biggest crowd I had ever been around."[15]

Dean gave up more than his share of San Antonio's seven "crowd-rule" doubles, allowing ten hits and five runs in five innings. Muncrief gave up eleven hits, but he pitched a complete game and got a 7-3 win.

Diz was pictured on the front of the *Light*'s sports section the next day, looking dejected in the Tulsa dugout. "It makes me mad," he told the *Light*. "I'd like to do better for all these people." The paper's sports editor Harold Scherwitz was not impressed. "The name of Dean still pulls them into the parks, and Diz still knows HOW to pitch, but that sidearm stuff he's throwing is the bunk. It has no speed, and a good ball club, unimpressed by the great man's game, can punch holes in the fences hitting against him."

Dean pitched just twice more in the big leagues, then went on to a legendary career as a broadcaster. And what of Bob Muncrief? He finished the 1940 season with twenty-two wins, the most in his professional career, and was promoted to the majors in 1941. He was 80-82 in twelve seasons.

Between the visits of the Babe Ruth and Dizzy Dean to San Antonio, the nation was battling to come out of the Great Depression. But for San Antonio, in many ways, it turned out to be the best years in the city's pro-baseball history.

Depression Ball,
1932–42

THE GREAT DEPRESSION hit baseball hard as disposable income—and crowds—dwindled. Attendance in the Texas League dropped from 828,091 in 1929 to 690,874 in 1930, and it sagged all the way to 522,512 three years later. The majors were no better off—the mighty New York Yankees drew just 8,826 a game in 1935, and from 1930 to 1939 the St. Louis Browns averaged more than 2,000 fans a game just in one season. San Antonio's attendance sank as well, with the Indians (so renamed in 1929) and Missions (starting in 1932) going from 106,517 fans in 1928 to just 31,761 in 1932.[1]

Still, the depression was good to San Antonio in some ways. A couple of players with longtime connections to the city started their careers during this period. Attendance started to climb after bottoming out in 1933. And the team made the playoffs six times from 1933 to 1940 and won the title in 1933, the most successful period in San Antonio pro-baseball history. But it almost ended before it began.

Perhaps Ellen Flaskamper should have stayed a little longer at League Park on the evening of June 18, 1932. During the Saturday afternoon game between the San Antonio Indians and the Dallas Steers, the wife of Indians infielder Ray Flaskamper stamped out a small fire in one of the box seats at the ballpark. It was not the first blaze at the stadium, which was built almost entirely of wood and had been the home of the Texas League club since 1925. It had taken a bucket brigade to save the press box during the summer of 1930.

But a bucket brigade was not going to save League Park this day. The first alarm came in to the San Antonio Fire Department at 6:47 P.M., barely an hour after the day's game had ended in front of a crowd of five hundred. The two newspapers with Sunday editions, the *Light* and the *Express,* had differing reports on who made the first call to firefighters—one reported it came from a neighbor across the street, while the other said it was from a worker at a soft-drink stand next door. In any case, Marville Gill, the team secretary, was the only person left in the stadium. He scooted out of his office upon spotting the flames, though not before stashing the day's gate receipts and team records in a safe. (They later were recovered, soggy but usable, by firemen from nearby Fort Sam Houston.)[2] Groundskeeper Chick Alvarez and former player George Bischoff spotted the fire early enough to race to the club-houses and rescue most of the teams' uniforms and equipment.

Three minutes after the fire was reported, it had spread throughout the wooden grandstands, which were topped with a freshly tarred roof. At the fire's height, flames and smoke could be seen for miles, and a crowd estimated at twenty thousand—bigger than any that had ever been inside the park—milled around the neighborhood, watching the spectacle and making it difficult for more fire crews to get to the burning structure.

Strong winds from the southeast spread sparks toward nearby Brackenridge Park, endangering the sets at the outdoor theater and leading to an impromptu bucket brigade at the Brackenridge Park Tourist Court, where a large tree caught fire. Grass fires were doused up to a quarter mile from the stadium.

Most residents in the area around the stadium soaked down the wood-shingle roofs on their houses with water hoses. But the closest neighbor did not have time. "So rapid was the spread of the fire to the home of John Boehler, 204 Isleta Street adjacent to the park, that Mrs. Boehler and her daughter had time to save only a bird cage before fleeing for their lives," the *Light* reported. "Their home was destroyed at a loss of about $3,400." Luckily, it was the only home destroyed that day. Even more fortunate, no one was hurt, though the other losses were spelled out two days later in the *Light*: "Sunday and Monday check-ups disclosed that, among the fire losses, were all the bats of the Dallas baseball club, half a dozen spare pair of uniform pants belonging to the Indians, two pair of shoes belonging to [San Antonio catcher Arthur] Bradbury, the typewriter owned by 'Kid' Reyes, La Prensa sports writer, and the scorebook belonging to The Light in which all the official scores of the first third of the season were kept."

One survivor was the Western Union ticker, which was in the team's offices under the stands. The solid-as-a-tank steel contraption, which produced a steady stream of scores and news on ticker tape during normal use, was still clicking away the morning after the fire, sitting amid the smoking rubble.[3]

The park was a total loss—estimated at just under sixty thousand dollars—and club president Homer Hammond had only thirty-three thousand dollars in insurance. Hammond, who had been losing his shirt with the team since he bought it from Harry Ables in 1929, kept the schedule going by playing the Sunday game at Eagle Field, a small ballpark next to Brackenridge High School, then making a deal with the school district to finish the season at Tech Field. (The headline on the story of the move in the *Evening News,* in an era before political correctness, was "Tribe Pitches Tepee on New Camping Ground.") Tech Field was the athletic facility of the newly designated San Antonio School of Technology, which was the successor to San Antonio High, the city's first public high school. The field had been built in the vicinity of one of the city's first minor-league stadiums, Electric Park, and near the San Pedro Springs.

While it had a certain pedigree—one of the first games played under artificial lights in Texas had been contested at Electric Park in 1897—Tech Field was not anywhere close to League Park. The grandstands held less than four thousand spectators and were built in the wrong corner of the property, forcing fans to look into the sun during afternoon games. In addition, they were topped by a metal roof that resounded like artillery fire under foul balls. The team had to work around the school's athletic schedule, pushing back game times during the spring and fall. But worst of all, the right-field fence was barely two hundred feet from home plate. To prevent a farce like Corsicana's 51-3 rout of Texarkana in 1902—played in a similarly undersized park in Ennis—the Indians' management placed a marker in right-center field. Any ball hit over the fence to the right of the post would be a ground-rule double; to the left was still a home run.[4]

It stayed that way until 1935, when the school board coughed up fifty thousand dollars, and Tech Field essentially was torn down and rebuilt in the sixty days before the start of the season. A crowd of ten thousand schoolkids crammed into the new park for its dedication. Hammond had unloaded the team by then, and the new owners, the St. Louis Browns, had little interest in spending money on the club during the depression. With skittish neighbors insisting that any replacement for League Park be constructed with far-less-flammable steel and concrete, the team wound up playing at Tech Field through 1946; a new park, Mission Stadium, opened in 1947.

San Antonio was lucky in one way in 1932—a similar fire had wiped out the ballpark in Shreveport earlier in the season, but instead of finding temporary quarters, the franchise simply picked up and moved to Tyler.[5] The source of the League Park fire was never pinned down, but firefighters blamed it on either a cigarette or a match dropped under the stands during the game.

Too bad Ellen Flaskamper was not there to stomp it out too.

The 1933 season brought even more changes. Following a trend started by the St. Louis Cardinals, a major-league organization bought the San Antonio franchise from the local owners, and with the sale came the promise of at least a few good "farm" players. But it was the other St. Louis club—the hapless Browns—who bought the team. Even during the early 1930s, the Browns were famous for their ineptitude. Since finishing second to the New York Yankees—by one game—in 1922, St. Louis had been pretty much on the skids, trailing the American League pennant winners by double digits every year, including an amazing 50½ games behind the 1927 Yankees. So San Antonio was not exactly ready to hold a welcoming parade for the new owners that spring (the Browns cooperated by not coming to the city for spring training until 1937).

But the Browns did bring a couple of improvements to their new organization. First, the St. Louis management assigned L. C. McEvoy as president of the team. McEvoy, who was a devout Catholic, decided the team needed some divine inspiration. He dumped Indians as a nickname and reached way back into local baseball history—back to 1895 and before—for a new name: Missionaries, Missions for short.[6] San Antonio's 1895 team had been one of the worst in local history, finishing 21-72 and employing six different managers, including two named Gus. But there had been a series of successful semipro teams in San Antonio nicknamed the Missions, and after the 1932 season, the town needed all the change it could get (the inept Indians finished 57-91, 41½ games out).

McEvoy, in addition to his religious bent, had a little better nucleus of a team than previous owner Homer Hammond, who had the bad luck of taking over the club from Harry Ables just before the stock market crashed in 1929. McEvoy had a handful of players under contract to the Browns and picked up several more Texas League veterans to fill out the roster.

The Browns also brought in a new manager, former big-league catcher Hank Severeid. Severeid had broken into the majors in 1911 with the Reds, not long after most of his players were born, and had played in 1,390 games, almost all of them with the Browns. (Somehow, fate shone on Severeid, though. In 1926, his final season in the majors, he was traded to the Yankees.) He even made a few playing appearances for his San Antonio club, though his legendary ability to jerk the ball down the left-field line at Tech Field produced only a .233 batting average. He was much more valuable to the team in the dugout, where his big-league experience could command respect from the five Missions who already had been to the big leagues as well as the collection of younger players on the roster.

Among the veterans were pitcher Hal Wiltse, who had played parts of four seasons with the Boston Red Sox, Philadelphia Phillies, and the Browns, and Larry Bettencourt, who had been with the Browns in 1931–32. San Antonio also had Charlie "Cholly" Engle, who had been with the Philadelphia A's in 1925–26 and the Pittsburgh Pirates in 1930, and Everett "Pid" Purdy, who had been with the Chicago White Sox in

1926 and the Cubs in 1927–29. The club had several young players on the way to the majors as well—nineteen-year-old infielder Harlond Clift, twenty-three-year-old pitcher Jim Elton Walkup, and twenty-five-year-old second baseman Ollie Bejma among them.

One player who fit into both categories was pitcher Fabian Kowalik, who had pitched for San Antonio in 1931–32 and was called up for two games with the Chicago White Sox in 1932. Kowalik, who was twenty-five in 1933, was the only big-leaguer ever from Falls City, a small Polish-American town forty miles southeast of San Antonio. And the right-hander had the season of his life for the Missions in 1933.

Actually, a number of the Missions had career-best seasons in 1933, which was one of the main reasons the team surged from the second division into the Texas League's first Shaughnessy playoffs. The Shaughnessy system was devised by Frank Shaughnessy, the president of the International League, to boost interest in games during the dark early days of the depression. It matched a league's first-place team against the fourth-place team and second against third in a best-of-five first round, with the winners from those series playing a best-of-seven series for the pennant.[7]

Fabian Kowalik of Falls City helped lead the Missions to the Texas League pennant in 1933. University of Texas at San Antonio Institute of Texan Cultures; illustration no. 0116-B

Kowalik was 21-13 during the regular season, from all indications his career high. Purdy roared back in August to hit .358 and win the league batting title (preventing Dallas's Zeke Bonura from claiming the hitting "triple crown"). Bejma and Cap Crossley tied for the league lead in doubles at forty-eight each. Walkup topped the league in strikeouts with 146, despite not being a regular member of the pitching rotation.

Even though they finished fourth, the Missions were definitely the league's hottest team heading into the postseason. The last day of the regular season, they pounded Beaumont 9-3 and 11-4 at Tech Field in an afternoon and evening of adventures. Crossley, the team's regular right fielder, played every position on the field in the first game, then pitched a complete game in the second—a game that also saw him come up with four doubles in four at-bats. Bejma went 6 for 8 in the two games, with six runs batted in, three doubles, and a home run. Purdy, who had struggled to even find a job in the off-season, went 3 for 4 in the first game to clinch the batting title, then sat out the second.[8]

Severeid made sure he had his best pitcher, Kowalik, ready for the first playoff game in Houston, and Kowalik spread out nine Houston hits to deliver a 3-1 victory. Wiltse gave up six hits in beating the Buffs 4-1 the next night in a game that saw the Missions wind up acting as a police force for umpire Frank Coe.

Coe ejected Houston manager Casey Selph in the ninth inning, and the Buffs' fans responded by littering the field with seat cushions and soda bottles. "After the game the crowd swarmed on the field with apparent mob spirit," the *Daily Express* reported. "The San Antonio players, led by Pid Purdy and Manager Hank Severeid, raced into the mob to protect Coe from possible injury. Many pop bottles were thrown but none touched Coe, who never flinched and displayed iron nerve."

The Missions returned to San Antonio to discover that extra seats had been erected at Tech Field, increasing capacity to an estimated five thousand (San Antonio had one of the smaller parks in the league and apparently griped about it—to no avail—to the Browns all season.) San Antonio finished off Houston 10-5 in Game Three, with Abe Miller surviving a three-run first inning by the Buffs to get the win (not sur-

1933 ROSTER

Missions with major-league experience, either before or after 1933:

Hal Wiltse, pitcher: Boston Red Sox, 1926–28; St. Louis Browns, 1928; Philadelphia Phillies, 1931.

Tommy Heath, catcher: St. Louis Browns, 1935, 1937–38.

Ollie Bejma, second base: St. Louis Browns, 1934–36; Chicago White Sox 1939.

Jim Elton Walkup, pitcher: St. Louis Browns, 1934–39; Detroit Tigers, 1939.

Larry Bettencourt, outfielder: St. Louis Browns, 1928, 1931–32.

Fred Tauby, third base: Chicago White Sox, 1935; Philadelphia Phillies, 1937.

Harlond Clift, infielder: St. Louis Browns, 1934–43; Washington Senators, 1943–45.

Cholly Engle, shortstop: Philadelphia Athletics, 1925–26; Pittsburgh Pirates, 1930.

Fabian Kowalik, pitcher: Chicago White Sox, 1932; Chicago Cubs, 1935–36; Philadelphia Phillies, 1936; Boston Braves, 1936.

Pid Purdy, outfielder: Chicago White Sox, 1926; Chicago Cubs 1927–29.

prisingly, Houston had opposed the idea of the Shaughnessy playoffs in 1933, and the club would continue to fight the idea for years). A crowd of 6,295, the biggest of the season, packed into Tech Field to see the game; hundreds more were turned away.

The championship round started two days later in front of 6,319 at Tech Field, and Galveston took a 2-0 lead through the first 6½ innings. But San Antonio exploded for seven runs in the bottom of the seventh, and Kowalik—by now the "Falls City Flash" in the newspapers—got the victory.

Yet another record crowd, this time 6,659, saw Wiltse shut down the Buccaneers 5-1 in Game Two. The teams went to Galveston—where the only thing more numerous than the mosquitoes in the damp evening air was the steady stream of abuse from the fans—and the Buccaneers won the next two games, 6-5 and 7-0.

Kowalik—pitching to his manager for the second time in the post-season—earned his third-straight victory in the playoffs the next night, as San Antonio won 2-1. "Kowalik was magnificent in winning his twenty-fourth game of the season," wrote Harold Scherwitz of the *Light*. "He allowed five hits, all singles, and pitched out of three holes. Ollie Bejma's sparkling work around second saved him from another, in a shaky fifth inning in which a walk and two hits gave Galveston its lone run."

Then, for the first time in local newspaper history, the ball club jumped onto the front pages. "San Antonio Missions Win League Pennant Beat Bucs 12 to 5," the *Express* declared the next morning. "Champions For First Time in 25 Years." The *Evening News* was only slightly less bold, proclaiming "Missions Win Texas League Championship Flag" across the top of the sports page that afternoon.

Wiltse got the win in front of another record crowd, this time more than eight thousand fans. The newspapers were practically breathless over the team's first pennant since 1908 and first-ever trip to the Dixie Series, a best-of-seven showdown against the champion of the Southern Association.

"Hooray! Who says the 'good old days' are not back again?" wrote *Evening News* columnist Jack O'Brien.

> Not since the memorable days of Cap. Leidy has this town sniffed the aroma of the throne room of baseball.
>
> The remarkable part of the Missions' victory is that they did it practically under their own power, without aid from the parent organization, the St. Louis Browns.
>
> Many a time, HELP, in a big way, was needed, but when hurling help and a first baseman were needed, St. Louis fired back the 'sorry-can't-help-you' line.
>
> A less hardy ball club would have folded under the pressure, but 'Pa Hank' Severeid, the ol' skipper himself, builded [*sic*] himself a machine of co-operating ballplayers who went out to win, in spite of St. Louis.[9]

Daily Express writer Ward Burris got in his own "I-told-you-so" the day after the pennant-clinching victory:

Since the first game in Houston, the writer has been anxious to call your attention to the "shot heard 'round the world" in the series. The score was 0-0 in the first game, Payne and Kowalik. Fred Tauby drove a home run over the left field fence for the first score of the series and it started San Antonio on the way.

From that moment on Houston was a whipped baseball club. From that moment on the Mission power accelerated and became the talk of the South. Had that first home run, with a 0-0 score, come from a Houston bat, the story might have been different.[10]

After the first Texas League pennant in twenty-five years, the Dixie Series did not seem quite as significant, though even more temporary seats were added to Tech Field to accommodate a crowd of ten thousand. Kowalik won for the fourth time in the playoffs in Game One, spreading out nine hits in a 3-1 victory against Andy Messenger, who had survived on some of the worst San Antonio teams of the 1920s. But Kowalik came up with a sore leg after the game. New Orleans beat Wiltse the next night when Bettencourt dropped what should have been the final out in the ninth inning, eventually allowing three unearned runs to score in a 7-4 loss.

The Missions won the final game in San Antonio, 6-3, but Texas League president J. Alvin Gardner got the locals worked up when he called San Antonio the "cheapest" city in baseball because of the small turnout at Tech Field, just thirty-two hundred. Considering the contest had been matched against a well-attended high school football game—and the Missions wound up topping one hundred thousand in attendance for the year, including the playoffs—the newspapers spent more than a little ink grousing about Gardner, especially after a crowd of two thousand showed up in New Orleans. "Looks like Prexy Gardner will have to add New Orleans to his list," Ward Burris cracked. "Those who were at the circus yesterday in the rain will not agree with Alvin Gardner in his statement that San Antonio is a cheap town and always has been. They rather agree with the writer in his statement made time and again, that if it's a good show and priced right, San Antonio will go and pay money to see it. If it is not, they will stay away in numbers."[11]

A limping Kowalik gave up two home runs to the Pelicans' Eddie Rose in Game Four as New Orleans—playing in the daytime for the first time in the series—won 5-2. Wiltse lost by the same score the next day, and the Pelicans finished off the series with a 2-0 win over Abe Miller.

Still, the team's first trip to the Dixie Series started a string of playoff appearances for San Antonio. The club fell to Galveston in the league championship series the next year, lost to Oklahoma City in the first round in 1937, lost to Beaumont in the league championship series in 1938, lost to Dallas in the first round in 1939, and fell to Beaumont in the first round in 1940. The run of four straight playoff appearances from 1937 to 1940 is the only time in San Antonio history that the team has made the postseason four years in a row, and six playoff teams from 1931 to 1940 marks the most successful period in local baseball history.

One of the reasons for that success was a husky young catcher from St. Louis named Sam Harshaney. In the spring of 2000, he was one of the few remaining members of the Missions of the 1930s. Even at the age of ninety, his mind was sharp, full of vivid details about his days on the ball field. He remembered opening day in 1935, when he hit a grand slam for the Missions but had it wiped out when thunderstorms arrived before the end of the fifth inning, after which the game would be official. In those days the first player of the season to homer for the Missions won an assortment of prizes, from cash to cigars. Because the game was not official, however, he missed out on the big package. "The headline in the Light next day, right above my picture, was 'Hard Luck Harshaney,'" he recalled with a chuckle.

He also remembered his days as a minor-league player-manager after World War II. Harshaney would teach school in San Antonio—which he adopted as his hometown after his third term with the Missions in 1946—until the last week of May, then take off for Harlingen, Brownsville, or San Angelo and manage a Class D club for the summer. Come September 1, he was back in San Antonio, ready for another school year. "I don't think I had a day off for six years," he said.

Sam Harshaney's lifetime in baseball began in the 1920s, growing up in Madison, Illinois, just across the Mississippi River from St. Louis. He spent more than his share of time at Sportsman's Park, home to both the Cardinals of the National League and the Browns of the

American League. Even when he graduated from high school—going sixteen miles up the road to Shurtleff College in Edwardsville, Illinois—he was a regular at the ballpark. That is, on days when he was not crushing the ball for the Shurtleff squad.

In the spring of 1934, the Browns' front office heard about Harshaney's skills and offered him a tryout. "They issued me a uniform and they hit me some ground balls," he said. "They apparently were pretty impressed." The Browns offered him a contract on the spot. But before he could sign, he had to check with his college coach. "He said 'Sam, do you like baseball?'" Harshaney said. "I said 'I eat baseball.' He said 'Well, I think you need to follow your wishes.'" Harshaney signed, and the Browns assigned him to their Class A affiliate, the San Antonio Missions, as an outfielder. "For that, they paid me the magnificent sum of $150 a month," he said with a chuckle.

He earned it. In one of his first games, Harshaney was in the outfield for an exhibition game against the University of Texas at Clark Field on the UT campus. Clark Field was an adventure for outfielders, especially visitors. Center field ended rather abruptly with a gravel-sided cliff less than 360 feet from home plate, and balls hit on top of "Billy Goat Hill" were still in play. "One day a guy hit a fly ball out to me, and I was running hard to get it—and I ran straight into that hill," Harshaney said. "I didn't even see it. I was following the flight of the ball. I wound up pulling pebbles out from under my skin. But they really appreciated me going out there and running into that hill." The *San Antonio Light* saw it just a little differently: "Viebig got a homer and so did Priebisch when the latter's drive landed on top of a cliff and outfielder Harshaney, chasing it, knocked himself cold by running into said cliff."[12]

By opening day, Missions manager Severeid was talking about making Harshaney a third baseman. Instead, the young player sat on the bench as the Missions opened the season against Galveston at Tech Field, which actually was filled and had fans literally hanging on for dear life to see the game.

Just outside the infamously short right-field fence, in the yard of one of the ballpark's neighbors, was a sprawling live oak tree. On game days the family that owned the house would collect money from fans

Sam Harshaney's Statistics
(Major League Numbers in Italics)

YEAR	TEAM	LEAGUE	GAMES	AB	R	H	2B	3B	HR	RBI	AVG.
1934	San Antonio	Texas	128	418	70	135	32	4	10	84	.323
1935	San Antonio	Texas	143	508	77	147	39	5	5	70	.289
1936	San Antonio	Texas	135	457	80	148	25	3	14	77	.324
1937	San Antonio	Texas	99	299	61	93	14	2	11	59	.311
1937	*St. Louis*	*American*	*5*	*11*	*0*	*1*	*0*	*0*	*0*	*0*	*.091*
1938	*St. Louis*	*American*	*11*	*24*	*2*	*7*	*0*	*0*	*0*	*0*	*.292*
1938	Toronto	International	68	132	7	30	3	0	1	13	.227
1939	Toronto	International	44	122	14	40	5	0	1	18	.328
1939	*St. Louis*	*American*	*42*	*145*	*15*	*35*	*2*	*0*	*0*	*15*	*.241*
1940	*St. Louis*	*American*	*3*	*1*	*0*	*0*	*0*	*0*	*0*	*0*	*.000*
1940	San Antonio	Texas	92	294	41	98	16	4	4	30	.333
1941	Toledo	Am. Assoc.	71	181	34	45	4	0	0	19	.249
1946	Toledo	Am. Assoc.	9	22	0	9	0	0	0	0	.409
1946	San Antonio	Texas	27	52	3	14	4	0	0	5	.269
1947	Austin	Big State	106	317	51	93	13	1	6	48	.293
1948	Del Rio	Longhorn	101	329	55	119	27	3	7	76	.362
1949	San Angelo	Longhorn	103	275	52	89	18	2	7	58	.324
1950	Harlingen	Rio Grande Valley	119	409	88	141	22	1	16	93	.345
Minor league totals			1,245	3,815	633	1,201	222	25	82	650	.315
Major league totals			61	181	17	43	2	0	0	15	.238
Career totals			1,306	3,996	650	1,244	224	25	82	665	.311

to sit in it—the higher the perch, the more expensive, with seats starting at a nickel each. (Tickets to get into Tech Field ranged from one dollar for box seats for men and sixty cents for women to twenty-five cents for kids to sit anywhere.)

Beyond the left-field fence was a big frame house owned by, as Harshaney put it, "a good ol' Texas gal" named Goldthorp. Every summer Goldthorp would rent rooms in the house to five or six San Antonio ballplayers, including Harshaney. "The family always had season passes to the ballpark, just for the inconvenience of baseballs landing in the yard all the time," he said. "They always had good seats in the grandstands"—in the noisy-but-shady box seats, no doubt.[13]

Harshaney started the season on the bench, behind a young third baseman named Carl Dorley and an outfield that returned intact from 1933. In fact, he did not even appear in a game until a week into the season, and then just as a pinch hitter. Two days later Severeid used his strong arm to pitch 1⅔ innings in relief during a blowout loss to Houston.

It was not until the end of May that he got his chance. With regular right fielder Mel Mazzera "ailing with a charley horse," Harshaney got his first start. He went 2 for 4 and drove in two runs in an 11-7 loss to Oklahoma City. Mazzera's leg did not improve over the next few days, and Harshaney seized the opportunity to move into the everyday lineup. Two days later, on May 25, he went 4 for 5 and scored four runs in a 19-5 romp over Tulsa. "Sam Harshaney, subbing for Mazzera in right, had the big Ladies Night crowd on his side from the start, and they went wild as he slashed out the line safeties," the *Light* reported. Mazzera's "charley horse" wound up being his downfall. By the end of June, Harshaney was hitting .421 and Mazzera just .226, and Sam was in the lineup for good.

Harshaney wound up playing 128 games, almost all in the outfield, and hit a team-high .323, with ten homers and eighty-four runs batted in. One of those home runs was particularly well timed. On July 14 he hit a two-run shot in the ninth inning to tie a game 11-11 at Tulsa. Four innings later an Oklahoma dust storm blew through town, and the game had to be stopped. It eventually was declared a tie, significant because the Missions wound up the regular season tied with Galveston for first place. They won their first-round playoff series, then lost to the Buccaneers in the championship series. "The last day of the season . . . [Severeid] paid me a big compliment in front of the team," Harshaney said. "He came into the clubhouse and gave me a personal tribute for the season I had. That meant a lot coming from an old war horse. It turned out to be a very enjoyable year."

The 1934 season also earned him mention from *The Sporting News,* which offered him fifty dollars or a set of golf clubs in exchange for an autographed bat. "Of course, the money was a whole lot more impor-tant than a set of golf clubs in 1934," he said. "You couldn't eat golf clubs. And they gave me a couple more bats anyway."

Harshaney made a major career change following that season. While on a barnstorming tour—as a way to stretch his moneymaking power into the fall—he took over behind the plate when the team's catcher quit. The next spring the Browns' general manager came to him during spring training with an offer. "He said they would buy me some catching equipment and give me a $50 [a month] raise if I'd go into catching," Harshaney recalled. "Heck, for that $50, I'd have cleaned up the grandstands for them." In 1937 he made it to the big leagues as a catcher. He wound up playing in sixty-one games for the Browns between 1937 and 1940.

After World War II, Harshaney earned a master's degree and began working as a coach and physical-education teacher—and a minor-league manager during the summer. In his last year as a player-manager, he hit .345 for Harlingen—at the age of forty—and retired with a professional career average of .311. He taught school and coached youth teams for years afterward. He participated in a dozen old-timers' games and still was promoting the game and remembering his days as a player and a manager years later. Sam Harshaney died in February, 2001, two months short of his ninety-first birthday. "I was looking forward to making it to the millennium, and I did," he had said the previous summer.[14]

The 1934 Missions went deep into the playoffs again, beating Beaumont in the first round before falling to Galveston in six games in the league championship series. The star was a pitcher from Texas A&M named Ash Hillin, who won twenty-four games and was the Texas League pitcher of the year. He also won the first and last games of the series with Beaumont and the second game of the championship series.

The next season San Antonio slumped to 75-84 and missed the postseason. The Missions were also on the losing end of the first perfect game in Texas League history, pitched by Tulsa's Al Shealy on June 23. But there were still highlights that season, including Sam Harshaney's only hit of the night on June 2—a single in the bottom of the twenty-first inning that scored Cholly Engle and beat Dallas 4-3.

San Antonio again made the postseason in 1937, but the Missions were eliminated by Oklahoma City. Hillin, who had moved to Oklahoma City after three years with San Antonio, beat his former team in the playoff opener and lost the third game. Hillin, who won thirty-one games and appeared in sixty-seven, was again the Texas League pitcher of the year.

The Missions came within one out of their second title in the decade the following season, taking a 3-2 lead into the bottom of the ninth of Game Seven in Beaumont (San Antonio led the series 3-2, with one tie). But the Exporters' Frank Croucher hit a two-run homer to give Beaumont a 4-3 win, and they clinched the championship the next day with a 3-2 victory.

Tech Field was the site of the Third Texas League All-Star Game in 1939, with the North defeating the South 7-2 in front of a crowd of 8,998. The Missions made the playoffs again, but after winning the first two games of their best-of-five series with Dallas, they lost three in a row.[15]

San Antonio had two of the best pitchers in the league in 1940, Bob Muncrief and Maury Newlin, but the Missions were swept out of the playoffs in the first round by Beaumont.

It was not apparent at the time, but a significant period in San Antonio baseball history ended in the spring of 1941. On April 1 the St. Louis Browns and Boston Braves wrapped up spring training and headed north on a barnstorming tour. They were the last two teams to conduct spring training in San Antonio. The day before, the New York Yankees' Joe DiMaggio gave the city a hint of what was to come that season, going 5 for 5 with three triples as the Yankees beat the Missions 16-4. That game also might have been a sign for the local franchise—the Missions finished last, with a record of 58-96. But in 1942, the last year before the league shut down for World War II, the Missions made their fifth playoff appearance in six years. Beaumont eliminated them four games to two in the first round.

Life Changes after the War,
1946–56

JUST ELEVEN DAYS after the end of World War II, directors of the Texas League voted in Dallas to resume play for the 1946 season.

The war had scrambled the league, with most teams starting over from scratch with their rosters. San Antonio had the added difficulty of being a lame-duck team at Tech Field when it was sold, to be demolished after the 1946 season. But baseball-starved fans packed the old ballpark one last time, setting a franchise attendance record of 295,103 for the year, almost double the previous mark. They also turned out in force to see San Antonian Ruth Lessing play for Fort Wayne against Peoria in an All-American Girls Professional Baseball League exhibition game.

The Browns—who made the World Series for the only time in their history in 1945—managed to put together a solid team for San Antonio in 1946, and the Missions finished third in the league, though losing to eventual champion Dallas in the first round of the playoffs. The Missions continued to be successful in the early 1950s, including the franchise's only Dixie Series title in 1950.

The war had started the country—and baseball—toward integration, though the Texas League would not have its first African American player until 1952 and San Antonio would not have its first until the

Fans sit on folding chairs and makeshift bleachers for the opening day at Mission Stadium, 1947. University of Texas at San Antonio Institute of Texan Cultures; illustration no. 3644

next season. By then, though, the advent of televised baseball and air conditioning had started the minors on a descent that nearly killed them. But there was no sign of decline on opening day, 1947.

When Al LaMacchia hurried to the mound—and he was famous for hurrying anytime he was on the diamond—on the sunny afternoon of April 18, 1947, he was greeted by a crowd of more than four thousand people who had come out to see the San Antonio Missions and Beaumont Exporters. Among them were several hundred in folding chairs, several hundred more on lawn chairs and blankets, and at least a few dozen straddling girders and wearing hard hats.

The Missions had played their last game at Tech Field on September 16, 1946, topping off a season of record turnout with another 15,416 fans for three playoff games. But the postwar boom that boosted attendance throughout baseball was going to have to continue elsewhere.

During the 1946 season, the San Antonio Independent School District, which owned Tech Field, sold the property to the City Transit Authority for a bus yard and maintenance complex. And transit needed the land sooner rather than later.

Plans called for the city to provide $200,000 and the St. Louis Browns, which owned the Missions, another $100,000 to build a facility south of Alamo Stadium, not far from the site of old League Park.[1] But the deal fell through. Instead the Browns had to go it alone, coming up with a reported $700,000 to build what would—eventually—be one of the finest minor-league facilities in the country, Mission Stadium, at Mitchell Street and Mission Road south of downtown.

Because of these delays, the stadium was not ready when the team arrived in town from spring training. It was not ready while the team played eight road games to start the season. It still was not ready when Al LaMacchia took to the mound on April 18 for the Missions' home opener. "The construction workers would stop working while we played," he said. "You could see them straddling those girders, sitting there eating their lunches."[2]

Very little of the main grandstands were in place for that game. A few lucky season-ticket holders were able, for $1.50, to sit in folding chairs—clearly identified on the back as belonging to Alamo Stadium—in the concrete portions of the grandstands already poured. The builders had managed to install twenty-five hundred seats in the ballpark using bleachers, some of which were scavenged from Tech Field. The rest of the overflow crowd sat on chairs or blankets they brought from home, lining foul ground beyond the player benches—the dugouts were not ready yet—and spilling onto the warning track in the outfield. Everyone else in the park got in for sixty cents, thirty cents for kids.[3]

But it was not just the fans who were sitting in unfinished territory. Players from both teams had to dress in locker rooms at Pittman-Sullivan Park four miles away. Ironically, they were carried to the new stadium in City Transit Authority buses.

"Signs are going up on the fences and most will be painted by Friday," the *Light* reported in a story headlined "Here's Real Dope on the Ball Park."

Mission Stadium, one of the finest facilities in the minor leagues when it opened in 1947, was the home of Texas League baseball in San Antonio until 1964. University of Texas at San Antonio Institute of Texan Cultures; illustration no. 3644

Frank Brothers' clock again will occupy a prominent place on the scoreboard.

Light towers were going up Tuesday afternoon but the lights will not be turned on until May, according to [Missions] President Bill Osley. Getting transformers is a new difficulty. The light system will develop more than 300,000 watts.

The park, when finished, will seat about 9,500. This includes 1,220 box seats, give or take a dozen, 3,000 bleachers, 500 of which haven't arrived yet, the rest grandstand seats. New and modern chairs have been ordered and will be installed in three center sections, the old chairs from Tech Field going into the far ends of the stands.[4]

By the time it was finished in May—and finally dubbed Mission Stadium—it was the best park in the Texas League. It had symmetrical fences, 325 feet at each foul pole and 400 feet in center. It offered cheap bleacher seats with lots of sun and shaded grandstands for day games. It was oriented so southerly breezes would kick up around dusk each night and cool the fans in the grandstands. And framing the main entrance behind home plate were two towers, modeled after the design of nearby Mission Concepcion. Sitting along Mission Road, the stadium fit into the trail of five Spanish missions that started downtown with the Alamo.

It was appropriate that LaMacchia started the team's home opener since he was the veteran pitcher on the staff. He had been in the major leagues with the St. Louis Browns in 1943, 1945, and part of 1946 before being traded to the Washington Senators—for an outfielder named Jeff Heath, LaMacchia recalled—at midseason. The Senators wanted to send him to Chattanooga in the Southern League, but he balked and asked for a trade. So in August the team dealt him back to the Browns, who sent him back to San Antonio—which had been his adopted hometown since his wedding to a local girl in 1944.

He arrived in San Antonio as the Missions were wrapping up a third-place finish and preparing for the first round of the playoffs against the second-place Dallas Rebels. He pitched twenty-eight innings down the stretch and was declared eligible for the playoffs in a deal with Dallas that allowed Rebels outfielder Al Carr—who had joined his team late in the season as well—to play in the postseason.[5]

AL LAMACCHIA'S CAREER HIGHLIGHTS

Al LaMacchia's playing career lasted from 1939 to 1953, including sixteen games in the majors with the St. Louis Browns and Washington Senators. It was, for the most part, uninspiring.

But it is not his playing career that distinguishes LaMacchia, who has lived in San Antonio since 1944. In 1956 he took a job as a scout for the Philadelphia Phillies, the only thing he has done since. "I've worked for 46 years in this game as a scout, and I must be doing a pretty good job because you don't keep a job like this for 46 years by just being a friend of somebody," he said in a 2000 interview.

In addition to the Phillies, he has worked for the Atlanta Braves, Toronto Blue Jays, Tampa Bay Devil Rays, and Los Angeles Dodgers. Among the players he discovered and signed are Dale Murphy, the National League Most Valuable Player in 1981 and 1982; Dave Stieb, a converted college outfielder who went 176-137 during a sixteen-year pitching career in the majors; and Cito Gaston, who managed the Toronto Blue Jays to back-to-back World Series titles in 1992 and 1993. In 1984 LaMacchia and Bobby Mattick, another scout, were named vice presidents of the Blue Jays, the first time scouts had been promoted to a team's board of directors. They threw out the ceremonial first pitch at Game One of the 1992 World Series. LaMacchia worked for the Devil Rays from 1996 to 2002, but when his duties were reduced, he took a job with the Dodgers—at the age of eighty-one—covering the American League West, the Houston Astros, the St. Louis Cardinals, and the Texas League.

"I'm a guy doing a job I really like, and I can't see stepping aside," he said. "I don't think I could retire. If I didn't have anything to do, I'd age in a hell of a hurry."

Carr scored two of Dallas's four runs in the first game of the playoffs as the Rebels won 4-3 at home. A homer with two outs in the bottom of the ninth gave Dallas a 2-0 lead in the series the next night and sent the series back to Tech Field. The Missions committed six errors behind Fred "Jelly" SoRelle and LaMacchia in the first game in San Antonio and lost 2-1, but then they came back with a 4-1 decision to stay alive. But Dallas won the next game 4-0, routing San Antonio starter Ned Garver with three runs in the second inning, and took the series. LaMacchia pitched five scoreless innings in relief in what turned out to be the last game at Tech Field.

Besides pitching in the last contest at the old ballpark and the first at Mission Stadium, LaMacchia has one other small place in San Antonio baseball history. On August 20, 1942, he was the winning pitcher in a game that took sixty-seven minutes to play, the second-fastest in San Antonio and league history (the shortest was forty-nine minutes on the final day of the 1913 season, when Galveston shut out San Antonio 4-0). "I just got into my stride," LaMacchia later said, noting that his opponent, H. K. Perry, also was a very fast worker. "In those days, people might decide to come to the game late, and if they showed up twenty minutes late they might miss the first couple of innings. If they had been twenty minutes late that night, they would have gotten there in the fifth inning." LaMacchia gave up just four hits and did not walk a man in the 2-1 victory. He retired seven in a row at one point and 12 in a row at another. "When I was at Birmingham, the guy who was the general manager told me the concessions manager didn't like me pitching on Friday, Saturday, or Sunday," he recalled. "The games would only last an hour and a half, and they didn't get to sell anything."

"I was just a fast worker," he said. LaMacchia did not want the infielders throwing the ball around after outs. He ran out to the mound to start innings. And he had a system with his catcher—he would only throw a fastball or a straight changeup if he did not get a signal. There were entire games when he did not get a sign. "Today you sit through games that are 3½ hours long. I could have pitched two games in that time. I can remember walking into the clubhouse the day I was pitching a game and hearing the infielders talking about who was pitching that night. They'd say LaMacchia, and then they'd say 'We're getting out of here fast tonight.' Looking back on it now, I consider that a hell of a compliment."[6]

For the record, the Missions' 8-7 loss to Beaumont on April 18, 1947, took two hours and two minutes to play. But Al LaMacchia only threw six innings.

Procopio Herrera was a South Texas legend who helped the Missions during their championship 1950 season. Courtesy San Antonio Missions

San Antonio finished out of the playoffs in 1947, 1948, and 1949, but interest continued to grow. Once Mission Stadium was finished, attendance topped two hundred thousand in 1948 and 1949, and several major-league clubs came through the city. One of the biggest turnouts came on March 31, 1949, when Jackie Robinson went 3 for 5 to lead the Brooklyn Dodgers to an 8-1 win over the Missions. Charlie Grant had two of the club's biggest hitting days ever that year, hitting three home runs in an 11-0 win over Tulsa on May 6 and driving in nine runs in a 26-7 victory over Dallas on June 16.

San Antonio returned to the playoffs in 1950, just squeezing in as the fourth-place team. The race through the postseason turned into one of the biggest in Missions history.

Much of what Procopio Rodriguez Herrera accomplished on the ball fields of Texas and Mexico has been lost to the dust of time and the fog of memory. His major-league career was shorter than the drive from San Antonio to his birthplace in Nuevo Laredo, Mexico. He pitched in three games for the St. Louis Browns in 1951. In 2⅓ innings he gave up six hits—two of them home runs—walked four, hit a batter, and allowed seven earned runs. His records are hard to find because, inexplicably, he is called "Bobby" or "Tito" Herrera in the records of baseball.

He was a sub-.500 pitcher in the Texas League. His records in the Mexican League, many of them now lost, probably were no better. But when his best days were behind him is when he earned his real reputation, pitching for semipro and company teams. He would pitch on a Saturday, soak his arm in ice all night, rub Ben-Gay all over it, and then pitch again on Sunday.

When players would gather behind the third-base stands at Mission Stadium to barbeque chicken, eat tamales and barbacoa, and drink beer after games on Sunday afternoons, Procopio Herrera was a legend. "He was a workhorse," said his son, Daniel. "He used to hang out at a place called Joe's Ice House. I had some of those guys come up to me and say 'Man, he could throw fire.'"

When he was living in San Antonio, Herrera labored at Alamo Iron Works three days a week, then went to play baseball. It was always baseball first, his son said, sometimes even at the expense of his family. "For my old man, baseball was a religion," Daniel Herrera said. "By Tuesday, he was getting ready for Saturday's game. He would pitch Saturday morning, pitch again Sunday evenings. They played on Sundays at 3:30, and to go to the ballpark at 3:30 on a Sunday in the summer, you really had to love the game. It would be very still and very hot. You have to love the game to do that."[7]

Herrera pitched thousands of innings on the dusty diamonds of the border and inside the familiar fences at Mission Stadium, on big-league fields and small-town sandlots. But the apex of all those games came on a chilly, foggy night in the fading innings of a championship series.

The Sulphur Springs bottom had never been an ideal location for a ballpark—not since Union soldiers occupying Nashville, Tennessee, brought the game of baseball to the city, not since professional baseball was first played there in 1885, and not since a young sportswriter

SAN ANTONIO MISSIONS...1950

Back row, left to right: Frank Mancuso, catcher; Procopio Herrera, pitcher; Eddie Albrecht, pitcher; Dr. William Cole, Trainer; Joe Lutz, infielder; Wes Hamner, infielder; Joe Frazier, outfielder; Walter Brown, pitcher.
Middle row, Jim Dych, outfielder; Frank Saucier, outfielder; Mel Held, pitcher; Rocco Ippolito, outfielder; Frank Biscan, pitcher; Johnny Sullivan, infielder; Louis Sleater, pitcher.
Front row, Hal Hudson, pitcher; John Gibson, pitcher; John Pavlick, pitcher; Don Heffner, Manager; Dan Baich, catcher; Andy Anderson, infielder; Charles Grant, infielder.
Batboys: Frank Castilla and Thomas Hatfield.

The 1950 Missions were the only team in San Antonio history to win the Dixie Series, the playoff between champions of the Texas and Southern Leagues. Courtesy San Antonio Missions

named Grantland Rice had dubbed the grounds Sulphur Dell. The playing field, which was below street level, was less than a quarter mile from the Cumberland River. Fog—as well as smoke from burning at the city dump, which lay beyond the right-field wall—often filled the park, especially during the cooler months of the season. That right-field wall was just 262 feet from home plate, and it was at the top of a grassy, slanted embankment that surrounded the entire playing field. Right fielders often played on a ledge cut into the embankment, and Casey Stengel once joked that he had bunted for a home run there.

Players hated it. They referred to it as "Sulphur Hell."[8]

Into Sulphur Hell walked Procopio Herrera on the night of October 5, 1950. It was Game Seven of the Dixie Series. The San Antonio Missions, who at one time had trailed three games to one in the best-of-seven series, were leading 6-3 in the bottom of the sixth. But their third pitcher of the game, Hal Hudson, walked the first two hitters and gave up a single to load the bases. Another single made it 6-4 and sent Manager Don Heffner out to the mound.

Herrera was not the obvious choice to come into the game. Just two days before, he had pitched nine innings in Game Five, giving up four runs and six hits in San Antonio's 7-4 victory. He also had walked seven. "Procopio Herrera picked the most opportune time possible to pitch one of his periodical masterpieces," observed *Evening News* sports editor Harry Reckner in his story about that game. Herrera had gone to spring training as a starter for the Missions, but he had not pitched well enough to keep that job and was sent to the bullpen. In forty-two appearances, he was 7-12 with eighty-nine walks and 113 strikeouts in 160 innings. In the playoffs he was just 1-2, and in two of his starts he had not been able to get out of the second inning.

San Antonio had several other solid starters in 1950, including Lou Sleater, who was 12-5 during the regular season, and Homer "Hoot" Gibson, who was 12-6. Johnny Pavlick, just 8-6 during the season, was 4-1 in the playoffs. What they lacked in pitching they made up at the plate, led by the league's top hitter, Frank Saucier at .343, and Jim Dyck, who was third in the league at .321.

The Missions trailed 3-0 going into the sixth inning, but they scored on a bases-loaded walk, a two-run single by Saucier, run-scoring singles by Wes Hamner and Rocky Ippolito, and a run-scoring groundout by Joe Frazier. But Nashville came back in the bottom of the inning against Hudson. Herrera then entered the game.

"Of all the hurlers on the staff, Herrera seemed less likely to come through in that spot," wrote *Express* sports editor Dick Peebles. "Last spring when Procopio went to spring training with the Browns, he complained about the cool weather. He said he couldn't get loose. He wanted to come back to San Antonio and pitch when it was hot. But when the hot weather came, Herrera wasn't much help. It was only when the weather started to cool off in the late weeks of the season that he hit his stride." (In fact, that was true of the entire team—San Antonio was in fifth place and out of the playoffs until August 31, when the Missions swept a doubleheader from second-place Fort Worth. They went 8-5 the rest of the way to make the postseason, then swept regular-season champion Beaumont in the first round and topped Tulsa four games to two for the Texas League pennant.)

The first batter up against Herrera, Bob Dant, grounded out to Dyck at first base, allowing the third run to score and make it 6-5. Herrera got Bob Mauldin to pop up for the second out and walked Tom Neill to load the bases again to set up a force play. He then got John Liptak to fly out to left to end the inning. Herrera retired the side in order in the seventh. San Antonio scored three more runs in the top of the eighth to make it 9-5, then after a one-out walk in the bottom of the inning, Herrera got Dant to ground into a double play. In the ninth he struck out Mauldin and got Neill to pop up. Missions third baseman Charlie Grant came over to Herrera after the second out. "You know how many pesos ride on this next out, don't you?" Grant said, his story related in the next day's *San Antonio Evening News.* "Then blow that ball by this guy." Herrera struck out Liptak on four pitches.

A photo in the *Evening News* shows Herrera surrounded by his teammates, tousling his hair and patting him on the back. "Procopio Herrera's relief pitching was a thing of beauty, Heffner said," the evening paper reported. "The Mexican fireballing right-hander got his dander up for the Dixie Series and made up for his erratic performances through the season."

Herrera was among ten members of the traveling party who came back to San Antonio from Nashville. A crowd of four hundred greeted them at the depot. "Most attractive, for more reasons than one, was Herrera, the hero of the final game," reported the *Express,* which had carried the Game Seven story on the front page. "The handsome Mexican from Nuevo Laredo was the winner of Thursday night's game after the official scorers huddled and decided his four-inning stretch outdid Gibson's."

That foggy night in Tennessee remains as the clearest in a haze of memories.

In the middle of their run of five straight titles, the New York Yankees came to San Antonio in 1951 for an exhibition game. A crowd of 11,807 showed up at Mission Stadium on April 5 to see, among others, the

Yankees' "18-year-old phenom" Mickey Mantle. The Yankees won 13-10, but Mantle had just one hit in six at-bats.

San Antonio went on to get much better pitching in 1951, including a seven-inning no-hitter by Tommy Fine against Tulsa. Fine walked the first batter of the game, which was part of a doubleheader, then retired the next twenty-one in a row. Later in the summer Bob Turley pitched sixteen innings and struck out twenty-two Tulsa hitters, but he did not get a decision, for the game ended in a 3-3 tie.[9] The team's pitching was the main reason the club finished second in the standings, 13½ games behind the Houston Buffs. San Antonio beat Dallas four games to three in the first round but were swept by the Buffs in the championship series.

The Missions finished fifth in 1952, but the buzz was about Dave Hoskins, the Texas League's first African American player. Dallas owner Dick Burnett, a millionaire oilman, ran his team as a hobby—but he hated to lose. His bold step worked out, for Hoskins—a former outfielder—won a league-high twenty-two games as a pitcher. His presence boosted attendance throughout the league, and it spurred similar moves by every other club but Shreveport. The Louisiana legislature nearly passed a law banning interracial sports in 1952, discouraging that franchise from integrating (the law eventually passed in 1956, and the Sports were forced to drop out of the league).

With help from the parent St. Louis Browns, the Missions wound up with two black players, men who would lead the way for generations of African American players in San Antonio, including future Hall of Famers Billy Williams and Joe Morgan. But leading the way was not always easy.

In the early 1950s Dunedin, Florida, proudly proclaimed itself the "spring training site of the San Antonio Missions" on the scoreboard at Grant Field, its baseball stadium. Merchants welcomed the team to town with signs in their windows. Townsfolk referred to the players as "our team." *Express* sports editor Dick Peebles reported that "Emma Friz, the lady who operates the Jersey House where the Missions stay, has become so attached to the boys that she cried for several minutes the other morning when George Hausmann and nine of the players left for the [St. Louis] Browns' minor league camp at Thomasville,

Ga." Jim McLaughlin, the Browns' farm director, told Peebles that he liked the setup so much that he expected the team to keep going back each spring.

But there was one thing—actually two—that fouled the relationship. Their names were Harry Wilson and Charlie White, the Missions' first African American players. They could not stay at Emma Friz's place; they had live with black families in Dunedin, on the other side of town from the ballpark. They were not allowed to eat in most of the same places as their teammates. There were even places in Florida where they were not allowed to play.[10]

It had been six seasons since Jackie Robinson had broken baseball's color line with the Brooklyn Dodgers and just under six since Larry Doby had integrated the American League, joining the Cleveland Indians, owned by Bill Veeck at that time. Veeck, who owned the Browns during the 1950s, signed a number of African Americans in an attempt to attract fans and get out of the American League's second division. But it took until 1953 for any of these players to make it to San Antonio, which was the next-to-last step before the big leagues for aspiring Browns.

Wilson, a left-handed pitcher from Tennessee, had signed with the organization in 1950. He played in the Class-C Canadian-American League in 1950 and Class-C California League the next year. In 1952 he led the Class-B Interstate League with eighteen wins, going 18-8 with a 2.05 earned-run average.[11] That earned him a shot at Double-A San Antonio. "[Missions manager Jim] Crandall and the big brass of the St. Louis organization are sold on Wilson as a future big-league hurler," the *Express* reported. "They say he only needs more experience."

White had started out in the Negro Leagues, playing with Philadelphia of the Negro American League in 1950 before signing with the Browns. He was with Toronto in the Triple-A International League for two seasons, splitting time between third base and catcher, but was sent down to San Antonio in 1953 to become a catcher full time.[12] "Marty Marion of the Browns is just as high on White, who has had a season and a half pro experience, all at Toronto," the *Express* said.

Their assignment to the Missions caused only a slight stir in the mainstream newspapers, the *Express,* the *News,* and the *Light.* "The arrival of Wilson and White assures the Missions of the first Negro battery in the history of the Texas League," the *Express*'s Peebles reported matter-of-factly six paragraphs into a report from Dunedin on March 24. (The two were posed for a photo together in the *Express* when the team arrived in San Antonio, but there was no story, just the caption "Pitcher Harry Wilson . . . Catcher Charley White . . . The Missions first Negro battery in history.")

With the door opened, the rest of the league (except for Shreveport) began adding black players. Tulsa signed two-sport star Chuck Harmon, who had led his high school to two Indiana state basketball titles, and Oklahoma signed pitcher Bill Greason.[13]

Fortunately for everyone, the Missions did not spend that much time in Dunedin in 1953. The team left Florida on March 27 for a series of exhibition games against military teams in Panama and arrived in San Antonio on April 10 after opening the season on the road. The arrival of the two black players was greeted with much fanfare by San Antonio's relatively small African American community; its newspaper, the *Register;* and its radio station, KCOR. And while there was still widespread segregation—Mission Stadium had a Jim Crow section down the right-field line—the city was considered the most liberal in the league.

Their teammates, most of whom had been in the Browns organization for several years, accepted them. "Wilson and White were regular guys, pretty popular with the team," said pitcher Ryne Duren. "They were just like any other guy on the club. Of course, they had to stay at different hotels at the places we stopped. We liked 'em and enjoyed being around them. I didn't see any prejudice. It was a non-issue as far as the players were concerned." Wilson became friends with South Texas legend Procopio Herrera and later pitched against and with his friend on the semipro fields of San Antonio. "They would go over to Houston Street, on the East Side, over to places like Hackberry Street," recounted Daniel Herrera. "They would walk a long, long way over to Hackberry Street, just having fun and going to bars."[14]

There was pressure on the young black players, though. Teams expected the same production from their own young African Americans players as the Dodgers had gotten from Robinson and the Eagles had gotten from Hoskins—not to mention the success of players like Willie Mays and Monte Irvin with the New York Giants.

Both Wilson and White began the season strong for the Missions. In his first start Wilson pitched all ten innings and spurred the winning rally with a single in a 2-1 win over Houston. He won his first four games, with the fourth coming on a historic night—the first meeting in Texas League history between teams with all-black batteries. White was the Missions' top hitter in June, even winning a $25 prize from the team's booster club for having the top batting average for the month. He was hitting .311, and Wilson was 8-4 when they were named to the Texas League All-Star Game on July 10.

But the pressure, the hot Texas summer—both had played in the North in 1952—and an assortment of nagging injuries began to slow them down in July. White, taking a daily battering behind the plate, slumped below .300 in July and finished the year at .274. Wilson improved his record to 9-4 the day he was named to the all-star game but did not win again until his last start of the season. White limped through the second half of the season on a badly injured toe. "He had a big toe oozing blood from a smashing foul tip and paining him so much he cut the front out of his shoe," the *Light* reported. Another report said he had suffered a broken thumb as well.

Wilson tailed off badly too, like a pitcher with a sore arm. Bill Norman, who replaced Crandall as the Missions' manager in July, used both players less and less down the stretch, even moving White back to third base for a while. "If Harry Wilson hurt his arm, nobody ever knew about it," Duren said. "At that time, you didn't say anything about that kind of thing. It was the kiss of death. That's probably what happened, though."

They were popular in the community from beginning to end. The city declared June 30 as Harry Wilson Day, including a proclamation from Mayor Pro Tempore Henry B. Gonzalez. "Wilson's admirers, with the Negro chamber of commerce as sponsor of the party and Brooklyn pitcher Don Newcombe [who was stationed at Fort Sam Houston's Brooke Army Medical Center] doing the honors, loaded Harry down with a couple of dozen gifts, mostly wearing apparel, and gave all the other Missions ties in ceremonies before the game," recounted the *Light*.

Ryne Duren was a wild, hard-throwing pitcher for the Missions who went on to harness his abilities and win the American League Cy Young Award. Photo © 2003 San Antonio Express -News. Reprinted with permission

On August 18 it was White's turn. He got a parade from the central library to the stadium, accompanied by a jazz band, and was given a brand-new Chevrolet "in appreciation for his fine play throughout the season, his sportsmanship and his contributions to race relations," the *Register* reported.

They finished the season with strong performances—Wilson won his tenth game, throwing a five-hit shutout against Houston, and White went 2 for 3 with three runs batted in two days later in the season finale. White earned his shot at the majors the next season, and he spent 1954 and 1955 with the National League's Milwaukee Braves as a part-time catcher. He went on to play eleven seasons in the minors after that and retired to the Seattle area. He died in 1998. Wilson's career was all but over in 1953. He came back to San Antonio the next season but was ineffective in twenty-four appearances—1-5 with a 6.93 earned-run average. He pitched two games for Wichita in the Western League in 1955. He died in 1993.

San Antonio finished out of the playoffs again in 1953, fading to seventh place.

In 1954, San Antonio had its first change of big-league affiliates since 1932—but in name only. During the off-season, the Browns moved to Baltimore and became the Orioles. Little changed at the big-league level—the Orioles struggled just as the Browns did—but San Antonio continued to get the occasional star and the occasional big performance. On May 2 Jim Pisoni hit a three-run home run in the fifth inning, a grand slam in the eighth, and a solo shot in the ninth for eight runs batted in that night.[15]

The next year San Antonio rode tremendous pitching back into the playoffs, as the Missions finished just a ½ game behind Dallas in the standings. Mel Held got credit for a five-inning no-hitter on May 11 in a game stopped by rain. On June 28 Ryne Duren struck out eighteen Beaumont hitters in a 1-0 win in his first start. And then on August 10, Dan Ferrarese began a streak that has never been matched in San Antonio baseball history. On that night he beat Tulsa 1-0. In his next start, on the fourteenth, he shut out Oklahoma City, 4-0. Four days later he beat Beaumont 7-0. And on August 24 he topped Houston 13-0. In all he pitched 38⅔ consecutive innings without allowing a run in the middle of a streak that saw him win nine games in a row.[16] But the Missions fell to Shreveport four games to two in the first round of the playoffs.

San Antonio slid back to a sub-.500 record in 1956. The season opened with a wild 20-18 win over Austin that saw the Missions hit six doubles in the first inning and twelve for the game. Wind gusts of up to thirty-eight miles an hour made pitchers on both sides miserable.

The off-season following the 1956 season was perhaps more notable than the season itself. A new regime took over in Baltimore, and the club wanted to sell off some assets, chief among them its money-losing minor-league teams, including the Missions.

The Long Farewell,

1957–64

PERHAPS THE only thing worse than the hellish conditions in Texas in the 1950s—the state was suffering through its worst drought in years, even worse than the Dust Bowl days of the 1930s—was the utter decline of baseball in the state. The Longhorn League, West Texas–New Mexico League, Rio Grande Valley League, and the Big State League had dried up and blown away like so much dried-out Texas topsoil. Longtime Texas League cities like Beaumont lost their teams.

The survivors struggled. Dallas and Fort Worth bolted for Triple A. In San Antonio the Orioles were looking for buyers after years of financial losses. As efforts dragged on through 1957, there was talk that San Antonio would not even have a team in 1958.[1]

But a group of local businessmen finally came together, putting together the money to buy and operate the team, along with Mission Stadium. Chief among them was Dan Sullivan, a local real estate investor whose athletic ties included his father, who raised race horses, and his uncle, Barlow Irvin, a former athletic director at Texas A&M. "Our general manager at the time, Marvin Milkes, took it upon himself to try and keep the team in San Antonio," Sullivan told Harry Page of the *Express-News* in 1988. "Before I knew it, I was selling box seats and putting up fence signs."[2]

Billy Williams was a powerful but raw young player for the Missions in the spring of 1957. He left the Missions after an incident in Victoria, Texas, but came back to the team for a week, then went on to a career that landed him in the Baseball Hall of Fame. At left, University of Texas at San Antonio Institute of Texan Cultures, illustration no. 5094. Above photo © 2003 San Antonio Express-News. Reprinted with permission

The Missions were unable to land a full-fledged affiliate for the 1958 season, but they did get a handful of players on loan from the Orioles, who apparently had forgotten that they needed a Double A team when they bailed out of San Antonio. The club, managed by future Houston Astros manager Grady Hatton, went 74-79 and finished sixth in the eight-team league.

During the off-season, Milkes signed a deal with the Chicago Cubs, who sent some of their top young players to San Antonio in the spring of 1959. Among them were nineteen-year-old third baseman Ron Santo, twenty-three-year-old pitcher Ron Perranoski, and twenty-four-year-old shortstop J. C. Hartman, who had been the Kansas City Monarchs' shortstop after the Cubs had signed Ernie Banks.

The Cubs also sent a tall, skinny nineteen-year-old from the little town of Whistler, Alabama, named Billy Williams. Williams had long arms and powerful wrists, and he could hit the ball hard to every corner of the ballpark. The problem was the Cubs could not figure out where to put him in the field. "They wanted to make him into an outfielder, so Grady Hatton and I would go to the park early to work with him," Hartman said. "Billy was so bad in the outfield at first that he had to wear a hard hat. I guess they had a surplus of first basemen, so they made him an outfielder."[3] Williams eventually warmed to the assignment and quit trying to catch balls with his head.

But playing in the outfield was not his biggest problem. While San Antonio had a reputation for racial tolerance, the rest of the league was not quite as accommodating to the team's two African American players, Williams and Hartman. "We were always the last one off the bus at night," Williams said. "They would take the white guys to their hotel, then take us to the private homes where we had to stay. And then we were the first ones picked up. The hardest thing by far was when the other guys would get off the bus to eat, and we had to wait for them to bring us some food. It was tough to see your teammates able to sit down to a nice meal and you had to wait for them on the bus." (During the 1959–61 seasons, the Texas League played a schedule that included a series of games against teams from the Mexican Leagues. In Mexico the players were treated equally—equally miserable. "Those places were awfully hot, and you could feel it the minute you got off the plane," Williams said. "It was like 100 degrees when we were down there, and the hotel didn't have any air conditioning.")[4]

Williams had never been far from his Alabama home before the 1959 season, and he had not suffered as many of the indignities as Hartman, who was his roommate both in San Antonio and on the road. Hartman suspected he was getting a little homesick about midway through the season, but it really came through one night on the road. "We went to Victoria, Texas, for a road game one night, and after the game there wasn't anything for us [Hartman and Williams] to eat," said Hartman, who also was from a small town in Alabama, Cottonton. "Grady

Hatton had to come downstairs and make them cook us something, and we had to eat out behind the kitchen. Billy was really mad about that, and he said he was going home." Williams asked Hartman to drive him to the train station when they got back to their room at San Antonio's Manhattan Hotel. "He said he wasn't going to let me do it, so I said I'll just call a cab," Williams said. "So he broke down and took me."[5]

At the time Williams was the top hitter on the team. Rogers Hornsby, who was working as a roving instructor for the Cubs, saw him hit one day and sent a message to the front office in Chicago: "Get that kid Williams up there as fast as you can. He's wasting his time here." Williams got on the first eastbound train. "That was a sad day at the ballpark," he said with a chuckle. "Grady Hatton didn't see me come in with Jay [Hartman], and we always came in together. He asked Jay where I was, and Jay was talking real sad, and he said you could find me in Mobile, Ala. Well, Grady Hatton was really sad over that."[6]

The Cubs called Williams at home, but they could not get him to go back to the Missions. They sent scouts and even their general manager, without success. They had Sullivan, who had become friends with Williams, call him. No luck. Then they sent former Negro Leaguer Buck O'Neil, who was working for the club as a scout. The persuasive O'Neil convinced Williams to go back to the Texas League. "Buck O'Neil took me to the park in town, where I could see some of the friends I had grown up with," Williams said. "We started talking about what I was doing—and what they were doing—and saw things a little differently. I realized I had a pretty good deal going on."

He rejoined the Missions for a series in Houston, then the Cubs sent him to Triple A—where he hit .670 the first week. Williams played in eighteen games for Chicago in 1959 and twelve more in 1960. He was in the majors for good in 1961 and wound up in virtually every game the Cubs played for the next decade.[7]

While in San Antonio, Williams and Sullivan's friendship grew strong—so much so that Sullivan would be Williams's guest at least once a season at Wrigley Field, and Williams would be Sullivan's regular guest on his hunting ranch near Falfurrias, Texas. Sullivan also was an invited guest the day Williams was inducted into the Baseball Hall of Fame in 1987. The two remained friends until Dan Sullivan's death in 1992.

The 1959 Missions went on to make the Texas League playoffs as the fourth-place team, and they surprised Victoria in the first round before getting swept by Austin in the finals. Sullivan and his group owned the team for one more season before selling to John Monfrey. "I was in the right place at the right time," he told the *Express-News*. "We almost broke even financially in four years."

In many ways it was the same for Williams. "The 1950s were a tough time in baseball, but my situation wasn't nearly as bad as it had been," he said. "I signed in '56. I can't imagine what it was like for those guys who played right after Jackie Robinson, or the guys who played in the 1940s in the minors. They had it a lot tougher than I did."[8] Sullivan was one of the big reasons Williams did not struggle as much as some of his predecessors. The owner, in fact, befriended a number of the players during the time he led the Missions.

During spring training in 1959, Sullivan was sitting with *San Antonio Light* sports writer John Trowbridge, watching the team work out. One of the few holdovers from the Missions' independent team of 1958 was there, a Cuban pitcher named Jose Santiago, who had become friends with Sullivan. "All these rookies were doing exercises to get into shape, but Jose didn't want to do all that," Trowbridge said. "He would sit up in the stands and talk to me. Jose played baseball all winter in the Caribbean, and he didn't need to work out to get into shape."

Grady Hatton, who had managed the Missions in 1958 and was yet another friend of Sullivan, came over and asked the owner for help with the recalcitrant pitcher. "Well, Danny is this little guy and kind of crippled up, but he went over and all but took Jose by the hand and says 'Come on Jose, let's run,'" Trowbridge said. "Well, they run a little bit and then Jose comes back over and sits down. Grady comes up and says, 'Well, let's see if you're in shape,' and he puts Jose in an exhibition game. He throws nine innings, a complete game, and wins. Then he comes back over and sits down in the stands again."[9]

One of the youngest players on the 1959 Missions also became friends with Sullivan—nineteen-year-old third baseman Ron Santo. Santo was as green as he could be—he showed up in San Antonio with yellow shoelaces in his spikes, a violation of the unwritten dress code—and was still rather easily distracted. "I remember one time, he was batting during a game and an Air Force XC-99 was passing above Mission Stadium," Sullivan told the *Express-News* in 1988. "Since he had come from a small town in Colorado, the six-engine plane fascinated him and he looked up at it during the game, as the pitcher was throwing. The pitch whistled by his ear and nearly hit him. Grady Hatton was so infuriated that he took Santo out and played third base himself." Hatton, who actually played in twenty games for the Cubs the next year, probably helped his club a little when he saved Santo from himself. The third baseman led the Texas League in doubles that year with thirty-five.

"There isn't any question that Williams, Santo and [pitcher Ron] Perranoski gave me my greatest pleasures as an owner," Sullivan told the *Express-News*. "It gave me great satisfaction watching them progress to the majors and go on to do quite well."

While San Antonio was sending some good players to the majors, attendance continued to shrink. An announced crowd of 840 watched a twenty-four-inning, six-hour marathon against the Rio Grande Valley Giants on April 29, 1960. The team drew 106,273 fans in 1960, less than half of what it had attracted in 1949. The biggest crowd of the season, more than 8,000, came out to Mission Stadium for the game between the all-stars of the Texas and Mexican Leagues. The Texas Leaguers won 7-2, beating future big-league star Luis Tiant.

The parent club, the Chicago Cubs, did not seem to care much about attendance, though. Owner Phillip K. Wrigley wanted a winner, and the Cubs had not been to the World Series since 1945 and had not won one since 1908. They finished seventh in 1960, far closer to the last-place Phillies than the first-place Pirates. The organization had some good young players, including Williams, Santo, and pitcher Jack Curtis, who had won nineteen games for the Missions in 1960. But Wrigley thought the Cubs needed something else, something unusual, something so radical that it might just shake up a franchise that had become something of a joke.

His solution was the "college of coaches." Rather than have a single manager running his team the entire season, he would have a set of nine coaches who would rotate in and out of the job.[10] Nine baseball minds might work better than one, he figured. And he also would apply the principle to the minor leagues, including Double-A San Antonio. The idea set off a round of laughter that probably was heard from Los Angeles to New York, and it had more holes than the typical infield in the low minors. Besides the mere logistical nightmare of rotating men between the big-league manager's job, coaching jobs, and like positions in the minors, there also was the matter of sharing information and scouting reports on both Cubs players and opponents as well as tracking the progress of young players in the farm system.

But this was the Cubs, after all, and anything was worth a try after a decade of looking up at the rest of the league. Besides, it would provide jobs for some old-timers, including Rip Collins, a member of the Cardinals' old Gas House Gang who had been selling sporting goods the year before becoming one of the chosen nine. His first assignment for 1961 was the Missions. "You know, there's been a lot of kidding about the Cubs having nine coaches and no manager," Collins told *Express* sports editor Johnny Janes before the start of the season. "We don't know ourselves whether it will bring the team up from seventh place, but we do know this—if we happen to have a good year there'll be some other clubs without managers this season."

But while making the postseason in the National League had been tough for the Cubs—especially with the Dodgers and Giants around—teams barely had to have a pulse to make the playoffs in the struggling Texas League. The league had gone from eight robust and stable franchises to six mostly sickly ones with the loss of Oklahoma City, Houston, Dallas, and Fort Worth during the late 1950s, but it had stuck to a four-team playoff system.

The league was fading as attendance plummeted from 2,041,043 in 1948 to 489,547 in 1960. In an attempt to pump up interest, it had resorted to a limited schedule of games against teams from the Mexican League, thirty-six in 1959 and 1960 and a scheduled twenty-four in 1961. The Pan American Association produced more interest on the Mexico side than in Texas, attracting big crowds for all-star games and playoffs south of the border and big yawns across the state. The schedule also produced a hellish series of trips for the Texas Leaguers, amounting to hundreds of travel miles in rickety planes and broken-down buses to forsaken outposts like the oil-boom city of Poza Rica on the Mexican gulf coast.

But optimism was high on opening day, April 16. League president Dick Butler predicted attendance would rise to 525,000, and he pointed to ownership changes in Tulsa, Victoria, and San Antonio as good signs. Butler was optimistic that Sports Incorporated, the new San Antonio ownership group led by businessman John Monfrey, could reverse sliding interest in the league's biggest remaining city.[11] It had a long way to go. San Antonio Community Baseball Incorporated, led by Dan Sullivan, had gone broke trying to break the trend in the three years it owned the team. Butler also predicted that the Cubs' college of coaches would give the Missions an edge. The *Express* quoted him as saying:

> The Texas League is fortunate that the Chicago Cubs have se-lected San Antonio for their experiment This means that their fin-est young talent will be on display at San Antonio and, correspond-ingly, the other clubs will have to be well-staffed in order to remain competitive.
>
> On this basis, San Antonio must be picked as the pre-season fa-vorite. But because of the number of outstanding young prospects signed by all the other clubs, the race should remain close through-out.

Butler, as it turns out, was an optimist of the highest order. Atten-dance in 1961 was terrible again. The media—including all three news-papers in San Antonio, the league's largest city—preferred to focus on the major leagues throughout the season, especially the pursuit of Babe Ruth's single-season home-run record by Mickey Mantle and Roger Maris. It took just forty-one days for the first franchise to move, Victoria's transferring to Ardmore, Oklahoma, which had not been in the Texas League since 1904, on May 27. On June 10 Victoria got base-ball back when the even-more-struggling Rio Grande Valley Giants moved there.[12]

The best team in the Texas League turned out to be Amarillo, which benefited from the big checkbook of the parent New York Yankees. The Gold Sox had five of the top ten hitters in the league, including eventual batting champion Phil Linz (.349), hits leader Don Brummer (174), and runs-batted-in leader Dick Berardino (ninety-three) as well as future big-league star Joe Pepitone. Amarillo hit a league-high .284 as a team. The Gold Sox also had the best pitching staff in the league, with four ten-game winners: Hal Stowe (14-1), Tom McNulty (14-5), Jim Bouton (13-7), and Robert Lasko (11-4). Tulsa was a solid second, led by outfielder Johnny Lewis and nineteen-game winner Paul Toth. San Antonio was left to hold off Austin for third under the college of coaches.

The Missions went 15-15 under Collins to start the season, then were 12-6 for Harry Craft, 15-17 for Bobby Adams, and 32-27 for Rube Walker, a total record of 74-65, 15½ games behind the Gold Sox. (At least they finished closer than the Cubs, who were 64-90 and once again finished seventh. Craft, the only coach to run both the Cubs and the Missions, was 7-9 in the National League.) San Antonio had the league's top home-run hitter in Craig Sorsensen, who belted an all-but-unnoticed twenty-seven during the summer of the Maris-Mantle-Ruth frenzy. But the Missions' lineup was so nondescript that it did not place a player on the postseason all-star team.

The newspapers yawned at the prospect of the playoffs, just a decade after the Missions had made front-page news during their run to the Dixie Series title. The preview of the series with second-place Tulsa in the *Express* was nine paragraphs long, wedged in with results from the major leagues as well as football stories of assorted lengths and topics. The quaintness of the college-of-coaches idea apparently was a distant memory.

But then an assortment of fates intervened. Austin, which had to beat Victoria in a one-game playoff to even make the postseason, shocked Amarillo with a split of their doubleheader, starting the best-of-five first round. San Antonio lost to Toth in the opener with Tulsa, but Harvey Branch and reliever Jack Warner led the Missions to a 2-1 win in the second game of the night. At the same time, something bigger than baseball was churning in the Gulf of Mexico. Hurricane Carla began spinning off storms early in September, as the playoffs were getting under way, and slowly began a crawl through the warm waters toward the Texas coast.

The Missions and Oilers were rained out the first night in Tulsa, and they barely got in a third game, a 7-2 San Antonio victory in seven innings. The teams played seven innings the next night before the rains came again, but they were tied at 3-3, so the game was called a draw. It cleared enough for a full game the next night, and the Missions beat their nemesis Toth with an unearned run in the sixth inning. Warner pitched the final 1⅔ innings, striking out Lewis to end the 3-1 victory and giving the Missions a couple of days off at home while Amarillo and Austin tried to dodge the rain.

The Gold Sox and Senators had split their second doubleheader, this one in Austin, to set up a deciding game at Disch Field on September 6. It turned out to be one of the wildest playoff games in league history. The Senators, led by a young Phil Niekro, took a 4-2 lead into the seventh inning. The Gold Sox tied it, then Austin went back up 6-4 in the bottom of the inning. Amarillo scored single runs in the eighth and ninth to make it 6-6, then went up 7-6 in the top of the eleventh. But the Senators scored twice in the bottom of the eleventh for the victory, with their ace, Larry Maxie, getting the win in relief.[13]

With the Mexican League champions from Vera Cruz already in San Antonio—the entire best-of-seven Pan American Association Series was scheduled for the Texas League winner's ballpark, with the teams alternating as "home" and "visitor"—the Missions went to Austin to open the best-of-five series with a doubleheader. None of the San Antonio papers even bothered to make the trip.

San Antonio's pitchers gave up eleven hits in the two games, with Branch winning the first game 3-1 and Don Prince and Fred Burdette topping the Senators 5-3 in the second contest. Sorensen drove in four runs with a three-run homer and a sacrifice fly in the second game. The Missions eliminated Austin the next night, winning 4-1 on the strength of a three-run homer by Nelson Mathews in the fourth inning.

But with Carla bearing down on Corpus Christi, the Missions ran into trouble against Vera Cruz in the championship series opener. San Antonio committed six errors, including a bizarre one in the ninth that led to the go-ahead run for the Eagles. With Mike Gaspar breaking for second on a 3-2 pitch to Pablo Bernard, Warner missed for ball four. But San Antonio catcher Ralph Holding did not hear the call, and his hasty throw to second bounced into center field, allowing Gaspar to trot to third. Felipe Montemayor then hit a fly to short center that Mathews dropped in his haste to make a throw to the plate. He recovered in time to throw out Bernard, saving San Antonio from a seventh error, but Gaspar scored easily to give the Eagles a 4-3 win. San Antonio—which got two triples from Mathews—also lost half its infield that night, as first baseman Don Davis reinjured a bruised hand in the first inning and shortstop Daryl Robertson aggravated a sore ankle in the third.[14] As it turned out, they had plenty of time to recover.

San Antonio routed 9-5 Vera Cruz the next night, with strong winds whipping through the 878 faithful fans at Mission Stadium. Paul Popovich went 4 for 5 for San Antonio, and Mathews and leadoff man Elder White both were 3 for 4. It is a wonder there were not more runs scored—Vera Cruz committed five errors on the night.

The rest of Carla arrived the next day, after causing millions of dollars in damage in the Corpus Christi area. The rains and high winds— gusts reached seventy miles an hour as far inland as Austin—forced postponements on September 10 and 11. With five more days of rain in the forecast, the Missions' and Eagles' owners on September 12 talked Butler into moving the rest of the series to Vera Cruz, which everyone thought was far enough south to have missed the storm.[15] Game Three was set for September 14. But then, after just over two innings, the rains arrived in Vera Cruz too, forcing another postponement.

Wet or not, the series was scheduled to continue the next night with a doubleheader. San Antonio won the first game 5-3 in the bottom of the ninth—the teams again were alternating as the home team, only adding to the confusion—on a triple by Holding and a two-run homer from Popovich. Vera Cruz took the second game, extending the series yet another day. Mathews hit a long home run and Jim Schandevel spread out seven Eagles hits to give the Missions a 3-1 win the next night. And finally on September 16—more than two full weeks after the postseason began—the Missions clinched the last Pan American Association Series ever played with an 8-2 victory. Mathews hit yet another home run to lead a ten-hit San Antonio attack. The center fielder/first baseman was 11 for 25 (a .440 average), with three triples, two home runs, and six runs batted in during the championship series.

The frenzy in the media was underwhelming. The *Express* reported on the game with a four-paragraph wire story, two mug shots, and a box score. The *Light* had a slightly longer version of the same story. There was no welcome-home party for the soggy victors, though a number of them got a shot at the big leagues in 1962 (and whether they had the college of coaches to thank or not is a matter for debate), seven with the Cubs and one with the Cardinals. Popovich, who spent two more seasons in the minors, was the only member of the 1961 Missions to wind up with a long career in the majors. He played parts of eleven seasons with the Cubs, Dodgers, and Pirates and hit .233. Prince had the shortest big-league career—it lasted just one inning, late in the 1962 season.

The 1961 season turned out to be the peak of the affiliation with the Cubs. The team finished fifth in the six-team league in 1962, with the highlight coming on June 1. That night a record crowd of 12,946 crammed into Mission Stadium to see the home team play El Paso. The National League expansion team Houston Colt .45s bought the Missions and their stadium following the 1962 season. One of the first moves was to come up with a new nickname befitting an affiliate of the state's first big-league team. Among the suggestions were the .22s and the BBs, but eventually the name "Bullets" was selected (as in providing ammunition for the Colt .45s).[16]

Houston general manager Paul Richards had a good eye for talent, and he was armed with the big checkbook of Judge Roy Hofheinz, the team's dominant owner. So the 1963 Bullets were stocked with a number of good players, including Texas League all-stars Mike White (a second baseman) and Joe Hoerner (a pitcher) and future big-leaguers Jim Wynn and Jerry Grote, a native San Antonian. Pitcher Cliff Davis, who threw a no-hitter against El Paso on June 1, led the league that year with a 13-7 record. The 1963 Bullets were good enough to bring home the city's first first-place finish in fifty-five years, topping the standings with a 79-61 record. They were declared co-champions with Tulsa after falling to the Oilers in the championship series.

But that three-games-to-one loss just set up the Bullets for another run for the title in 1964. It would be a memorable season, one that included one of the most memorable characters in San Antonio baseball history filled with memorable characters, including: Irishman Charley O'Leary, who had outfit his 1917 team in green and named them the Shamrocks to break a string of bad luck; team president Harry Ables, who had activated himself as a player and pitched in a game in 1925—twenty years after his first appearance in the Texas League— and then did it again in 1926; and right-handed pitcher Tiny Owens, who had entertained fans by climbing the wires behind home plate during the 1920s. But none of them could match Clint Courtney.

The American League rookie of the year for the St. Louis Browns in 1952, Courtney established his real reputation the next season, when he fought the Yankees' Billy Martin, Phil Rizzuto, and Allie Reynolds— more or less all at once—over a play at second base. He was a regular in on-field fights—as well as serious poker games and ping-pong matches— and usually lost. (One former teammate said Courtney spent his life overestimating his abilities.)[17] His personality earned him a less-than-endearing nickname, "Scrap Iron." Short and squat—five feet, eight inches tall, weighing 180 pounds—as well as bald, he wore Coke-bottle-thick glasses and spoke with an almost incomprehensible Cajun accent. His idea of packing for a road trip was to put a toothbrush in his pocket.

But at some point during his eleven-year career in the major leagues, he became friends with Paul Richards. In 1963 Richards hired him as a backup catcher—mostly in name—and coach for the Bullets. He was a perfect foil for Lou Fitzgerald, a low-key Tennesseean who was the Bullets' manager in 1963 and 1964. "Courtney was a real character," said Don Bradey, a career minor-leaguer whom the Colts signed in 1963 to help the young pitchers in their system. "He was up to something all the time, and he kept the team real loose all the time."[18]

Courtney was with San Antonio part of the 1963 season, including one brief appearance as interim manager. In that game he decided to use himself as a pinch hitter, as the *Express* reported later:

When he walked from the dugout the public address man announced "now batting, former New York Yankee, Chicago White

Lou Fitzgerald was the manager of the San Antonio Bullets in 1963–64. Photo © 2003 San Antonio Express-News. *Reprinted with permission*

Sox, Washington Senator, and veteran minor-league player Clint Courtney."

Duly impressed by his fanfare, Scraps swung mightily at the first pitch, fell halfway down the first base line while his batting helmet sailed in the other direction, and the ball dribbled weakly back to the pitcher.

In the spring of 1964, he was sent to the Bullets again, and Fitzgerald assigned him to umpire an intrasquad game at the training camp in Moultrie, Georgia. "But the other day, he just walked off to get a ciga-rette," Fitzgerald told the *Express* that spring. "When he got back the catcher told him he had missed two pitches, and Scraps just said, 'Well, let's make it one ball and one strike 'cause I don't want to beat anybody.'"

It did not take Fitzgerald and Courtney long to realize that the 1964 Bullets had a chance to be even better than the 1963 team. The Bullets were loaded, including the double-play combination of Sonny Jackson and Joe Morgan. "Those little boys are so fast I can't believe it,"

Fitzgerald told the *Express* about Jackson and Morgan, who had played together the previous season in Class A. "And both of them can hit the ball, too. They're definitely major-league material."

The pair also were extremely dedicated—they would go to the stadium early on game days and work on turning double plays. Fitzgerald hit them a hundred ground balls a day, with Courtney scooping them out at first. The extra work paid off. In addition to having the best team in the league, the Bullets led the league in double plays with 150. "When you were pitching, you let balls go up the middle, because you knew they would turn a double play," pitcher Don Arlich said. "If the pitcher got involved, he usually messed it up."[19]

Morgan got off to a slow start at the plate that season, struggling through the first week without a hit. "The way the clubhouse was at Mission Stadium, you had to walk through the crowd to get to the dugout," Fitzgerald said. "Well, you know Joe Morgan got off to that bad start, and this guy comes up to me in the stands and says, 'Lou, you're never going to win a pennant like we did last year with that little black kid at second base.' I said I'd check with Paul Richards about getting us another second baseman. Joe hit two home runs into the wind and stole three bases that night. I saw that guy the next day and I said, 'Well, I got ahold of Paul and he's sending us another second baseman.' And the guy looks at me and said, 'Oh no! He'll be just fine.'"[20] Morgan recovered enough to hit .323 with forty-two doubles, eight triples, twelve home runs, and ninety runs batted in, and he was named the league's most valuable player.

Courtney, meanwhile, was leading the league in adventures, some of them intended and many of them not. "[That summer] Clint was building a house back in Louisiana, and he found out that you could get that Mexican floor tile pretty cheap in Juarez," said Chris Zachary, who was the Bullets' top pitcher in 1964. So on the team's next trip to El Paso, Courtney rented a truck and followed the team bus on the 550-mile drive out west. "He took that truck across the border and filled it full of tile," Zachary said. "And then when he tried to come back into the country, they hit him with a big ol' tariff. It turned out when he was done with that and renting the truck, it had cost him more than if he had just bought the tile in Louisiana."[21]

Statistics for the San Antonio Bullets' Regulars, 1964

PLAYERS IN NINETY OR MORE GAMES

Pos.	Player	AB	R	H	2B	3B	HR	RBI	BB	SO	SB
C	Dave Adlesh	474	55	96	15	2	14	54	4	**156**	0
OF	Brock Davis	473	49	118	23	5	4	47	54	81	22
1B	Chuck Harrison	494	94	147	24	3	**40**	119	65	92	4
SS	Sonny Jackson	575	97	164	22	5	2	30	61	68	45
3B	Von McDaniel	405	61	106	27	3	17	74	52	74	1
2B	Joe Morgan	496	113	160	**42**	8	12	90	105	56	47
OF	Aaron Pointer	323	50	75	17	3	7	45	54	60	17
OF	Leo Posada	397	83	108	19	7	22	90	66	119	12

Note: Six San Antonio players led the Texas League in fielding percentage at their positions: catcher Dave Adlesh, .991; first baseman Chuck Harrison, .994; second baseman Joe Morgan, .967; third baseman Von McDaniel, .955; outfielder Brock Davis, .985; and pitcher Darrell Brandon, 1.000.

PITCHERS IN TEN OR MORE APPEARANCES

Pitcher	W-L	ERA	G	GS	CG	ShO	IP	H	R	ER	BB	SO
Don Arlich	7-3	3.00	27	15	3	0	111	93	44	37	43	79
Don Bradey	12-5	2.88	46	7	2	0	125	122	50	40	34	109
Darrell Brandon	15-7	3.25	32	23	8	1	180	160	79	65	77	103
Ray Cordeiro	0-1	2.35	12	1	0	0	23	24	12	6	9	8
John Goetz	2-5	3.04	22	3	1	0	77	73	32	26	21	74
John Harms	8-2	2.41	36	0	0	0	82	64	34	22	42	63
Jesse Hickman	5-6	4.38	27	8	2	1	78	69	46	38	58	86
Jim Ray	4-4	3.72	16	16	3	2	92	76	47	38	55	77
Chuck Taylor	8-8	4.19	28	22	6	2	146	132	79	68	61	111
Chris Zachary	16-6	3.20	26	25	**16**	3	194	155	74	69	71	188

Bold indicates led league.

But their catcher-coach's adventures were not much of a distraction for the Bullets, who benefited from Richards's ability to find and sign young talent as well as his extensive connections throughout baseball. The Bullets got outstanding pitching, both from young arms like Zachary—who as a "bonus baby" had spent the 1963 season with the Colts as required by baseball rules—to veterans like Bradey. Zachary went 16-6 and struck out 188, and Darrell Brandon, another young starter, was 15-7 with 103 strikeouts. Bradey was 12-5 with 109 strikeouts.

The team also had a core group of young hitters. First baseman Chuck Harrison, who had played for San Antonio the previous season, led the Texas League in home runs with forty. Morgan led the league with forty-two doubles. Jackson led the league in singles with 135.

In addition, catcher Dave Adlesh set a league record that probably never will be broken—he caught 130 games in a row, topping a fifty-year-old mark. "I lost 20 pounds that season, but I broke that 50-year-old record, and I'll probably keep that record," he said. "No one will ever be stupid enough to try that again. I broke my finger a couple of times, but they kept sending me out there."[22]

Courtney, it seems, was his backup, and he did not want to catch anymore. He had his role, though, as a pinch hitter, batting .324, including a big hit one evening when he went up for Harrison. "Chuck Harrison hit quite a few homers for us, but he also was a big swinger," Fitzgerald said. "One night I took Harrison out and pinch-hit Courtney for him. Harrison was mad, but the bases were loaded and I was afraid Harrison would strike out. So Courtney goes up there and gets a hit and wins the game. He didn't say anything to me afterward, but he walks right by Harrison in the clubhouse and says, 'Buddy boy, I've hit for better players that you—in the big leagues.'"[23]

The Bullets wrapped up their second straight regular-season title September 1 in El Paso and beat the Sun Kings three games to one in the first-round playoffs as Tulsa was eliminating Albuquerque. San Antonio beat Tulsa 1-0 in sixteen innings to start the best-of-five finals, as Jackson delivered a bases-loaded sacrifice fly to score Von McDaniel.

But Adlesh, broken down by a summer behind the plate, could not play in Game Two, so Fitzgerald had to use Courtney behind the plate. "Clint had been out all day buying cattle or something, and he comes in about half-drunk," Fitzgerald recalled. "Well, I have to play him, and he can't do anything (Tulsa stole six bases off him in a 6-3 win). The trainer finally came to me and said that Clint was cutting out between innings and sticking his head in the whirlpool. He thought that might just be making it worse."[24]

The Colts sent the Bullets a new catcher, Joe Wooten, for the next game, and he caught Brandon's two-hitter in Tulsa to give their team a

2-1 advantage. Then San Antonio pounded out fourteen hits and whipped the Oilers 10-5 for the title, the city's first combination of regular-season and playoff championships and the first double title in the league in eight years.

But few in San Antonio enjoyed it because a story the newspapers began reporting in mid-August came true at the end of the season—the Colts sold the team to a group from Amarillo, leaving San Antonio without minor-league baseball for the first time since World War II. Richards blamed poor attendance for the move.[25] The Bullets, who along with Mission Stadium were owned by the Colts, drew just 85,808 fans in 1964, by far the worst in the league. Richards said he had lost between $100,000 and $150,000 a year on the team. He also blamed the three local newspapers for poor coverage. The Colts also did not help their San Antonio affiliate much. Hofheinz owned a radio station in the city, but it carried Bullets games only when there was not a Colts game scheduled.

There were other theories as well, though the truth may have died with Hofheinz. One was simple—he did not want baseball competition in the closest major market to Houston, especially with the Astrodome opening in 1965. That idea gained some credence when Richards spoke to the *Express*. "Of course, the real reason for the minor leagues' failure is chain store baseball," he said. "It simply is not a saleable product in a minor-league city." There also were rumors that the site of Mission Stadium had been determined to be perfect for a radio transmission tower for a station to reach all of South Texas. But the stadium actually stood empty from the last game in 1964—Clint Courtney's last appearance behind the plate—until 1974, when it was torn down.

It would take a crisis in the Texas League and a community effort to get baseball back, but this did not happen until after three long years had passed.

The Welcome Back,
1968–77

THE TEXAS LEAGUE was in serious trouble in 1967. It had lost Houston, the state's biggest market, to the major leagues. Longtime member Tulsa had bolted for Triple A. The next-biggest market in the region, Dallas–Fort Worth, had the worst team in the league for the second straight year. Owners in Austin folded their club at the end of the season. Leaguewide, attendance dropped for the third straight year, to 609,890.[1]

Of course the 1960s were a rough decade for anyone in minor-league baseball—especially considering the years followed the 1950s, when the minors went from fifty-nine leagues drawing forty-two million fans to twelve million fans watching twenty-one leagues. But times had been particularly tough for the Texas League, which was under the leadership of former big-league player and manager Bobby Bragan. The league had been stuck at six teams since 1959. Attendance had crept up slightly, but mainly because of the newness of teams in El Paso, Dallas–Fort Worth, and Amarillo and the strong efforts in Tulsa through 1965. Bragan and former Texas League president Dick Butler, who was working for the American League at the time, came to the same conclusion: the league needed San Antonio back.

The city had been without a team since the Bullets had won the pennant in 1964, after which the Houston Colt .45s, which had owned the team and their home park, Mission Stadium, sold the franchise to Amarillo. Mission Stadium was just twenty years old in 1967, and even after three years of neglect, it would have been better than many of the minor-league parks in use at the time. But there was no convincing Colts owner Roy Hofheinz to let anyone in San Antonio use it for professional baseball.

Bragan called the man with the only other stadium in town—Elmer Kosub, baseball coach and athletic director at St. Mary's University, a small Catholic college on the city's West Side. "At the time, we had a little stadium at St. Mary's, and it wouldn't have seated 3,000 if you had pushed them in," Kosub said.[2] But Bragan and Butler were persistent. So Kosub, already a veteran of the local baseball scene, started calling his former players, St. Mary's alumni, and local business leaders for ideas. A group of a dozen or so met in the fall of 1967 and decided on a plan—they would organize and put enough renovation into the little ballpark on campus to make it usable for a Texas League team.

Local attorney Henry Christopher, who had played baseball for Kosub, was one of the leaders of the group. He and Kosub went to the Major League Baseball winter meetings in Mexico City in December and cornered Chicago Cubs owner Phillip Wrigley, who had had a farm team in San Antonio from 1959 to 1962 and apparently liked the city. Wrigley also liked the idea of having his minor-league players based on a college campus, where they could attend school during the off-season. "That's just how the deal originated," Christopher said. "We just wanted to get pro baseball back in San Antonio."[3]

Landing an affiliation was critical because of a year-old change in the relationship between the majors and the minors. Beginning in 1966, big-league organizations had to draft amateur players to sign them instead of simply scouting and signing as many as they could afford wherever they were found. The minors were going to be the training grounds for all those young players.

But an affiliation was not going to do San Antonio any good if it did not have an adequate facility. That's where Kosub, Christopher, and the San Antonio Sports Association came in. They signed a landmark agreement with the university for use of the stadium and the parking lot—the first time a professional team had ever made such a deal with a school. (One of the reasons it was so rare was that NCAA rules forbade it. But St. Mary's was in the NAIA, a competing organization for smaller colleges.)[4]

"The first thing we had to do was build up the stadium," Christopher said. Bill Sebera, a local contractor, agreed to coordinate the effort. There was not much money available, though. V. J. Keefe, a local cement contractor, agreed to supply surplus concrete, to donate some of the budget, and to cosign a loan. Keefe died soon afterward, but his widow maintained the agreement, and the association operated on a budget of less than $100,000.

Fortunately, Kosub was skilled at scrounging up equipment and facilities thanks to years of working with a tight athletic budget at St. Mary's. First, he located the owner of Burnett Field in Dallas, which had been abandoned ("The city had condemned it—they were afraid somebody was going to get murdered there," Kosub quipped), and found out that the ballpark was in the process of being torn down. "We went up there and talked to the salvage guy, and they sold us the lights," he recalled. "He sold me the light towers and the reflectors for $5,000. They even took them down and loaded them onto our trucks." The trucks, of course, were donated too—by the Wolff family, which owned a building-supplies business in San Antonio.

LaGrave Field in Fort Worth, another former Texas League ballpark that had fallen into disrepair, was being dismantled at the same time. Kosub drove there and got in good with the head of the salvage crew. He bought another set of lights—which he subsequently sold to Pan American University in Edinburg—as well as a large number of seats.

And while Hofheinz would not let anyone use Mission Stadium, he had no problem with Kosub salvaging anything he could from the park. "The owners of the Astros gave us—the university—as much of the equipment as we could take out," he said. "They even gave me the grandstands. I didn't have any use for them, though, and eventually a salvage guy bought them for the steel." But bleachers from the park—as well as coolers, seats and turnstiles—wound up at St. Mary's. The San

Antonio Sports Association even got equipment from an existing Texas League park, picking up more turnstiles and other equipment no longer needed at Turnpike Stadium in Arlington, the home of the Dallas–Fort Worth Spurs and later the Texas Rangers' first ballpark.[5]

San Antonio building contractors donated everything from drilling services to set up the lights to cranes to hoist large sections of seats into place. The Wolff family donated building materials too. Members of the sports association did virtually all of the labor on the park, which was renamed V. J. Keefe Field in time for the season opener in 1968.

The Cubs and White Sox played the first professional game at the park, an exhibition on March 31 that attracted a packed house of 4,500. The Missions arrived from spring training in Arizona the next week. "The boys are very pleased with the park," Manager Harry Bright told the *Light* after a workout that attracted between 200 and 300 fans. "The field is in good condition, the lighting is very good and the distances to the fence are major-league."

On April 16 Councilman Felix Trevino threw out the ceremonial first pitch to City Manager Jerry Henckel. Actually, he had to throw out five first pitches since the ceremonial batter, U.S. representative Henry B. Gonzalez, refused to swing at anything out of the strike zone. The men who had built the stadium were there that night. "We were the ushers, we worked the ticket booth, the concession stands," Christopher said. "We did everything." Kosub also was there, serving as the team's general manager in addition to his duties at St. Mary's.

A crowd of 3,037 showed up on opening night to see a team the Cubs promised had "many of the organization's top prospects." San Antonio beat Amarillo 3-2 in ten innings, with Archie Reynolds pitching a three-hitter for the Missions and Jerry Jestadt singling in the winning run.[6] The new team was not an immediate hit, though. The Missions were last in the league in attendance, drawing 40,069 to seventy home games, and they finished with the worst record in the league, 53-86 (last in the Western Division during the first year the league played in two divisions).

But professional baseball was back in San Antonio to stay. And the Texas League was on its way back too. "[Bragan and Butler] really went out on a limb, but fortunately Bobby Bragan had that personality that

1968 SALVAGE

In addition to everything from soda machines to seats and lights, the San Antonio Sports Association also salvaged a piece of history from one of the Texas League's most-historic ballparks in 1967.

Elmer Kosub, the baseball coach and athletic director at St. Mary's University and a member of the association, was at the site of Fort Worth's LaGrave Field during demolition work, looking for one more bit of salvage for V. J. Keefe Field. Amid the ruins he spotted a large mirror—one with the names of some of the Fort Worth Cats greatest players from the 1920s engraved on it. "I grabbed that mirror out of the wreckage and brought it down here," Kosub recalled in 2000. "One night we presented it to a widow of one of the players. That was a tremendous thrill."

Kosub's salvage work also extended beyond Keefe Field. In the process of dismantling Mission Stadium, the light standards were taken down and sold to the New Braunfels Independent School District for its football stadium. Bleachers were dismantled and rebuilt at football fields in New Braunfels and Marion as well as Turnpike Stadium in Arlington—home of the Dallas–Fort Worth Spurs of the Texas League.

he could help sell anything," Kosub remembered. "And they had the idea that the Texas League wasn't going to make it without San Antonio. Fort Worth and Dallas were on the way out, and San Antonio was gone. There wasn't going to be any Texas left in the Texas League without us."[7] The reincarnated Missions struggled to attract 38,024 the next year, despite the presence of future big-leaguer Oscar Gamble, who went 7 for 8 in a midsummer doubleheader against Shreveport.

The San Antonio Sports Foundation ran the team until 1971, doing virtually all of the work with volunteer labor, but attendance topped out at just 47,113. The team was sold to local businessmen following the 1971 season, and the affiliation was changed from the Cubs to the Milwaukee Brewers (the local club became the Brewers as well, thanks in part to the presence of two major breweries in town). The San Antonio Brewers were little better than their parent club, going 53-87, and the affiliation ended after one season. The next spring, a new club, the Cleveland Indians, were welcomed to San Antonio like the second coming of Babe Ruth.

But the excitement of getting a new franchise in 1968 had worn off quickly, due to some truly awful squads sent to South Texas by the parent teams—San Antonio had finished with the worst record in the Texas League in 1968, 1969, and 1972. Only the marketing genius of John Begzos had gotten the fans out in 1972, when the Brewers drew a league-high 253,139.

Begzos used every angle he could to get fans to the park, from throwing special nights for players and coaches—manager Tony Pacheco got a new car—to dozens of giveaways and promotional nights. He also got a promise from Indians farm director Bob Quinn. "If the local ballclub can better itself by acquiring one or two ball players whom Begzos and Pacheco feel can help the club, then we will cooperate in every way," Quinn was quoted as saying in the *Light*. "Pacheco will be under no orders to play anybody. He can play anybody he wants. We're not going to interfere in what our managers do."[8]

San Antonio fans had grumbled for four years about the young and inexperienced players the Cubs and Brewers sent to town (the 1972 season was, in fact, Milwaukee's first season to have a Double A team, and the players were mostly inept except for a slugger named Gorman Thomas). The Indians sent San Antonio a good team to start the season, one that included future big-league pitchers Jim Kern and Rick Sawyer, plus infielder Duane Kuiper, outfielder Larry Johnson, and catcher Jeff Newman. Kern, Sawyer, Kuiper, and Newman all made the postseason all-star team, along with twenty-nine-year-old reliever Luis Penalver, who had twenty saves, and Joe Azcue, a player-coach with eleven years of big-league experience.

But Begzos was not satisfied. With the Brewers still chasing defending champ El Paso in the Western Division, he convinced San Antonian Joel Horlen—who had retired the previous year after pitching for the Oakland A's in the World Series—to come play for the Brewers. "I wasn't doing too much at the time, just building a few houses, so I had some free time," Horlen later recalled.

Coming off a big-league career, Joel Horlen helped lead San Antonio to the Texas League Champion-ship Series in 1973. Photo © 2003 San Antonio Express-News. Reprinted with permission

At first, Horlen agreed to just pitch home games, and he threw in relief. "But the team went on the road, and I said, 'Heck, I wasn't doing anything,' so I got in my car and drove to Little Rock to be with the team. I got into a game and got bombed, gave up three or four runs, and I got in the car and drove back home." As it turned out, that was the only game he lost.

When the Brewers returned to San Antonio, Pacheco asked the vet-eran if he could start since one of the young pitchers had hurt his back during the road trip. Horlen threw five innings and got a win. The next time he threw six innings and got a win. Then it was seven in-nings and another win. "The team went on the road again, to Ama-rillo, and they needed a starting pitcher up there," Horlen said. "I had an airplane at the time, so I figured I'd fly up there a day ahead of time to work out, pitch in the game and then come home. So of course I go up there and throw nine innings."[9]

San Antonio used its strong pitching—Sawyer won a league-high eighteen games, Kern won eleven, and Horlen went 6-1—to overtake El Paso down the stretch. The Brewers won fifteen in a row at Keefe Field in August.

The division title set up a championship series against the Memphis Blues, who were 4-10 (1-6 at Keefe) against the Brewers during the regular season and hit just .186 against San Antonio pitching. The first two games of the best-of-five series were rained out in Memphis, so the entire series was moved to San Antonio, beginning September 8. Horlen and Penalver combined to give up six hits and one run in the first game, which San Antonio won 3-1. Memphis beat Sawyer 3-2 in Game Two, but the Brewers came back to take Game Three 5-2, thanks to a grand slam from Danay Covert and a complete game from Kern. Memphis forced a deciding game when Wayne Kirby threw a three-hitter, allowing just one San Antonio runner to reach second base in a 1-0 victory.

Horlen was scheduled to start in Game Five. He had beaten Memphis three times already, and the young team always seemed to play well behind him. But Begzos got a phone call the afternoon of the game from Quinn, the Indians' farm director. San Antonio was to start Bob Grossman, a hard-throwing right-hander who was 5-11 during the regular season instead of Horlen. "This puts them right at the bottom of my list," Begzos told the *Light*. "I worked too long and too hard these past two months to take this crap anymore. I hold Cleveland farm director Bob Quinn directly responsible. . . . There's no way I'm going to put up with this tin-Jesus routine any longer. If we stay with Cleveland, I'm leaving."[10]

Horlen sat in the picnic area at Keefe with Begzos during the game, which Memphis won 3-2. "I was disappointed, but the kids on the team were really upset," he later recalled. "They were ready to play, and they had confidence in me. They kind of had the wind taken out of their sails. I don't know that we would have won if I had pitched—I might have gotten bombed—but they had a lot of confidence in me. That's just the way baseball is sometimes."[11] (It is certainly the way of the minors, where teams are at the mercy of their parent clubs—just ask the San Antonio Dodgers seven seasons later, when they lost Fernando Valenzuela before the deciding game of the 1980 playoffs.)

It took twenty-four more years before San Antonio won another Texas League pennant.

San Antonio completed its three-year affiliation with the Indians, not coming close to the playoffs in 1974 or 1975. Begzos did indeed quit as general manager after the 1973 season, taking his marketing expertise to the new sports kids in town, the San Antonio Spurs of the American Basketball Association. Horlen went on to serve as a minor-league manager and coach for the San Francisco Giants for fifteen years. He retired—this time for good—in 1999. The highlight of the 1974 season was a no-hitter against Victoria by future big-leaguer Larry Andersen. Andersen saved his performance for a big night—there was an overflow crowd of more than 5,800 at Keefe for the game. Tom McGough threw a no-hitter for San Antonio the next season, walking one and striking out eight against Shreveport.

The team signed a one-year agreement with the Texas Rangers during the off-season, but the bicentennial year was no better on the field. The Brewers finished 63-71, and on October 28, 1976, the team was sold to former big-league player Wally Moon, who signed an agreement with another major-league organization. While Moon would not last as owner, the affiliation endured—more than two decades, in fact—and it brought some of the game's best young players to San Antonio. It also brought more than a little heartache for local fans.

Days of the Dodgers,
1977–93

IN 1977 the Los Angeles Dodgers were among the top organizations in baseball. Since the end of World War II, the Dodgers had broken the game's color barrier, expanded the major leagues to the West Coast, and won the National League pennant eleven times. They also had produced some of the greatest players, including Jackie Robinson and Sandy Koufax. So when new San Antonio owner Wally Moon signed an affiliation deal with the Dodgers, the prospects looked good for the city.

In their first year the San Antonio Dodgers finished 61-67. In 1978 they were 79-57 and just missed the playoffs. In 1979 pitcher Rick Goulding threw a no-hitter against Amarillo, retiring twenty-seven in a row after the leadoff man reached on an error, and the Dodgers made the postseason. They advanced to the league championship series by beating Midland two games to none but were swept by Arkansas in the finals.

At first things looked good for Moon too. He was able to get the Texas Rangers and Houston Astros to play an exhibition game at Keefe Field in 1978, drawing 3,267 fans. But the Dodgers never would come to town—in fact, in the entire twenty-four-year affiliation, the big-league club never played in San Antonio. Regular-season attendance sagged too, topping out at 74,420 in 1978 and dropping to 63,990 the next year.

That started talks between Moon and Tom Turner Sr., who had made his fortune in convenience stores, trucking, and gasoline sales. Turner was looking for a new challenge, and he got it when he bought the team in 1979. He added a patio seating area at Keefe, built more concession stands, increased the number of promotions, and created a team of cheerleaders, the Dodger Dollies.[1] Attendance jumped by almost 100,000 in 1980, thanks in part to Turner's efforts. The players who came to San Antonio from spring training did not hurt matters, either.

The San Antonio Dodgers roster that year had some of the organization's top prospects, including a skinny pitcher named Orel Hershiser and two guys who would go on to manage in San Antonio, Tom Beyers and John Shoemaker. It also included a pudgy, rumpled-looking kid from Mexico with a bad haircut and virtually no idea about getting along in a foreign country.

Fernando Valenzuela had spent the 1979 season at Lodi, the Dodgers' Class A outpost in the California League, but he had not spent much time getting acclimated—that or everything was too much to take in. Valenzuela's hometown, Navajoa, had neither paved streets nor indoor plumbing while he was growing up. On top of being from the Mexican equivalent of the boondocks, the nineteen-year-old was exceedingly shy, whether conversing in Spanish or his exceedingly limited English.[2]

In today's minor-league-baseball system, teams make a special effort to accommodate their Spanish-speaking prospects. They sign sixteen-year-olds and send them to "academies," where they learn everything from managing a bank account to English vocabulary. When they arrive in the United States, their minor-league teams set them up with apartments and arrange niceties like transportation and occasionally even translators.

But in the 1970s and early 1980s, players were on their own. There were three Spanish-speaking prospects on the 1980 San Antonio Dodgers—Valenzuela, infielder Alex Taveras, and pitcher Ubaldo Heredia. Taveras was a Venezuelan who had been to the major leagues briefly

Fernando Valenzuela came to San Antonio as an untested nineteen year old, but by the end of the 1980 season, he was in the major leagues. Photo © 2003 San Antonio Express-News. *Reprinted with permission*

with the Houston Astros in 1976, and Heredia was a Mexican who had pitched in the Mexican League and at Triple-A Albuquerque the year before. "Whenever I went out to the mound, I had to call [Alex] over so Fernando could tell me how he felt, or so I could ask him something," said Don "Ducky" LeJohn, the San Antonio manager at the time. "Anything you had to do on the mound with a pitcher had to go through Alex."[3]

No one thought to have either of the Spanish-speakers actually living with Valenzuela, though. He was on his own, though he had gotten some counseling before leaving home. "The first paycheck they got when they were in town, I was trying to get him to endorse it so I could cash it for him," said Steve Ford, at the time the assistant general manager of the San Antonio Dodgers. "He wouldn't sign it. I tried and

CHAPTER 9

Fernando Valenzuela's Season at San Antonio

Date	Opponent	W-L	IP	H	R	ER	BB	SO
Apr. 14	@Midland	L	2.2	7	5	5	4	1
Apr. 17	El Paso	W	6.2	7	1	1	2	6
Apr. 22	@Amarillo	W	7.2	6	2	2	5	11
Apr. 27	@Amarillo	W	7	2	0	0	0	7
Apr. 30	@El Paso	W	1.1	1	0	0	0	0
May 3	Amarillo	L	2.2	2	4	0	5	2
May 7	Midland	L	9	5	3	3	5	6
May 11	Midland	ND	7	6	4	4	5	4
May 22	@Shreveport	ND	6	4	1	1	2	5
May 27	Jackson	W	6.2	9	1	1	2	10
June 1	Shreveport	L	9.1	9	3	3	6	7
June 13	Midland	L	9	8	2	2	3	6
June 18	Amarillo	L	2.2	6	4	4	3	2
June 23	@Amarillo	ND	1.2	5	6	3	3	1
June 28	El Paso	W	10	4	1	1	4	5
July 3	@Midland	L	5	9	6	6	2	2
July 10	Tulsa	L	9	8	2	2	1	8
July 15	Arkansas	W	7	8	3	3	1	5
July 21	@Tulsa	L	6.2	11	5	5	3	9
July 28	@Arkansas	L	7	3	1	1	2	7
Aug. 2	Midland	W	9	4	0	0	3	12
Aug. 6	El Paso	W	7	8	5	4	3	9
Aug. 13	@Amarillo	ND	5	1	0	0	0	9
Aug. 17	@El Paso	W	7	9	2	1	1	4
Aug. 22	Amarillo	W	9	2	0	0	1	15
Aug. 27	@Midland	W	9	3	0	0	2	9
Totals		13-9	170	147	61	52	68	162

TEXAS LEAGUE WESTERN DIVISION PLAYOFFS

Date	Opponent	W-L	IP	H	R	ER	BB	SO
Sept. 2	Amarillo	W	9	2	0	0	2	12

tried. They finally had somebody come in and translate for him, and then he signed it. People back home had told him to never sign anything that looked official, and this check was probably the most official-looking thing he'd ever seen."[4]

Beyers and Hershiser, who lived in the apartment next door to

Valenzuela's, began to keep an eye on their teammate. One day, they checked the refrigerator to find only water and Twinkies, resulting in a trip to a nearby grocery store. Another time, they dragged him along on a team outing—a dozen or so players rented inner tubes and floated down the Guadalupe River on an off day. "We were always trying to think up ways to get him out of the apartment," Beyers said. "We had a blast. I think he lost his shoes, though, and I don't think he had but one pair of shoes and a couple of outfits to his name."

The two were constantly checking up on their teammate. One day, in the middle of a typically blistering South Texas day, they noticed the windows were open next door. "Orel and I walked by and looked in the window, and he was sitting there on the couch, just sweating like a pig," Beyers said. "The air conditioner had gone out, and he didn't know how to tell anyone it needed to be fixed. I'll never forget that sight of him, sitting there looking all sad and sweaty on the couch."[5]

But Valenzuela was more than just sweaty, he was homesick. "One night, he was ready to go home," Taveras said. "He had his bags packed outside the stadium. I said, 'Hey, what's wrong with you?' He told me he had some problems. He missed his girl." Taveras relayed the message to the Dodgers.[6] The future Mrs. Valenzuela showed up soon afterward—and so did the real Fernando Valenzuela. He had started the season as "an average Double-A pitcher," LeJohn remembered. Before she arrived, he was 5-6. Valenzuela finished the season 14-9. "By that time, he had learned that screwball, and he really got it under control the second half of the season," Beyers said. "He was pretty tough to beat after that."

San Antonio had clinched a playoff berth by winning the first half of the Western Division race, but it was Valenzuela who carried the team in the second half and gave it momentum headed into the playoffs. In his last seven starts, he gave up six earned runs, including four in one game at windblown El Paso. He finished the season with a two-hit shutout against Amarillo—with fifteen strikeouts—and a three-hit shutout against Midland. In the first game of the best-of-three Western Division playoffs, he did not allow a hit through the first six innings and wound up with a two-hit complete-game win over Amarillo. He struck out twelve. San Antonio clinched the series the next night.

*Orel Hershiser helped
Fernando Valenzuela
survive the 1980 season
in San Antonio.
Courtesy Texas League*

Arkansas won the first two games of the best-of-five championship series in Little Rock. The teams and a steady fall rain arrived in San Antonio almost simultaneously.

But Los Angeles manager Tommy Lasorda had been pestering the Dodgers' front office to promote Valenzuela to the majors ever since he had found out the pitcher had been 6-0 with a 0.99 earned-run average in August. When the rains twice delayed Valenzuela's scheduled start in Game Three, Lasorda could wait no longer. The Dodgers, who were fighting the Astros for the National League West title, promoted Valenzuela to the majors on September 10. "I don't know what we're going to do with him," Lasorda said when Valenzuela joined the Dodgers during a series in Houston. "He just got here today."[7]

Valenzuela sat and watched, mostly. His big-league debut did not come until September 15 in Atlanta, when he pitched two innings.

When it finally quit raining in San Antonio—two days after Valenzuela was gone—Arkansas finished off the series sweep. "They called him up on us, and that left a pretty big hole in our ballclub," LeJohn said. "It seemed like every year, we would be in the playoffs and have to give up one of our best players—[Mike] Scioscia, [Tom] Niedenfuer, Hershiser."

The next spring, "Fernandomania" took off in Los Angeles, as the pitcher was the National League's starter in the all-star game, the rookie of the year, and the Cy Young Award winner.

San Antonio made the playoffs the next season, in a year highlighted by the play of brothers Dave and Steve Sax. They hit three home runs each in a 34-8 win in Midland on April 13, and both wound up making the postseason all-star team. The Dodgers once again advanced to the league championship series but were swept by Jackson.

It would be six more years before the team would make the playoffs again and sixteen before San Antonio won another pennant. There were highlights, though. In 1983 Sid Fernandez won the pitcher's "triple crown," leading the league in wins (thirteen), earned-run average (2.82), and strikeouts (209). Three San Antonio pitchers—Vance Lovelace, Brian Piper, and Steve Martin—combined on a no-hitter against Beaumont in 1984. The Dodgers scraped up one run in the victory on June 19.

In 1986 Turner sold the team to BHK Investments, led by Ethan Blackaby. Two years later Blackaby sold it to Dave Elmore, who had made his money in the travel business but was rapidly expanding his holdings in minor-league sports.

The 1988 season brought more than just another change in ownership, though. That year the club—which went back to the Missions nickname for the first time since 1971—had a young manager, Kevin Kennedy, who was more aggressive than his predecessors and had a tendency to play to win instead of following the Dodgers' philosophy of developing players and not worrying about wins and losses.

Kennedy's team made the playoffs, falling to El Paso in the first round. But it was not that series that made history—it was a game that began

Sid Fernandez was the dominant pitcher in the Texas League in 1983, winning the pitchers' "triple crown" by leading in earned-run average, strikeouts, and wins. Courtesy Texas League

on just another warm, breezy day on July 16, 1988 at V. J. Keefe Field. A game that continued into a warm, breezy evening. And then a warm, breezy night. And then a warm, breezy morning. And then, two days later, into the record book. The Missions and the Jackson Mets began the twenty-fifth game of the second half in front of an overflow crowd of 3,792. They played nine innings without scoring a run. Then they played ten, then fifteen, then twenty, then twenty-five innings without a run.

Finally, at 2:25 A.M., umpire Joe Burleson, Missions general manager Burl Yarbrough, Kennedy, and Mets manager Tucker Ashford marched into the Missions' offices and called Carl Sawatski, the president of the Texas League, at his home in Little Rock. "I was quite surprised when the phone rang," Sawatski told the *Express* in 1988. "I was in bed and my wife grabbed the phone. I told her it must be a wrong number. But lo and behold, it was Burl Yarbrough calling to tell me they were in the 25th inning in San Antonio."

Without any guidelines for game length—and no curfew in San Antonio—the game had dragged out for seven hours and ten minutes. "He was kind of sleepy, and I told him I was sorry to bother him," Yarbrough said. "I told him we were still playing ball and he said 'Oh.' I told him it was the 25th inning, and he said 'Oh my.'" Sawatski, once he woke up, had no problem with the teams stopping for the night.

Even without a conclusion, the game set records. It already was the longest game in Texas League history and was tied for the most innings played.[8] It was the longest scoreless game in baseball history, topping the twenty-three innings the Houston Astros and New York

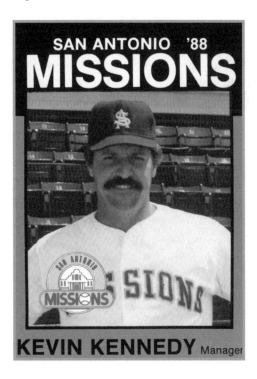

Kevin Kennedy, who went on to manage in the major leagues and work as a commentator on television, was the manager of the Missions in 1988. Courtesy Texas League

Box Score from the Twenty-Six-Inning Game
V. J. Keefe Stadium, July 14–16, 1988

JACKSON					SAN ANTONIO				
Player	*AB*	*R*	*H*	*RBI*	*Player*	*AB*	*R*	*H*	*RBI*
Hayden, lf	10	0	2	0	Santana, cf	6	0	0	0
Gardner, 2b	11	0	2	0	Torres, p	1	0	1	0
Salinas, 3b	10	0	0	0	Wetteland, ph	1	0	1	0
Cuevas, rf	10	0	2	0	Hickey, p	2	0	0	0
Shipley, ss	8	0	0	0	Wohler, p	1	0	0	0
Gideon, 1b	3	0	1	0	Huff, cf	10	0	3	0
Lindblade, 1b	8	0	1	0	Mitchell, 1b	8	0	1	0
DeButch, cf	9	0	2	0	McConnell, 3b	10	1	2	0
Jelic, c	7	0	0	0	Lopez, c	10	0	2	0
Givens, p	3	0	0	0	Batesole, 1b	4	0	0	0
M. Ramon, ph	1	0	0	0	Hartley, p	1	0	0	0
Rodriguez, p	0	0	0	0	Benitez, rf	4	0	0	0
Contreras, ph	1	0	0	0	Francois, 2b	10	0	3	1
J. Ramon, p	1	0	0	0	Bustabad, ss	8	0	2	0
Conley, p	3	0	0	0	LaFever, p	2	0	0	0
Jones, ph	1	0	0	0	Mata, ph	1	0	0	0
Tapani, p	0	0	0	0	Munoz, p	0	0	0	0
Beatty, p	0	0	0	0	Kirby, lf	7	0	1	0
Totals	**86**	**0**	**10**	**0**	**Totals**	**86**	**1**	**16**	**1**

Jackson   000 000 000 000 000 000 000 000 00 — 0

San Antonio   000 000 000 000 000 000 000 000 01 — 1

One out when winning run scored.

    E—Francois, Santana, Salinas, Lopez, Benitez. DP—Jackson 1, San Antonio 3. LOB—Jackson 17, San Antonio 20. 2B—Cuevas, Bustabad, Huff, Francois, Lopez. 3B—Huff. SB—Francois, Hayden 2, Gardner, Shipley, DeButch 2. Sacrifice—Bustabad.

JACKSON

Player	*IP*	*H*	*R*	*ER*	*BB*	*SO*
Givens	10	5	0	0	1	9
Rodriguez	2	0	0	0	1	3
J. Ramon	3 2/3	3	0	0	2	2
Conley	7 1/3	5	0	0	3	4
Tapani	2	0	0	0	1	0
Beatty (L, 10-7)	1/3	3	1	1	1	0

SAN ANTONIO

Player	IP	H	R	ER	BB	SO
LaFever	8	4	0	0	2	4
Munoz	2	1	0	0	0	3
Hartley	4	0	0	0	3	5
Torres	4	2	0	0	1	3
Hickey	6	3	0	0	4	1
Wohler (W, 4-2)	2	0	0	0	0	0

HBP—Shipley (by LaFever), Huff (by Ramon). WP—Hartley, Ramon 2. Balk—LaFever, Roman. PB—Lopez.

Umpires—Home, Burleson; first, Gutierrez; third, Jones. Time—7:23. Attendance—3,792.

Mets had played in 1968. (But extra-inning games and pitchers' duels were common at Keefe. Prevailing winds in the summer blew in from right-center field, and the later in the day it got, the stronger the winds became. Balls that were crushed were held up by the wind and became long outs. Even in the era before shortstops were hitting forty home runs a season, the home run was the quickest way to end an extra-innings game.)

Jackson's best chance to score early in the game came in the fifth inning, when Mike DeButch tried to score from third base on an infield grounder. But San Antonio third baseman Walt McConnell fielded the ball cleanly and fired home to Luis Lopez, who tagged out the runner. "He came up to me on his sixth at-bat and said, 'You should have called me safe, then we would all be home,'" Burleson, who called the entire game behind the plate, told the *Express.* "I said, 'I guess you're right.'" The Mets were 1 for 16 with runners in scoring position. They left seventeen runners on base. San Antonio left eighteen. "It was just an unbelievable job by both staffs," Missions pitching coach Pat Zachry told the *Light.* "Unbelievable."

It was unbelievable to a lot of people. As news of the game went out on the wires, the phone in the Missions' office began to ring. David

Oldham, at the time the team's assistant general manager, answered one call from an all-sports, all-night talk show in New York at 12:45 A.M. "They had picked it up on the ticker and wanted to know what was going on. They really treated me like a South Texas hick, and I kind of played along," said Oldham, who was from Kansas. "'We're just sittin' here drinkin' and trying to keep the players awake,' I told them."[9]

At first the extra-innings game had been an annoyance to the staff, which had come in that spring when Elmore bought the team and was still trying to get used to the city, the stadium, and the team. "When you first go extra innings, the first few innings you just want to get it over with," Yarbrough said. "But the further this one went along, the more we began to realize that we were becoming a part of history."[10]

The crowd dwindled quickly, and by the sixteenth inning, the sportswriters covering the game—Harry Page for the *Express* and Brad Townsend for the *Light*—were counting the remaining fans. At 1:00 A.M., the total stood at 321.[11] Around midnight, the team's front office brought in coffee, doughnuts, and breakfast tacos for the stalwarts.

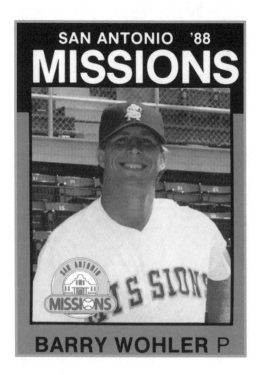

Barry Wohler napped in the bullpen through the later stretches of the longest game in Texas League history, but he eventually was the winning pitcher. Courtesy Texas League

Some of the players needed a dose of caffeine too. Missions pitcher Barry Wohler slept in the bullpen—which was out of Kennedy's view, far down the left-field line—from the sixteenth to the twenty-second inning. He had to be roused by his teammates to warm up, and he went into the game in the top of the twenty-fifth. The Mets' bats needed to be roused too. Jackson went from the sixth to the twentieth inning without a base hit into the outfield. "You could have a bad week on a night like this," Jackson play-by-play announcer Bill Walberg told his listeners, not long after he ran out of major-league scores to report and joked that "Japanese League scores will be coming in soon."[12]

The later it got, the more ludicrous it became. Pitchers stayed in the game to hit because there were no more pinch hitters left. San Antonio's Mike Huff led off the twenty-first inning with a double but was thrown out trying to stretch it into a triple. Two innings later he managed to make it to third with a triple but was stranded there. In the twenty-fourth McConnell threw out another Jackson runner trying to score from third on a ground ball.

The few insomniacs remaining at 2:30 A.M. booed when they heard the game had been suspended, but their persistence was rewarded with free tickets to another game.

The teams played a nine-inning game the next night, then came back an hour early on Saturday to pick up where they had left off. Wohler—who pantomimed a game-winning homer at 3:00 A.M. on Friday—retired the Mets in order to start the twenty-sixth. With one out in the bottom of the twenty-sixth, McConnell singled off Jackson's Blaine Beatty. Lopez doubled to move him to third, and Manny Benitez was walked intentionally to set up a force play. Instead, Manny Francois lined a single to center field and McConnell trotted home with the winning run. It had taken just thirteen minutes. "I feel like this was the World Series," Francois told the *Express*. "However, I don't want to play a game like this again." Kennedy, who had sat through a suspended game that lasted thirty-three innings when he was a player, joked that it was the quickest victory he had ever gotten. "If you're going to be in the record books, it's great—as long as you win," he told the *Express*.

The game may have worn out the players, but it was a godsend for the new management. It earned the franchise national publicity as offi-

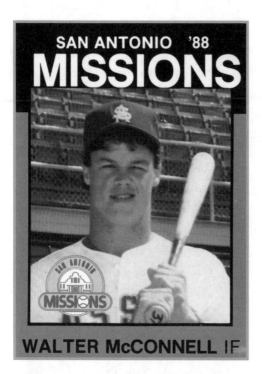

WALTER McCONNELL IF

Walt McConnell had a number of key plays in the Missions' twenty-six-inning victory over Jackson in 1988, and he scored the winning run on Manny Francois's single. Courtesy Texas League

MANUEL FRANCOIS IF

Manny Francois's single in the bottom of the twenty-sixth inning gave San Antonio a victory over Jackson in the longest game in league history. Courtesy Texas League

cial scorekeeper Reed Switzer spent much of the time between games answering the phone in the press box and talking to media from one end of the country to the other. "I was just thanking God it was over," said Jackson's Chris Jelic, who caught all twenty-six innings for the Mets.[13]

Kennedy did not return the next season, and neither did most of the players who had made the Missions a playoff team. San Antonio sank to last in the West, going 49-87 for the season.

The Missions bounced back in 1990, though, with a powerful young lineup and the best overall record in the league. Among the stars were first baseman Eric Karros, who led the league in hitting (.352), hits (179), doubles (forty-five) and total bases (282); Henry Rodriguez, who was tops in home runs (twenty-eight) and runs batted in (109); and Tom Goodwin, who led the league in stolen bases (sixty). Steve Finken, who had a five-hit day on June 11, and pitcher Mike James also were postseason all-stars. Karros, who went on to be the National League Rookie of the Year in 1992, also had a five-hit day that season, going 5 for 5 against Midland on June 8.

But after beating El Paso in the first round of the playoffs and going up two games to one against Shreveport in the championship series, the young Missions lost their momentum in a series of rainouts. The Captains came back and won three straight games to take the first of back-to-back Texas League pennants.

San Antonio slipped to 61-75 in 1991, but there were some memorable moments and more future stars of the big leagues on the field. Among the players wearing San Antonio uniforms in 1991 were Pedro Martinez and Raul Mondesi, though only Mondesi stayed for the entire season (one of the cornerstones of the Dodgers' minor-league philosophy was moving players up to the next level of the minors when they excelled, no matter what the cost to the local team). On April 25 three Missions—Brett Magnusson, Eric Young, and Braulio Castillo— had four hits each in a 9-4 win over El Paso. Young, who set a franchise record with seventy stolen bases, went 5 for 5 and stole four bases in a 13-12 loss to El Paso in July.

The next season's team also had its share of future big-leaguers, including another brief stay by a future all-star. Catcher Mike Piazza,

Mike Piazza was in San Antonio for only a portion of a season en route to the major leagues. Photo © 2003 San Antonio Express-News. Reprinted with permission

zooming through the minors, played for the Missions briefly. Juan Castro, who went on to a long major-league career, went 5 for 6—all extra-base hits—in a doubleheader sweep against Shreveport. In July Todd Hollandsworth—another future rookie of the year—drove in seven runs in an 11-2 romp over Tulsa.

The 1993 season turned out to be the last for V. J. Keefe Field. Minor-league baseball had once again become a moneymaking business, not simply a civic enterprise, and what had been adequate in 1968 was no longer acceptable.

A New Home and a Title,

1994–2000

WHEN HE BOUGHT the team in early 1988, Dave Elmore also inherited the lease on V. J. Keefe Field, a facility where the locker rooms were too small, the lights were showing signs of age, the grandstands were rickety, and fan amenities were few. The new owner began to put money into the stadium for repairs and upgrades, and it took just over a year and a half for talk to start about a new home for the team.

Part of the call for the new stadium came from the Los Angeles Dodgers, which wanted better facilities for its young prospects. "There's no question they are concerned with the facilities we have," Elmore told the *Express-News* in 1988. "They have talked to me about the facility, and I don't know if they will give me an ultimatum or not."

By the next year, the pressure from the Dodgers was building and talk about a ballpark increasing. One story reported on possible sites at the University of Texas at San Antonio, Sea World of Texas, and on land owned by the Harlandale Independent School District.[1] But nothing happened, and by the fall of 1990, the Dodgers were ready to pull out of San Antonio. The organization went into negotiations to move to El Paso, which was closer to the Dodgers' Triple A team in Albuquerque and had a brand-new city-owned stadium.

At the same time, confusion about a new agreement between the majors and the minors left San Antonio thinking it had a two-year extension with the Dodgers. An arbitration panel eventually worked out a compromise, with the San Antonio–Los Angeles deal extended for two more seasons. But the compromise came with a warning. "While Burl [Yarbrough, the Missions' general manager] and the Missions might be pleased at the moment, if they are going to keep the Dodgers during the long term, some things will have to be done to repair their relationship," said Peter Kirk, the spokesman for the arbitration committee.[2]

The new agreement between the majors and minors also had laid down specific requirements for minor-league ballparks, including locker-room sizes and seating capacities—requirements that San Antonio was not going to meet at V. J. Keefe Field. "There were a lot of ballparks at that time all over America that weren't in good shape, or old, and Major League Baseball felt that there were a lot of inadequate facilities," Yarbrough said.[3] The agreement—along with a resurgence of the popularity of baseball, thanks in part to a series of movies (*Bull Durham, The Natural,* and *Field of Dreams*) in the late 1980s—helped spur a boom in minor-league attendance that continues today.

Nelson Wolff (center) was part of a group that helped bring the Texas League back to San Antonio in 1968 and was instrumental in getting a new stadium built in the 1990s. Photo © 2003 San Antonio Express-News. *Reprinted with permission*

The last little push for a new stadium came in May, 1991, when Nelson Wolff was elected mayor. Wolff had grown up in San Antonio, watching games at Mission Stadium and serving as a batboy for the semipro Texas Consolidated Transport team, which played across the street from Mission. He had played some semipro ball in the Spanish-American League in the early 1960s and was part of the San Antonio Sports Association, which brought the Texas League back to the city in 1968.

Wolff had served in the Texas House of Representatives and the Texas Senate in the 1970s and had been on the city council since 1987. One of his priorities was to get a new baseball stadium built. "I tried for three years when I was on the council, but I couldn't get anyone interested in building a new stadium," he said. "I was trying to figure out some way to build a ballpark, even if it was using some of the money from the [Alamodome, which had recently been approved by voters]."

The mayor revisited some of the sites previously mentioned for a stadium, including the Harlandale multisport facility and Sea World. He talked to officials from the San Antonio Livestock Show and Rodeo, which controlled the Freeman Coliseum and its grounds, about a ballpark (a feasibility study commissioned by the Missions had recommended building near the coliseum, but the idea never progressed). Then Wolff found a tract of land on the city's South Side across U.S. Highway 90 from city-owned Camargo Park and Kelly Air Force Base. The forty-acre lot was owned by Levi Strauss Company, which had a plant next door. "They didn't want to give it to us, but kept talking and talking," Wolff said. "We finally had to get a little rough with them," he said with a laugh. "They finally sold it to us for 40 cents a square foot, which was very cheap for land like that, on a corner."

Wolff got a break from the financial markets—interest rates were the lowest in years, meaning that the city was not paying as much as usual on bond debt. Working with City Manager Alex Briseno and his staff, the mayor came up with a way to build the stadium without selling bonds and without affecting cash flow. "I got it through the council in about a three-week period," Wolff said. "I knew that if I didn't work fast that we'd never get it done. In a three-week period it went through, bang, bang, bang."[4]

SAN ANTONIO'S STADIUMS

Nelson W. Wolff Municipal Stadium, 1994–, is a state-of-the-art minor-league facility that can seat 6,200, with a grass berm and standing space for 3,000 additional spectators.

V. J. Keefe Field, 1968–93, was the product of a one-of-a-kind agreement between a professional baseball organization and a school, in this case St. Mary's University.

Mission Stadium, 1947–64, in its prime one of the finest minor-league parks in the country, with shaded seating and twin towers designed in the style of San Antonio's Mission Concepcion, was located at Mitchell Street and Mission Road, south of downtown.

Tech Field, 1932–42 and 1946, an all-sports facility owned by the San Antonio Independent School District and expanded in 1935 to accommodate more fans, was at San Pedro Park, north of downtown. Maintenance facilities for VIA Metropolitan Transit are currently on the site.

League Park, 1923–32, an all-wood structure that was home to major-league spring training as well as the Missions, was located on Josephine Street south of the Brackenridge Park Golf Course and seated 7,000.

Block Stadium (renamed League Park after 1915), 1913–23, built on the southern edge of downtown by team owner Morris Block, was also home to big-league spring training. New owners of the club, thinking a facility north of downtown would be more convenient to fans, moved out following the 1923 season, but it was used for semipro baseball games as well as football and boxing matches until it was torn down in 1927.

Electric Park, 1906–12, part of the amusement-park facility of the same name, had a somewhat misleading name because it had no lights.

San Pedro Park, 1892–1905, was the original ballpark on the site north of downtown near the San Pedro Springs. Electric Park and Tech Field were on the same site, with modifications.

Muth's Park, 1888, was the first home to professional baseball in San Antonio, serving as the ballpark for the city's first Texas League team. It was located on Government Hill near Fort Sam Houston.

The next summer the Dodgers signed a four-year contract extension with the Missions, and Municipal Stadium opened April, 18, 1994, with a game between San Antonio and El Paso. Wolff threw out the first pitch. "Who knows where baseball would be here without him as mayor," Yarbrough said of Wolff. "If there hadn't been a stadium built here, I don't know if we could have continued to play here. We had gone as far as we could with [Keefe Field]. We wouldn't have been able to meet the standards. We probably would have lost the Dodgers, and I don't thing we would have baseball here without Nelson."[5] City leaders recognized that as well. In 1995 the ballpark was renamed Nelson W. Wolff Municipal Stadium.

Wolff considered minor-league baseball, despite its nature as a business, as a quality-of-life issue for the city. "There was no real political opposition to it, no big fight," he said. "I think people understood that this was for the people here. And for people of middle- and low-income means, this was something they could still go to. The tickets were still just a few bucks. It was a fan-friendly deal." San Antonio broke the all-time Texas League attendance record in 1994, attracting 411,959 fans, and the Missions drew 387,090 the next year, the second-highest attendance total in league history.[6]

But the team was not winning, failing to make the playoffs in the first three seasons in the new stadium despite the presence of some solid players. Wilton Guerrero, the slap-hitting brother of big-leaguer Vladimir Guerrero, led the league in hitting in 1995. Future American League all-star Paul Konerko had a fifteen-game hitting streak in 1996, then went on a week-long tear that saw him get ten hits, six home runs, and ten runs batted in. In fact, the years from 1991 to 1996 were among the worst in San Antonio history. The Missions had the worst record in the Texas League's Western Division four times and never finished above .500 for a season.

Managers came and went. Top-quality prospects came and usually went before the season was over. The minor-league front office, which operated independently from the major-league club, was restless. Attendance had begun to slip from the record numbers posted when Wolff Stadium was opened. There were rumblings from the fans and from the media for the Dodgers to take the focus off "player development" a little and give the city a winner. In 1997 they managed to do both.

Wolff Stadium replaced Keefe Field and helped boost attendance to a then–Texas League record of 411,959 fans when it opened in 1994. Courtesy Texas League

Paul Konerko led the Missions in virtually every offensive category in 1996.
Courtesy Texas League, photo by Tom Kayser

The team that flew into San Antonio from spring training on March 31, 1997, had a some good prospects, among them shortstop Alex Cora, younger brother of big-league veteran Joey Cora, and center fielder Kevin Gibbs, who had stolen sixty bases in 1996 in Class A. It also had a lot of veterans, players who had been in the minors for three or four years, some even at the Triple A level, and one, Garey Ingram, who had been to the major leagues in 1994–95. By the end of the season, a handful of players with at least some big-league experience would play for the team, including Mike Anderson, older brother of Missions broadcaster Brian Anderson. It had a veteran pitching coach, Guy Conti, who had been loyal to the Dodgers for eleven years, waiting for a chance to move up and working with virtually every pitcher on the Missions' 1997 staff in the process. And it had a bona fide big-leaguer as hitting coach, former Detroit Tigers catcher Lance Parrish.

But the most important part of what the Dodgers sent to San Antonio was the manager—Ron Roenicke. Roenicke, a former number-one draft pick for the Dodgers, had zoomed through the farm system as a player, but he had never been a standout in the majors. He played part-time for six big-league teams in eight seasons. He joked that with all the time he spent on the bench watching, he learned a lot about the game, watching different managers and the way they handled people as well as the game. When his playing career ended in 1988, Roenicke decided he wanted to be a manager. At first he was a scout for the Dodgers but eventually worked his way up to the manager's job at Great Falls, Montana, in the rookie-level Pioneer League in 1994. The next season he managed Class-A San Bernardino to the California League title and was the league's manager of the year.

Roenicke spent the 1996 season as hitting coach at Triple-A Albuquerque but jumped at the chance to manage again when the Dodgers shuffled their minor-league staff for 1997. His attention to detail impressed Parrish, a nineteen-year big-league veteran, who called him the best-prepared manager he had ever seen. "His handle on the game was amazing," Parrish said.[7]

Manager Ron Roenicke (left) and pitching coach Guy Conti helped lead San Antonio to the Texas League pennant in 1997. Courtesy Texas League, photo by Tom Kayser

Roenicke knew he had to strike a balance between player development and winning in San Antonio, and he knew coming into the season that the team had a chance to be successful. In 1995 he had pulled it off in San Bernardino, combining his knowledge of the game and of his players with a keen eye for strategy and momentum. "It felt like every game, we had a chance to win it," he said of that 1995 team the week before the 1997 season started. "We didn't win every one, but it seemed like we would always come up with a way to at least get the tying run to the plate late in the game."[8]

Soon the same thing happened in San Antonio. Blessed with a team that had speed, savvy, and lots of pitching, the Missions zoomed into first place on April 22 amid a streak that saw them win thirteen of fourteen games, including seven of eight from their main rival, El Paso. When they did not get hits, they got good pitching—nineteen-year-old Dennys Reyes, the skinny-legged, barrel-chested son of a former Mexican League star, started the season 8-0. Eric Weaver, who was in his third season in San Antonio, started 7-1. When the pitchers struggled, the hitters delivered. The biggest day came on a windy Sunday in Tulsa, when San Antonio scored a franchise-record twenty-two runs against the Drillers. Jay Kirkpatrick, a twenty-seven-year-old first baseman who had been at every level in the Dodgers' farm system, drove in eight runs.

And it seemed that at every turn, the Missions found a way to win in the late innings. They won in the bottom of the ninth on opening day. They scored six runs in the seventh inning against El Paso on the day they moved into first place. They beat Wichita in the bottom of the ninth on April 28 when J. P. Roberge looped a bases-loaded single just over the infield. On May 6 they shocked Tulsa 1-0 when Dan Melendez hit a homer just inside the right-field foul pole in the bottom of the ninth.

By the end of May, the Missions were 36-17, and eight different players had been honored: Roberge, Ingram, and Paul LoDuca had been named Texas League Player of the Week; Reyes and Weaver had shared pitcher of the week accolades; Roberge had been the league's player of the month in May; Ignacio Flores, who had started 6-2, had been the Dodgers' minor-league pitcher of the month in May; and Gibbs and third baseman Brian Richardson had been named the Dodgers' minor-leaguers of the week.

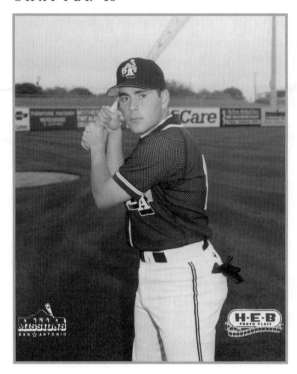

Paul LoDuca was the hitting leader of the 1997 Missions, who won the Texas League pennant for the first and only time during San Antonio's affiliation with the Los Angeles Dodgers. Courtesy Texas League

Roberge, who hit .355 in May, was Roenicke's kind of player—hard-nosed at the plate and able to do a lot in the field. The soft-spoken Californian played first base, second base, left field, and catcher during the season and always seemed to deliver at the plate in clutch situations. "He's not just a good hitter, he's a smart hitter," Roenicke said of Roberge after the April game in which his bloop hit drove in the winning run in the ninth.[9]

San Antonio clinched a playoff berth—the Missions' first since 1990—with ten games left in the first half. At 40-18, San Antonio had the best record in all of minor-league baseball. In their starting rotation Reyes was 8-1, Weaver was 7-2, Flores was 6-2 (and leading the league in earned-run average at 1.76), and Petie Roach, a converted first baseman, was 7-4. And with the playoffs clinched, the roster suddenly changed. On June 13 Reyes was promoted to Triple A. Weaver went up the next day, and Roach was gone on June 16. By the end of June, San Antonio was 6-10 and in third place.

The Double-A All-Star Game—in which Roberge, Gibbs, Flores,

and LoDuca all played—gave the team a two-day break in July. On the first day of the second half, San Antonio beat Jackson 4-3 in twelve innings to start a seven-game winning streak, topped off by one of those defining moments in a season.

San Antonio trailed Arkansas 4-3 in the bottom of the ninth on July 14, with the Travelers' Aaron Looper—and his ninety-eight-mile-an-hour fastball—on the mound. Cora led off the inning with a double just inside the first-base bag. LoDuca had been on deck to pinch-hit, but Roenicke called him back and sent up Gibbs, a switch-hitter, to bat left-handed. Gibbs was coming off the injured list and could not even swing a bat left-handed, but Arkansas did not know that. All the Travelers knew was that Gibbs was third in the league in hitting and a tremendous bunter. Gibbs squared around to bunt on the first pitch, forcing the third baseman to charge in and leave the base uncovered. Gibbs waved at the ball and missed, but Cora stole third without a throw. Roenicke then sent LoDuca up to hit for Gibbs, and he singled to score the tying run. San Antonio went on to win the game on a bases-loaded walk. "Sometimes you just try things and they work," Roenicke said after the game.

Some new pitchers began to throw well after the break, including Pat Ahearne, whom the Dodgers had signed out of independent ball in 1996, and Rick Gorecki, who had missed all of 1995 and 1996 with injuries. They added Will Brunson, a side-arm-throwing left-hander, on July 15 and screwball pitcher Jeff Kubenka, who had been a star at St. Mary's University the year before, on July 17.

The Missions stayed close to the front-running El Paso Diablos. By winning the second half, San Antonio could go straight to the Texas League Championship Series and avoid a playoff against the Diablos, who had been in the postseason six of the previous seven years. Even with improving pitching, San Antonio did not want to risk a best-of-five series with El Paso, which had a team batting average over .300 led by third baseman Mike Kinkade, who led the league in hitting at .385; Scott Krause, who was second at .361; and Danny Klassen, fourth at .331.

The second-half title came down to the last five games—all in El Paso. To win the second half, the Missions had to win four of them. El Paso scored two runs in the bottom of the ninth of the first game—off

1997 MISSIONS PLAYERS WHO WENT ON TO THE MAJOR LEAGUES.

Howard Battle: Braves, 1999

Alex Cora: Dodgers, 1998–

Rick Gorecki: Dodgers, 1998; Devil Rays, 1999

Matt Herges: Dodgers, 1999–2001; Expos, 2002

Garey Ingram: Dodgers, 1997

Keith Johnson: Angels, 2000

Mike Judd: Dodgers, 1997–2000; Devil Rays, 2001; Rangers, 2001

Jeff Kubenka: Dodgers, 1998–99

Paul LoDuca: Dodgers, 2001–2002

Dennys Reyes: Dodgers, 1997–98; Reds, 1998–2001; Rockies, 2001–2002; Rangers, 2002–

Ricky Stone: Astros, 2001–2002

Eric Weaver: Dodgers, 1998; Mariners, 1999; Angels, 2000

Jeff Williams: Dodgers, 1999–

Ron Roenicke is currently the third-base coach for the Anaheim Angels, and Lance Parrish is now the bullpen coach for the Detroit Tigers.

Kubenka, who had been all but unhittable since joining the team—to send it to extra innings. But in the tenth San Antonio rallied in typical fashion—Vernon Spearman led off with a single, reached second on a sacrifice, and went to third on a wild pitch. Brian Richardson brought him home with a single, and Kubenka finished off the Diablos in the bottom of the tenth. San Antonio won the second game 11-5, pounding out seventeen hits, including six doubles. Brunson gave up ten hits in six innings but just three runs. The Missions scored six runs in the third inning of game three and held on to win 10-6 when Kubenka struck out two El Paso batters with the bases loaded in the bottom of the ninth.

Then came the clincher. In front of one of the biggest crowds of the season at Cohen Stadium (7,090), the Diablos and Missions played a game for the ages. El Paso took a 5-1 lead into the top of the eighth, but San Antonio rallied. With the score at 5-2, two outs, and two runners on, Roenicke sent up Keith Johnson to pinch-hit for Cora.

Johnson, a sixth-round draft choice in 1992, was in his fifth year in the Dodgers' farm system but had played just four games above the Double A level. He had been moved out of his regular position, short-stop, by Cora and his splashy defense, but like Roberge he was one of Roenicke's favorite players because he would do anything the manager asked and play any position on the field. He had hit a career-best .274 in 1996, when he played 127 games for the Missions. He would wind up at .268 in 1997, but it was his two hits on that Friday night in El Paso that will be among his biggest.

Johnson had hurt his ankle running into the outfield fence at Wolff Stadium the week before, and he had been unable to play in the field since. But he had come up with a game-winning pinch hit the Sunday before against Wichita, so Roenicke went with a hunch. Johnson delivered a three-run homer to tie the game at 5-5. But El Paso rallied for two runs in the bottom of the inning for a 7-5 edge.

With one away in the top of the ninth, Kyle Cooney and Melendez were hit by pitches, bringing up Johnson again, who had faked his way in the outfield through the bottom of the eighth. He worked a 2-1 count against reliever Scott Garner, then hit the next pitch to the deepest part of left field for a two-run triple. Johnson came home moments later on Gibbs's sacrifice fly, and Kubenka held the lead in the bottom of the ninth as the Missions clinched the second half.

At the same time Shreveport—the first-half champion in the East—was knocking off Tulsa, which meant that the championship series would start immediately.

The Missions won the series opener, which was the first playoff game ever at Wolff Stadium, beating the Captains 6-0 behind seven innings of shutout pitching from Gorecki. Mike Judd, a young pitcher who had gotten hot for San Antonio after coming up from Class A at midseason, matched him the next night, also a 6-0 win for the Missions. The third game went to the bottom of the ninth tied at 1-1, but Roberge gave San Antonio its last final-at-bat win, hitting a line-drive homer off reliever Edwin Corps and sending the series to Shreveport.

Left-handed pitcher Will Brunson was the winner in the deciding game of the 1997 Texas League Championship Series. Courtesy Texas League

A night of stormy weather slowed down the Missions, though. Virtually the entire team was stranded in the Dallas–Fort Worth Airport the next night when their flight out of San Antonio was four hours late and the last flight to Shreveport was canceled.

The Captains won 1-0 the next day, then rallied in the eighth to take Game Five, 5-4. Troy Brohawn, the league's earned-run-average champion, shut them out the next night to force Game Seven. But on a late September afternoon at Fairgrounds Field, Brunson came through with the game of his life. The skinny left-hander threw eight shutout innings against the Captains, and San Antonio scored two runs—on an error and a wild pitch—in the fourth inning of the 2-0 victory.

The pennant was the Missions' first—and only—title during their affiliation with the Dodgers. The players gave much of the credit to their manager. "I owe a lot to Ron," Johnson said in 1999. "The years I played for him, I started paying a whole lot more attention to the game.

He had such a good eye about the game, things that most people would miss. I think playing for him made me a much more intelligent player. I became a player who would always be thinking about things that were going to happen, so I could react properly instead of everything being a surprise." Gibbs said it was Roenicke's work habits that made the difference. "The best thing about him is that he's always working, always looking for a way to give the team a chance to win. He does what it takes to make you a better player."[10]

Parrish benefited from working with his longtime friend as well. The next season, when Roenicke was promoted from San Antonio to Albuquerque at midseason, he took over the team—which won the first half—through a rebuilding period in July and August and a tough first-round playoff loss to Wichita.

Roenicke credited the good mix of players for much of the team's success. "You need those young guys who will come in and play, who have that raw talent. But a manager can tell a guy how to play, or a coach can tell a guy how to play, but if they see other guys playing the game how it's supposed to be played, it will mean a lot more."[11]

Ron Roenicke (left) and Gorman Heimueller were the manager and pitching coach respectively of the 1998 Missions. Courtesy Texas League, photo by Tom Kayser

CHAPTER 10

In addition to a second-straight playoff appearance in 1998, San Antonio also saw what is believed to be the only "homer cycle" in baseball history. Arkansas's Tyrone Horne, who never played a day in the major leagues, hit a solo homer, two-run homer, three-run homer, and grand slam in consecutive at-bats at Wolff Stadium. The Missions also had one of their biggest rallies ever in 1998, scoring twelve runs in the eleventh inning of what had been a scoreless game at Wichita. Angel Pena hit a grand slam and a solo shot in the inning, and Mike Metcalfe, Juan Diaz, and Glenn Davis also had homers.

The 1999 season saw the first appearance of big-league teams at Wolff Stadium, as the Houston Astros beat the Detroit Tigers 8-3 on April 3. And while the 1999 team did not make the postseason, it did have its share of big days. Luke Allen went 5 for 6 as part of a twenty-eight-hit attack in a 22-8 win over Midland and Hiram Bocachica. Eric Gagne, a French Canadian former hockey player, was the Texas League Pitcher of the Year as he led the league with 185 strikeouts and a 2.63 earned-run average as a starter. Matt Montgomery topped the league in saves with twenty-six, which was a team record until 2003.

The Missions sagged to the worst record in the West in 2000, at 64-76. And by the end of that season, the relationship with the Dodgers was over. Besides long-term problems like different ideas about winning at the minor-league level, the relationship had worsened when the Dodgers were sold to a group led by media baron Rupert Murdoch. There had been an almost complete turnover in the on-field staff, and budget cuts had affected the Missions operations as well.

San Antonio had more than its share of suitors, though. Having a farm team in a big city with a major airport located in the western part of Double A territory (there are no Double A teams west of El Paso) with a relatively new stadium and facilities was attractive to a number of teams. In the end the Missions signed up with the Seattle Mariners, thanks in part to the relationship between club president Burl Yarbrough and Mariners general manager Pat Gillick, who had given Yarbrough his first job in baseball. In the official announcement of the deal, both men were optimistic that it would be a good relationship for both parties.

As it turned out, they had reason for optimism.

The New Generation,

2001–2003

ON MAY 24, 2001, the Seattle Mariners did something the Los Angeles Dodgers, Texas Rangers, Cleveland Indians, Milwaukee Brewers, or Chicago Cubs never did—they came to town to play an exhibition game against their local farm club.

A crowd of 7,587—swollen by dozens of Japanese journalists covering the rookie season of Ichiro Suzuki—turned out at Wolff Stadium for the game, which the Missions won 14-2. And while the victory was not the first official act for the new parent club in San Antonio, it was a noteworthy start to a new relationship.

The Mariners did something else positive as well, sending a playoff-quality team to San Antonio. The Missions wound up losing to Round Rock in the divisional playoffs in a dramatic best-of-five series that came down to the last out of the last game. It turned out to be a prelude to one of the most dramatic seasons—and dramatic comebacks—in San Antonio history.

The day Greg Dobbs showed up in San Antonio, Missions manager Dave Brundage had him in the lineup.

San Antonio had been awful the first half of the 2002 season, finishing twenty games under .500 and seventeen games behind division-

Greg Dobbs came up from class A late in the 2002 season and played a key role the Missions' run to the Texas League pennant. Courtesy Texas League

winning Round Rock. When they had hit well, they had not pitched well (a trend that started three games into the year with a 12-11 loss at El Paso). When they pitched well, the hitting disappeared (they lost five games 2-1). The hitting seemed to be missing in action on a regular basis.

So when Dobbs—a tenth-round draft pick who had hit .324 in 2001, his first season in professional ball—showed up on July 19, Brundage put him to work. Dobbs singled in his first at-bat in Double A. First-base coach Terry Pollreisz, who had coached him in rookie ball the year before, patted him on the back and said, "Well, that didn't take you long, did it?"

"Even the first baseman congratulated me," Dobbs said.[1]

The fun did not last long, though. Later in the game, he pulled a calf muscle, an injury that put Dobbs out of the lineup for fifteen days. "I had to kid him a little bit about that one—I told him we got the worse end of that trade," Brundage said.[2]

But Dobbs put his time to good use. He quickly discovered the spiritual leader of the team, first baseman Andy Barkett, and spent as much time with him as possible. Barkett had played seventeen games with the Pittsburgh Pirates in 2001, and at twenty-six he was one of the veterans on the Missions. There had been no veterans in low Class A ball, where Dobbs had hit .275 but showed flashes of brilliance, including a sixteen-game hitting streak. "I thought, 'Hey, this guy has been to the big leagues,'" Dobbs said. "He's been where I want to go, and he obviously knows how to get there." They talked regularly, and when Dobbs got back into the lineup on August 4, one of their discussions came into play.

During the game at Round Rock, Dobbs came up with a runner at second base with nobody out. The obvious baseball decision was to give himself up to move the runner to third—hit the ball to the right side, even for an out. He tried, but the pitcher made a good play to stop the ball, freezing the runner at second. "When I got back to the dugout, he asked me what I had been thinking out there," Dobbs said. "I said I was trying to pull that fastball, I just was little late on it. With a guy on second in that situation, you move him over. "He looked at me and said, 'You're right. You just didn't get it done this time.'" You know, as a ballplayer, you know those things. But sometimes it helps for someone to reinforce it a little."[3]

Dobbs did not need many reinforcements, though. He went 2 for 4 that night against the Express and 3 for 4 the next against Midland, boosting his average to .545 and prompting Missions broadcasters Brian Anderson and Roy Acuff to dub him "The Natural."[4] As Dobbs got hot, so did the rest of the Missions. They won the series with Midland at home. They beat Wichita 3 of 4 on the road. By August 15 they were 32-22 in the second half. After a split in Tulsa, they won nine of their last twelve games, clinching the half on August 29 against the Express.

During August, Dobbs hit .366, including twelve multihit games and a 4-for-4 day against Tulsa. The thing that amazed everyone—including scout Al LaMacchia, who said Dobbs had the biggest effect of any player in the league the entire season—was how effortlessly he did it. Dobbs, who also had to adjust to playing right field after spending the first half of the season at third base, said:

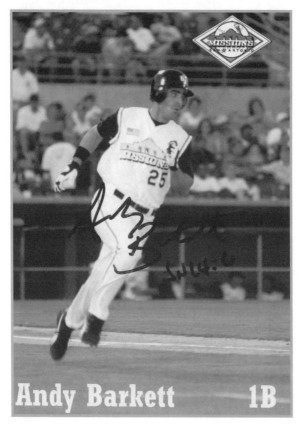

Andy Barkett 1B

Veteran Andy Barkett and Manager Dave Brundage played major roles in the Missions' turnaround from last place in the first half of 2002 to the Texas League pennant that year. Courtesy Texas League

It's funny to say, but I found it was easier to hit in Double A. You know what to expect at the plate. In low-A ball, the pitchers might throw three in the dirt and two to the backstop, then bust a fastball right down the middle of the plate on you like they've been doing it their whole lives. The pitchers were all over the joint.

But in Double A it just seemed easier. The guys were around the [strike] zone. They were older guys, guys who knew what they were doing and they knew how to locate their pitches. There were even some guys who had been to the big leagues.

I'm an aggressive hitter by nature. I like to hit the first pitch, and seeing that kind of pitching, it just all worked out.[5]

It continued to work out in the playoffs. In the opener at Round Rock, he hit a game-tying home run in the ninth (Barkett brought home Jamal Strong with the go-ahead run in the tenth). After the Express took the next two games of the best-of-five series, San Antonio's bullpen—which was the team's other strength down the stretch—kept the series going by shutting down Round Rock over the last four-plus innings. And in the deciding game, Dobbs went 3 for 4 with a triple as San Antonio won 4-2.

The opener of the championship series in Tulsa was one of the strangest games in Texas League playoff history. San Antonio went the first 9⅔ innings without a hit—the game went into extra innings at 2-2 thanks to seven walks—before Adrian Myers singled home Antonio Perez. Allan Simpson, part of the Missions' three-headed bullpen, then finished off the Drillers.

Tulsa won the next night when Doug Garcia slid around a tag by Missions catcher Scott Maynard—after a perfect throw from Dobbs in right field—in the bottom of the eighth. The Drillers went up 2-1 in the series when the Missions left thirteen runners on base the next night and won 4-3.

When the series moved to San Antonio, Dobbs got another big opportunity. He came up with the bases loaded and one out in the bottom of the ninth of a 3-3 game. Drillers manager Tim Ireland had five men in the infield, daring Dobbs to hit a game-winning sacrifice fly. The pitcher was left-hander Allen McDill, who had pitched in the majors for the Royals, Tigers, and Red Sox. Dobbs quickly got behind in the count at 0-2. "The first two sliders were dirty," he said. "I told myself that I had seen his slider and that I had to stay back and trust myself." He watched two more pitches drop out of the strike zone, then fouled off two more pitches. And then "He left a slider up and I was able to get it to the outfield," Dobbs said, remembering another bit of reinforcement from Barkett about doing anything it takes to get a run home from third with less than two outs.[6] Dobbs's sacrifice fly brought in Ruben Castillo with the winning run.

San Antonio won Game Five 9-6, as Antonio Perez went 3 for 4 and Dobbs was 2 for 2, with two runs batted in. And he appeared to have done his part the next night, hitting a double to left-center that scored Strong. But Ireland argued that the ball had bounced up and hit the chain-link fence above the outfield wall—and won. Strong was sent back to third base, and the Drillers won 4-3.

Broadcaster Roy Acuff, interviewing Missions manager Jimmy Johnson, was a big part of the celebration of the team's pennant-clinching victory in Game Seven of the Texas League Championship Series in 2002. Courtesy Texas League

ROY

To fans of the San Antonio Missions, Roy Acuff was more than just a play-by-play man on the radio—after fifteen years broadcasting, he was the voice of the team, its image. And to a dedicated home audience (and more than a few who listened to the radio while at the ballpark), Acuff's voice was the Missions. Being around the players virtually all the time as part of the traveling party, he also became a part of their intimate group, getting to know many of them personally.

So when he fell and broke his hip in the lobby of an Oklahoma City hotel on August 12, 2002—in front of the team—his well being was of major concern. He had surgery in Oklahoma and spent five days in the hospital there before going home for more physical therapy.

His return to Wolff Stadium late in August was a moment for celebration. His first night back on the air was something different. It was the final night of the regular season, a meaningless game at Wolff Stadium against Round Rock, the Missions' opponent in the first round of the playoffs. Acuff went into the radio booth in the seventh inning to do play by play for the rest of the game in preparation for the playoffs. But after nine innings, the score was 5-5, as it was after ten, eleven, and fifteen. Finally, Round Rock teed off on Missions second baseman Rob Gandolfo, who had become a pitcher in the thirteen inning, and won 12-5 in eighteen innings. Acuff did the play by play for every inning after the seventh. "After that, he knew he was ready," said his longtime partner, Brian Anderson.

And while the Missions did not plan to play a five-plus-hour game on the night of his comeback, the team did have something special for Acuff at the end of the season. "The players dedicated the playoffs to Roy," Anderson said. "They had a team meeting and made it a point to 'take care of business' if for no other reason than for Roy."

Acuff worked at all the Missions' home playoff games, including the pennant-clincher against Tulsa. The players, knowing he still was not mobile enough to get down to the clubhouse, carried the championship trophy up to the radio booth. "We were still on the air when most of the Missions came pouring into the booth," Anderson said. "It was a great scene."

That set up the seventh game, the first seventh and deciding game of a championship series ever played in San Antonio. The Missions scored two runs in the first inning against Drillers starter Travis Hughes, and San Antonio starter Rafael Soriano—who had pitched in eight games for the Seattle Mariners in the middle of the season—gave up two hits in seven innings. Aaron Looper, the final member of the bullpen triumvirate and who had been a set-up man all year, pitched the last two innings (of the closers, Aaron Taylor had been promoted to the major leagues, and Simpson had to sit out with numbness that, after the season, was diagnosed as lupus). Dobbs was 2 for 3 and finished the postseason with a .435 average.

Afterward he admitted he was as excited for players like Barkett—who made the game-ending putout at first base—and Strong as he was for himself.

> There was no better guy to make the final out. I'm sprinting in from right field, and I'm screaming and Jamal is screaming, and we can't hear each other because the crowd is screaming louder.
>
> It was just a wonderful feeling—you're overwhelmed—but I was so happy for the coaches and the guys who had turned it around from the first half. It was fulfilling for me, but I was as excited for everyone else.[7]

Among the most excited was Brundage, who won his first championship at any level. "You sure don't want to do it like that, worst to first," he said. "You'd rather win them all. You never think anything like this could happen to you, or anything better."[8]

Life just continued to get better for The Natural. Dobbs was married the next February and a week later went to spring training with the major-league club. But his luck ran out early in the 2003 season with the Missions—he suffered a season-ending injury, a torn Achilles tendon, the first week in San Antonio.

Conclusion

PROFESSIONAL BASEBALL has not always been a successful—or even profitable—adventure in San Antonio. The city has seen more than its share of mediocre teams, from the earliest days of the Texas League to well into its second century. And there have been more than a few times when the business of minor-league baseball in the city was a money-loser, most notably when the team left town after a pennant in 1964.

But in the long run, the sport has survived in San Antonio. Civic-minded leaders brought it back in 1968, and businessmen helped it grow. The arrival of the NBA's Spurs turned the attention away from the diamond for a while, but the construction of Wolff Stadium helped boost interest in the only charter member of the Texas League still in the league after 115 years.

The three-year-old affiliation with the Seattle Mariners has boosted the quality of the team as well. After making the playoffs in 2001 and rallying to win a pennant in 2002, the Missions dominated the Texas League in 2003, winning both halves of the Western Division race with ease and beating Frisco in the Texas League Championship Series four games to one. The club also delivered the city's first sweep of the league's three postseason awards, with Player of the Year Justin Leone, Pitcher of the Year Travis Blackley, and Manager of the Year Dave Brundage. Leone came to San Antonio in the spring as a utility player after a series of mediocre seasons in Class A, but he took over the third-base job when Greg Dobbs was injured early in the season and, eventually leading the league in doubles, on-base percentage, extra-base hits, and runs scored. Blackley led the league in wins and was second in earned-run average on a staff that also had three of the top four leaders in strikeouts. (Clint Nageotte was tops in the league; Bobby Madritsch, who won two games in the championship series, came in second; and Blackley was fourth.)

San Antonio's three straight postseason appearances under the Mariners marked the first time the team had made the playoffs more than two years in a row since the Great Depression, and the back-to-back playoff titles are a first in San Antonio baseball history. The 2003 Missions also broke one of the oldest records in franchise history, the seventeen-game winning streak by the 1908 Bronchos, by claiming eighteen in a row during the first half to vault from last place to first.

With the current structure of minor-league baseball—the movement of franchises is even more limited than in the major leagues—it is unlikely that San Antonio will move beyond the Double A Texas League. But in many ways, that is a good thing, for experts agree that the best young players in baseball are at the Double A level. With minor-league baseball, fans can afford to buy tickets and sit close to the action. And staying in the Texas League continues a lineage that began in the nineteenth century, something that not many organizations today can claim.

So in many ways San Antonio's future in professional baseball looks bright—much brighter than it did on that summer afternoon in 1888 when an overzealous fan pilfered the sportswriter's scorebook on the trolley.

Appendix 1

Year-by-Year Results and Highlights

The information provided below was compiled
by Scott Hanzelka and Chris Foltz.

1888
Nickname: None
Record: First team, 6-28; second team, 14-11
Managers: First team, John Cavanaugh, Robert Rose; second team, John McCloskey
Ballpark: Muth's Park
Notes: Gus Sherry of the second team led the Texas League in triples with six. Lew Whistler, who also played for Houston and Galveston, led the league in home runs with seven. Frank Hoffman of the second team led the league with 231 strikeouts and an 0.70 earned-run average; his record was 22-11.

1892
Nickname: None
Record: 11-20
Manager: Lou Sylvester
Ballpark: San Pedro Park

1895
Nickname: Missionaries
Record: 21-72
Managers: William Clare, George Reese, George Watkins, Red Cox, J. C. Sherry, Gus Land
Ballpark: San Pedro Park

1896
Nickname: Bronchos
Record: 57-71
Managers: Dan Crotty, Mike Lawrence, Mike O'Connor
Ballpark: San Pedro Park
Notes: O'Connor, who spent part of the season at Denison, was the Texas League batting champion at .395 and led the league in home runs with eighteen.

1897
Texas League co-champions with Galveston
Nickname: Bronchos
Record: 68-44
Manager: Mike O'Connor
Ballpark: San Pedro Park

1898
Nickname: Gentlemen
Record: 7-20
Managers: Tom Farley, Arthur Rutherford, Frank "Kid" Fears
Ballpark: San Pedro Park

1899
Nickname: Bronchos
Record: 35-39
Managers: Pete Weckbecker, Win Clark, Charlie Weber
Ballpark: San Pedro Park
Notes: Bill Clark led the league in stolen bases with fifty-eight.

1903
South Texas League champions
Nickname: Mustangs
Record: 69-54
Manager: Wade Moore
Ballpark: San Pedro Park
Notes: Pitcher Orth Thomas went 22-18.

1904
Nickname: Mustangs
Record: 32-88
Managers: Wade Moore, Ellis Hardy, Charles Blackburn
Ballpark: San Pedro Park

1905
Nickname: Warriors
Record: 69-60
Managers: Bill Morrow, Walter Morris, George Page
Ballpark: San Pedro Park

1906

Nickname: Bronchos
Record: 57-70
Managers: William Alexander, George Page, Ike Pendleton
Ballpark: Electric Park

1907

Nickname: Bronchos
Record: 81-58
Managers: Sam LaRoque, Pat Newnam
Ballpark: Electric Park
Notes: Buck Harris was 23-12, and E. M. Colgrove was 22-13.

1908

Texas League champions
Nickname: Bronchos
Record: 95-48
Managers: George "Cap" Leidy, Pat Newnam
Ballpark: Electric Park
Notes: Newnam led the league in home runs with eighteen. Buck Harris was 22-9, and Fred Winchell was 20-11. Edward C. Collins stole fifty-eight bases. The pitching staff threw a San Antonio–record twenty-two shutouts.

1909

Nickname: Bronchos
Record: 76-63
Manager: George "Cap" Leidy
Ballpark: Electric Park
Notes: George Stinson led the Texas League in triples with ten. Fred Winchell led the league in strikeouts with 260 and went 21-12. Harry Ables struck out 259, and Willie Mitchell struck out 215.

1910

Nickname: Bronchos
Record: 74-62
Manager: George "Cap" Leidy
Ballpark: Electric Park
Notes: George Stinson tied for the league lead in home runs with eleven. Harry Ables led the league in strikeouts with 310 and threw a seven-inning no-hitter against Waco. Fred Blanding was 20-9. Harry Billiard struck out 242.

1911

Nickname: Bronchos

Record: 77-68

Manager: George "Cap" Leidy

Ballpark: Electric Park

Notes: Frank Metz led the league in home runs with twenty-two.

1912

Nickname: Bronchos

Record: 84-57

Managers: George "Cap" Leidy, Frank Metz

Ballpark: Electric Park

Notes: Metz was the Texas League batting champion at .323 and led the league in home runs with twenty-one and doubles with thirty-three. Clyde Goodwin was 22-10, Brown Rogers was 21-9, and Frank Browning was 21-14.

1913

Nickname: Bronchos

Record: 74-78

Manager: George Stinson

Ballpark: Block Stadium

Notes: Dave Davenport tied for the league lead in strikeouts with 204. Roy Morton, who spent part of the season with Galveston, was 21-12.

1914

Nickname: Bronchos

Record: 46-103

Managers: Clyde Goodwin, Dred Cavender, John Kibler

Ballpark: Block Stadium

1915

Nickname: Bronchos

Record: 81-67

Manager: George "Cap" Leidy

Ballpark: League Park

Notes: Scotty Barr, who spent part of the season with San Antonio, led the Texas League in triples with nineteen. Emmett "Hick" Munsell led the league in wins with twenty-five. Ovid Mullins was 23-14.

1916

Nickname: Bronchos

Record: 66-79

Managers: George "Cap" Leidy, Jack Love, Dolly Stark, Harry Stewart
Ballpark: League Park

1917
Nickname: Bronchos
Record: 76-89
Managers: Charley O'Leary, Clay Perry
Ballpark: League Park
Notes: John Baggan led the Texas League in triples with thirteen.

1918
Nickname: Bronchos
Record: 43-45
Manager: Clay Perry
Ballpark: League Park

1919
Nickname: Aces
Record: 60-89
Manager: Mique Finn
Ballpark: League Park

1920
Nickname: Bears
Record: 79-71
Manager: John Nee
Ballpark: League Park
Notes: Bill Fincher was 21-11. Eddie Brown led the league in hits with two hundred. Eugene Cocreham pitched thirty-four complete games.

1921
Nickname: Bears
Record: 60-89
Manager: John Nee
Ballpark: League Park
Notes: Fred "Snake" Henry led the league in stolen bases with fifty-two. Bob Couchman, who spent part of the season with Galveston, was 20-15. Mutt Williams, who spent part of the season with Dallas, was 20-19 and struck out 206. Joe Connolly drove in 110 runs.

1922

Nickname: Bears
Record: 76-79
Manager: Hub Northen
Ballpark: League Park
Attendance: 41,874
Notes: Homer Ezzell, who spent part of the season with Shreveport, led the league in stolen bases with fifty-five. Kedzi Kirkham led the league with 114 hits.

1923

Nickname: Bears
Record: 81-68
Manager: Bob Coleman
Ballpark: League Park
Attendance: 78,783
Notes: Ike Boone was the Texas League batting champion at .402, the last hitter in the league to top .400; he also led the league with fifty-three doubles, twenty-six triples, and 135 runs batted in. Syl Simon had 116 runs batted in.

1924

Nickname: Bears
Record: 75-75
Manager: Bob Coleman
Ballpark: League Park
Attendance: 88,280

1925

Nickname: Bears
Record: 81-64
Manager: Bob Coleman
Ballpark: League Park
Attendance: 94,158
Notes: Danny Clark was the Texas League batting champion at .399 and led the league in stolen bases with twenty-nine; he also hit 31 home runs and drove in 143 runs. Lyman Nason led the league in triples with eighteen and drove in 109 runs. Si Rosenthal drove in 115 runs, and Jim Washburn drove in 101. The 1925 Bears set San Antonio records for total bases (2,522), home runs (171), and runs batted in (962).

1926

Nickname: Bears
Record: 86-70
Manager: Carl Mitze
Ballpark: League Park
Attendance: 148,533
Notes: Ray Flaskamper led the league in stolen bases with thirty. Tiny Owens tied for the league lead in wins with twenty-two. Frank Watt went 20-9. Ping Bodie, who spent part of the season with Wichita Falls, drove in 105 runs.

1927

Nickname: Bears
Record: 65-90
Managers: Carl Mitze, Bob Couchman, Ray Flaskamper
Ballpark: League Park
Attendance: 88,403

1928

Nickname: Bears
Record: 76-83
Manager: Frank Gibson
Ballpark: League Park
Attendance: 106,517
Notes: Ray Flaskamper led the league in stolen bases with forty-eight. Ray Grimes drove in 114 runs, and Lyman Nason drove in 104.

1929

Nickname: Indians
Record: 56-106
Managers: William Alexander, Pat Newnam
Ballpark: League Park
Attendance: 77,086
Notes: Bud Messenger, who spent part of the season at Wichita Falls, led the league in strikeouts with 138.

1930

Nickname: Indians
Record: 60-93
Manager: George J. Burns
Ballpark: League Park
Attendance: 59,828
Notes: Jo Jo Moore led the Texas League with eighteen triples.

1931
Nickname: Indians
Record: 66-94
Manager: Claude Robertson
Ballpark: League Park
Attendance: 55,202

1932
Nickname: Indians
Record: 57-91
Manager: Claude Robertson
Ballparks: League Park, Eagle Field, Tech Field
Attendance: 31,761

1933
Texas League champions
Nickname: Missions
Record: 79-72
Affiliation: St. Louis Browns
Manager: Hank Severeid
Ballpark: Tech Field
Attendance: 78,363
All-stars: Cap Crossley, utility; Pid Purdy, outfielder; Fabian Kowalik, pitcher
Notes: Purdy was the Texas League batting champion at .358. Ollie Bejma and
Crossley tied for the league lead in doubles with forty-eight. Jim E. Walkup
led the league in strikeouts with 146. Kowalik was 21-13. Larry Bettencourt
drove in 102 runs.

1934
Lost in league championship series
Nickname: Missions
Record: 89-65
Affiliation: St. Louis Browns
Manager: Hank Severeid
Ballpark: Tech Field
Attendance: 125,259
All-stars: Chet Morgan, outfielder (spent part of season with Beaumont); Tommy
Heath, catcher; Ash Hillin, pitcher
Notes: Hillin was the Texas League Pitcher of the Year and led the league in wins
with twenty-four. Morgan was the batting champion at .342 and had 216 hits.
Larry Bettencourt led the league with 129 runs batted in. Earl Caldwell was
20-14.

1935
Nickname: Missions
Record: 75-84
Affiliation: St. Louis Browns
Manager: Hank Severeid
Ballpark: Tech Field
Attendance: 109,665
All-star: Earl Caldwell, pitcher
Notes: Debs Garms led the league in triples with eighteen.

1936
Nickname: Missions
Record: 73-77
Affiliation: St. Louis Browns
Manager: Bob Coleman
Ballpark: Tech Field
Attendance: 97,743
All-stars: Sig Gryska, shortstop; Debs Garms, outfielder; Lefty Mills, pitcher
Notes: Gryska drove in 122 runs. Garms led the league in hits with 203.

1937
Lost in first round of playoffs
Nickname: Missions
Record: 85-76
Affiliation: St. Louis Browns
Manager: Zack Taylor
Ballpark: Tech Field
Attendance: 141,341

1938
Lost in league championship series
Nickname: Missions
Record: 93-67
Affiliation: St. Louis Browns
Manager: Zack Taylor
Ballpark: Tech Field
Attendance: 136,249
Notes: Bill Trotter was 22-9, and Jack Kramer was 20-11. Sig Gryska drove in 106
  runs.

1939
Lost in first round of playoffs
Nickname: Missions
Record: 89-72
Affiliation: St. Louis Browns
Manager: Zack Taylor
Ballpark: Tech Field
Attendance: 116,416
Notes: Emil Bildilli tied for the league lead in wins with twenty-two. Tony Criscola drove in 106 runs. John Lucadello led the league with 182 hits.

1940
Lost in first round of playoffs
Nickname: Missions
Record: 89-72
Affiliation: St. Louis Browns
Manager: Marty McManus
Ballpark: Tech Field
Attendance: 97,575
Notes: Bob Muncrief was the Texas League Player of the Year and had a record of 22-9. Pinky Jorgensen, who spent part of the year with Oklahoma City, led the league in home runs with twenty-three. Vern Stephens led the league with ninety-seven runs batted in. Maury Newlin led the league in wins with twenty-three.

1941
Nickname: Missions
Record: 58-96
Affiliation: St. Louis Browns
Manager: Marty McManus
Ballpark: Tech Field
Attendance: 34,010

1942
Lost in first round of playoffs
Nickname: Missions
Record: 80-68
Affiliation: St. Louis Browns
Manager: Ralph Winegarner
Ballpark: Tech Field
Attendance: 66,792
Notes: John Whitehead led the league with a 1.20 earned-run average.

1946

Lost in first round of playoffs
Nickname: Missions
Record: 87-65
Affiliation: St. Louis Browns
Manager: Jimmy Adair
Ballpark: Tech Field
Attendance: 295,103
Notes: The pitching staff set a record for team earned-run average (2.47).

1947

Nickname: Missions
Record: 60-94
Affiliation: St. Louis Browns
Managers: Jimmy Adair, Mark Carrola
Ballpark: Mission Stadium
Attendance: 152,605

1948

Nickname: Missions
Record: 75-76
Affiliation: St. Louis Browns
Manager: Gus Mancuso
Ballpark: Mission Stadium
Attendance: 263,959
All-star: Bill Sommers, second baseman

1949

Nickname: Missions
Record: 70-83
Affiliation: St. Louis Browns
Manager: Gus Mancuso
Ballpark: Mission Stadium
Attendance: 225,500

1950

Texas League champions
Nickname: Missions
Record: 79-75
Affiliation: St. Louis Browns
Manager: Don Heffner
Ballpark: Mission Stadium

1950 (*cont.*)

Attendance: 180,580

Notes: Frank Saucier was *The Sporting News* Minor League Player of the Year and was the Texas League batting champion with a .343 average.

1951

Lost in league championship series

Nickname: Missions

Record: 86-75

Affiliation: St. Louis Browns

Manager: Jo Jo White

Ballpark: Mission Stadium

Attendance: 180,577

Notes: Bob Turley was the Texas League Pitcher of the Year, going 20-8 and striking out two hundred; he struck out twenty-two in a sixteen-inning game. Jim Dyck was the player of the year and led the league with 127 runs batted in. Omer Tolson tied for the league lead in triples with twelve. The team set a San Antonio record for most complete games with eighty-three.

1952

Nickname: Missions

Record: 79-82

Affiliation: St. Louis Browns

Manager: Jo Jo White

Ballpark: Mission Stadium

Attendance: 110,001

Notes: Bud Heslet led the league in home runs with thirty-one and drove in 117 runs.

1953

Nickname: Missions

Record: 67-87

Affiliation: St. Louis Browns

Managers: Jimmie Crandall, Bill Norman

Ballpark: Mission Stadium

Attendance: 98,711

Notes: Ryne Duren led the league in strikeouts with 212 and threw a seven-inning no-hitter against Beaumont.

1954

Nickname: Missions

Record: 78-83

Affiliation: Baltimore Orioles

Manager: Don Heffner

Ballpark: Mission Stadium

Attendance: 149,065

Notes: Frank Kellert was the Texas League Player of the Year and led the league with 146 runs batted in; he also hit forty-one home runs. Joe Durham led the league in triples with seventeen and drove in 108 runs. Ryne Duren struck out 224.

1955

Lost in first round of playoffs

Nickname: Missions

Record: 93-68

Affiliation: Baltimore Orioles

Manager: Don Heffner

Ballpark: Mission Stadium

Attendance: 150,861

Notes: Jim Pisoni led the league with 118 runs batted in. Mel Held was 24-7 and threw a five-inning no-hitter against Fort Worth.

1956

Nickname: Missions

Record: 76-78

Affiliation: Baltimore Orioles

Manager: Joe Schultz Jr.

Ballpark: Mission Stadium

Attendance: 100,001

1957

Lost in first round of playoffs

Nickname: Missions

Record: 76-78

Affiliation: Baltimore Orioles

Manager: Joe Schultz Jr.

Ballpark: Mission Stadium

Attendance: 93,661

1958

Nickname: Missions

Record: 74-79

Affiliation: Baltimore Orioles

Manager: Grady Hatton

Ballpark: Mission Stadium

1958 (*cont.*)

Attendance: 101,305

Notes: Henry Moreno hit thirty home runs. Jim Archer led the league with nineteen complete games.

1959

Nickname: Missions

Record: 75-70

Affiliation: Chicago Cubs

Manager: Grady Hatton

Ballpark: Mission Stadium

Attendance: 111,487

All-star: Lee Handley, right fielder

Notes: Ron Santo led the Texas League in doubles with thirty-five.

1960

Lost in first round of playoffs

Nickname: Missions

Record: 77-68

Affiliation: Chicago Cubs

Managers: Grady Hatton, Lou Klein

Ballpark: Mission Stadium

Attendance: 106,273

All-stars: J. C. Hartman, shortstop; Duke Ducote, left fielder; Jack Curtis, pitcher

Notes: Curtis was the Texas League Pitcher of the Year and led the league in wins with nineteen. Ducote led the league in home runs with thirty-two.

1961

League co-champions

Nickname: Missions

Record: 74-65

Affiliation: Chicago Cubs

Managers: Rip Collins, Harry Craft, Bobby Adams, Rube Walker

Ballpark: Mission Stadium

Attendance: 91,493

Notes: Don Davis led the Texas League in doubles with thirty-three. Nelson Matthews tied for the league lead in triples with ten. Craig Sorensen led the league in home runs with twenty-seven.

1962

Nickname: Missions

Record: 68-72

Affiliation: Chicago Cubs

Manager: Walt Dixon

Ballpark: Mission Stadium

Attendance: 101,917

All-star: Don Eaddy, third baseman

Notes: Billy Ott led the league in triples with twelve. Harvey Branch led the league in strikeouts with 216.

1963

League co-champions

Nickname: Bullets

Record: 79-61

Affiliation: Houston Colt .45s

Manager: Lou Fitzgerald

Ballpark: Mission Stadium

Attendance: 84,965

All-stars: Mike White, second baseman; Joe Horner, pitcher

1964

League champions

Nickname: Bullets

Record: 85-55

Affiliation: Houston Colt .45s

Manager: Lou Fitzgerald

Ballpark: Mission Stadium

Attendance: 85,808

All-stars: Joe Morgan, second baseman; Sonny Jackson, shortstop; Chuck Harrison, utility; Leo Posada, outfielder; Clint Courtney, catcher; Chris Zachary, pitcher; Don Bradey, pitcher

Notes: Zachary was the Texas League Pitcher of the Year. Morgan was the player of the year and led the league in doubles with forty-two. Harrison led the league in home runs with forty and was second in runs batted in with 119.

1968

Nickname: Missions

Record: 53-86

Affiliation: Chicago Cubs

Manager: Harry Bright

Ballpark: V. J. Keefe Field

Attendance: 40,069

Notes: Archie Reynolds tied for the league lead in wins with thirteen.

1969

Nickname: Missions
Record: 51-81
Affiliation: Chicago Cubs
Manager: Jim Marshall
Ballpark: V. J. Keefe Field
Attendance: 38,024
All-stars: Brock Davis, outfielder; Oscar Gamble, outfielder; John Felske, catcher; Dean Burk, pitcher
Notes: Gamble led the Texas League in doubles with thirty-two.

1970

Nickname: Missions
Record: 67-69
Affiliation: Chicago Cubs
Manager: Jim Marshall
Ballpark: V. J. Keefe Field
Attendance: 44,271
All-stars: Adrian Garrett, outfielder; Pat Jacquez, pitcher
Notes: Garrett led the league in home runs with twenty-nine. Don Nottebart tied for the league lead in saves with fifteen.

1971

Nickname: Missions
Record: 63-77
Affiliation: Chicago Cubs
Manager: Walt Dixon
Ballpark: V. J. Keefe Field
Attendance: 47,113
All-star: Billy North, outfielder
Notes: North led the league in stolen bases with forty-seven.

1972

Nickname: Brewers
Record: 53-87
Affiliation: Milwaukee Brewers
Managers: Mike Roarke, Al Widmar, Jim Walton
Ballpark: V. J. Keefe Field
Attendance: 253,139
All-star: Gorman Thomas, outfielder.
Notes: Thomas led the league in home runs with twenty-six. John Begzos was the Texas League Executive of the Year.

1973

Lost championship series
Nickname: Brewers
Record: 82-57
Affiliation: Cleveland Indians
Manager: Tony Pacheco
Ballpark: V. J. Keefe Field
Attendance: 177,197
All-stars: Duane Kuiper, second baseman; Joe Azcue, designated hitter; Jeff
    Newman, catcher; Jim Kern, pitcher; Luis Penalver, pitcher; Rick Sawyer, pitcher
Notes: Sawyer led the league in wins with eighteen. Penalver led the league with
    twenty saves.

1974

Nickname: Brewers
Record: 68-64
Affiliation: Cleveland Indians
Manager: Woody Smith
Ballpark: V. J. Keefe Field
Attendance: 143,519
All-stars: Dennis Eckersley, pitcher; Larry Andersen, pitcher
Notes: Eckersley was the Texas League's right-handed pitcher of the year and tied
    for the league lead in wins with fourteen; he led the league with 163 strikeouts.

1975

Nickname: Brewers
Record: 50-85
Affiliation: Cleveland Indians
Manager: Woody Smith
Ballpark: V. J. Keefe Field
Attendance: 138,517

1976

Nickname: Brewers
Record: 63-71
Affiliation: Texas Rangers
Manager: Marty Martinez
Ballpark: V. J. Keefe Field
Attendance: 60,122
All-star: John Poloni, pitcher
Notes: Keith Chauncey led the league in stolen bases with thirty-one. Gary Gray
    drove in 109 runs.

1977

Nickname: Dodgers
Record: 61-67
Affiliation: Los Angeles Dodgers
Manager: Don LeJohn
Ballpark: V. J. Keefe Field
Attendance: 53,359

1978

Nickname: Dodgers
Record: 79-57
Affiliation: Los Angeles Dodgers
Manager: Don LeJohn
Ballpark: V. J. Keefe Field
Attendance: 74,420
All-stars: Mickey Hatcher, third baseman; Dave Patterson, pitcher
Notes: Dick Sander led the league in strikeouts with 159. Patterson led the league
in saves with nineteen.

1979

Nickname: Dodgers
Record: 69-62
Affiliation: Los Angeles Dodgers
Manager: Don LeJohn
Ballpark: V. J. Keefe Field
Attendance: 63,990
All-stars: Gary Weiss, shortstop; Ron Roenicke, outfielder
Notes: Tack Wilson led the league in stolen bases with fifty-six. Mickey Lashley
led the league in saves with nine.

1980

Lost championship series
Nickname: Dodgers
Record: 74-62
Affiliation: Los Angeles Dodgers
Manager: Don LeJohn
Ballpark: V. J. Keefe Field
Attendance: 153,355
Notes: Brian Holton tied for the league lead in wins with fifteen. Fernando
Valenzuela led the league in strikeouts with 162.

1981

Lost in championship series

Nickname: Dodgers

Record: 76-57

Affiliation: Los Angeles Dodgers

Manager: Don LeJohn

Ballpark: V. J. Keefe Field

Attendance: 134,668

All-stars: Steve Sax, second baseman; Dave Sax, utility; Dale Holman, outfielder; Mark Bradley, outfielder; Mike Zouras, catcher; Rick Rodas, pitcher; Tom Niedenfuer, pitcher

Notes: Steve Sax was the Texas League Player of the Year and led the league in batting at .346. Holman was the most valuable player of the all-star game. Greg Brock led the league in home runs with thirty-two and drove in 106 runs. Orel Hershiser led the league in saves with fifteen.

1982

Nickname: Dodgers

Record: 68-68

Affiliation: Los Angeles Dodgers

Manager: Don LeJohn

Ballpark: V. J. Keefe Field

Attendance: 138,024

All-stars: Dann Bilardello, catcher; Dean Rennicke, pitcher; Paul Voigt, pitcher

1983

Nickname: Dodgers

Record: 66-70

Affiliation: Los Angeles Dodgers

Managers: Terry Collins, Rick Ollar, Dave Wallace

Ballpark: V. J. Keefe Field

Attendance: 100,283

All-stars: R. J. Reynolds, outfielder; Sid Fernandez, pitcher

Notes: Fernandez won the pitching "triple crown" (lowest earned-run average, 2.82; most strikeouts, 209; tied for most wins, thirteen) and was the Texas League Pitcher of the Year; he also was most valuable player of the all-star game. Roberto Alexander led the league in saves with twenty-two.

1984

Nickname: Dodgers

Record: 64-72

Affiliation: Los Angeles Dodgers

1984 (*cont.*)

Manager: Gary Larocque

Ballpark: V. J. Keefe Field

Attendance: 125,542

All-stars: Joe Vavra, utility; Ralph Bryant, outfielder; Gilberto Reyes, catcher; Tim Meeks, pitcher

Notes: Mariano Duncan and Stu Pederson tied for the league lead in triples with eleven. Bryant led the league in home runs with thirty-one. Meeks tied for the league lead in wins with fourteen. Bill Pagani was the Texas League Executive of the Year.

1985

Nickname: Dodgers

Record: 59-75

Affiliation: Los Angeles Dodgers

Manager: Gary Larocque

Ballpark: V. J. Keefe Field

Attendance: 106,183

All-stars: Jeff Hamilton, third baseman; Jose Gonzalez, outfielder; Scott May, pitcher

1986

Nickname: Dodgers

Record: 64-71

Affiliation: Los Angeles Dodgers

Manager: Gary Larocque

Ballpark: V. J. Keefe Field

Attendance: 122,261

All-stars: Tracy Woodson, third baseman; Mike Devereaux, outfielder; Shawn Hillegas, pitcher

Notes: Ken Harvey tied for the league lead in triples with eight.

1987

Nickname: Dodgers

Record: 50-86

Affiliation: Los Angeles Dodgers

Manager: Gary Larocque

Ballpark: V. J. Keefe Field

Attendance: 122,277

All-stars: Mike Devereaux, outfielder; Joe Szekely, catcher

1988

Lost in first round of playoffs
Nickname: Missions
Record: 73-60
Affiliation: Los Angeles Dodgers
Manager: Kevin Kennedy
Ballpark: V. J. Keefe Field
Attendance: 130,899
All-stars: Domingo Michel, utility; Mike Huff, outfielder; Mike Munoz, pitcher

1989

Nickname: Missions
Record: 49-87
Affiliation: Los Angeles Dodgers
Manager: John Shoemaker
Ballpark: V. J. Keefe Field
Attendance: 158,402
All-star: Carlos Hernandez, catcher
Notes: Chris Nichting led the league in strikeouts with 136. Burl Yarbrough was
    the Texas League Executive of the Year.

1990

Lost in championship series
Nickname: Missions
Record: 78-56
Affiliation: Los Angeles Dodgers
Manager: John Shoemaker
Ballpark: V. J. Keefe Field
Attendance: 180,931
All-stars: Eric Karros, first baseman; Steve Finken, third baseman; Henry
    Rodriguez, outfielder; Tom Goodwin, outfielder; Mike James, pitcher
Notes: Rodriguez was the Texas League Player of the Year and led the league in
    home runs (twenty-eight) and runs batted in (109). Karros led the league in
    batting at .352 and in doubles with forty-five. Goodwin led the league in sto-
    len bases with sixty.

1991

Nickname: Missions
Record: 61-75
Affiliation: Los Angeles Dodgers
Manager: John Shoemaker
Ballpark: V. J. Keefe Field

1991 (*cont.*)

Attendance: 185,336

Notes: Pedro Martinez, who spent part of the season at Bakersfield, was *The Sporting News* Minor League Player of the Year. Eric Young led the league in stolen bases with seventy. Dennis Springer led the league in strikeouts with 138.

1992

Nickname: Missions
Record: 62-74
Affiliation: Los Angeles Dodgers
Manager: Jerry Royster
Ballpark: V. J. Keefe Field
Attendance: 177,365
All-star: Billy Ashley, outfielder
Notes: Ashley led the league in home runs with twenty-four.

1993

Nickname: Missions
Record: 58-76
Affiliation: Los Angeles Dodgers
Manager: Glenn Hoffman
Ballpark: V. J. Keefe Field
Attendance: 189,251
All-stars: Ben Van Ryn, pitcher; Rick Gorecki, pitcher
Notes: Van Ryn was the Texas League Pitcher of the Year, leading the league in wins with fourteen and in earned-run average at 2.21.

1994

Nickname: Missions
Record: 62-74
Affiliation: Los Angeles Dodgers
Manager: Tom Beyers
Ballpark: Wolff Stadium
Attendance: 411,959
All-star: Juan Castro, shortstop
Notes: Burl Yarbrough was the Texas League Executive of the Year.

1995

Nickname: Missions
Record: 64-72
Affiliation: Los Angeles Dodgers
Manager: John Shelby

Ballpark: Wolff Stadium

Attendance: 387,090

All-stars: Wilton Guerrero, shortstop; Oreste Marrero, designated hitter; David Pyc, pitcher; Gary Rath, pitcher

Notes: Guerrero led the Texas League in batting at .348. Rath tied for the league lead in wins with thirteen and led the league in earned-run average at 2.77.

1996

Nickname: Missions

Record: 69-70

Affiliation: Los Angeles Dodgers

Manager: John Shelby

Ballpark: Wolff Stadium

Attendance: 381,001

All-stars: Paul Konerko, first baseman; Eric Weaver, pitcher

Notes: Willie Romero led the Texas League in doubles with thirty-six.

1997

League champions

Nickname: Missions

Record: 84-55

Affiliation: Los Angeles Dodgers

Manager: Ron Roenicke

Ballpark: Wolff Stadium

Attendance: 336,542

All-stars: J. P. Roberge, utility; Kevin Gibbs, outfielder; Paul LoDuca, catcher

Notes: Roenicke was the Texas League Manager of the Year. San Antonio was the organization of the year. Brian Richardson led the league in triples with thirteen. Roberge drove in 105 runs. The Missions led the league in fielding percentage (.976).

1998

Lost in first round of playoffs

Nickname: Missions

Record: 67-73

Affiliation: Los Angeles Dodgers

Managers: Ron Roenicke, Lance Parrish

Ballpark: Wolff Stadium

Attendance: 387,715

All-stars: Adrian Beltre, third baseman; Peter Bergeron, outfielder; Angel Pena, catcher; Ted Lilly, pitcher

Notes: Pena drove in 105 runs.

1999

Nickname: Missions
Record: 67-73
Affiliation: Los Angeles Dodgers
Manager: Jimmy Johnson
Ballpark: Wolff Stadium
Attendance: 318,590
All-stars: Tony Mota, outfielder; Eric Gagne, pitcher
Notes: Gagne was the Texas League Pitcher of the Year and led the league in earned-run average at 2.63 and strikeouts with 185. Luke Allen led the league in triples with twelve. Mike Mctcalfe led the league in stolen bases with fifty-seven. Matt Montgomery led the league in saves with twenty-six.

2000

Nickname: Missions
Record: 64-76
Affiliation: Los Angeles Dodgers
Manager: Rick Burleson
Ballpark: Wolff Stadium
Attendance: 325,137
All-star: Luke Prokopec, pitcher

2001

Lost in first round of playoffs
Nickname: Missions
Record: 70-67
Affiliation: Seattle Mariners
Manager: Dave Brundage
Ballpark: Wolff Stadium
Attendance: 309,113
All-star: Jeff Heaverlo, pitcher
Notes: Heaverlo led the league in strikeouts with 173, complete games with four, and shutouts with four. Bo Robinson led the league in walks with eighty-one.

2002

League champions
Nickname: Missions
Record: 68-72
Affiliation: Seattle Mariners
Manager: Dave Brundage
Ballpark: Wolff Stadium
Attendance: 316,983

All-star: Craig Anderson, pitcher

Notes: Jamaal Strong led the league in stolen bases with forty-six. Aaron Taylor tied for second in the league in saves with twenty-four.

2003

League champions

Nickname: Missions

Record: 88-51

Affiliation: Seattle Mariners

Manager: Dave Brundage

Ballpark: Wolff Stadium

Attendance: 305,235

All-stars: Jose Lopez, shortstop; Justin Leone, third base; Mike Curry, outfield; A. J. Zapp, designated hitter; Clint Nageotte, pitcher; Bobby Madritsch, pitcher; Travis Blackley, pitcher

Notes: For the first time in San Antonio baseball history, the Missions swept the postseason honors: Dave Brundage, manager of the year; Justin Leone, player of the year; and Travis Blackley, pitcher of the year. Leone led the league in doubles, on-base percentage, extra-base hits, and runs scored. Blackley led the league with seventeen wins. Clint Nageotte led the league in strikeouts with 157, Bobby Madritsch was second with 154, and Blackley was fourth with 144. Jared Hoerman led the league in saves, with a franchise-record thirty-six. Mike Curry led the league in stolen bases with fifty-eight.

Appendix 2

Players Who Made It to the Major Leagues

Below are the names of San Antonio players who made it to the major leagues, with the years they played in San Antonio; compiled by Scott Hanzelka.

Fred Abbott, 1895
Harry Ables, 1908–10, 1925–26
Bert Adams, 1909
Dick Adams, 1948
Karl Adams, 1923
Dave Adlesh, 1963–64
Pat Ahearne, 1996–97
Raleigh Aitchison, 1916
Ed Albrecht, 1950–51, 1953
Matt Alexander, 1969
Luke Allen, 1998–2000
Mack Allison, 1911
Victor Alvarez, 1999–2000
Ed Amelung, 1981–82, 1988
Larry Andersen, 1974
Andy Anderson, 1946–47, 1950
Mike Anderson, 1997
Jim Archer, 1958
George Archie, 1948–49
Don Arlich, 1964
Tony Arnold, 1989
Billy Ashley, 1992
Pedro Astacio, 1991
Jim Atkins, 1956
Rick Austin, 1973
Joe Azcue, 1973

Tom Badcock, 1971
Floyd Baker, 1942
Neal Baker, 1929
Bobby Balcena, 1951–53
Frank Baldwin, 1958
Mike Balenti, 1915–16
Tony Balsamo, 1961–62
John Barfield, 1994
Clyde Barfoot, 1917–20
Red Barkley, 1939
Scotty Barr, 1915
Tony Barron, 1991–92
Billy Bartley, 1903
Howard Battle, 1997
Matt Batts, 1957
Trey Beamon, 2001
Robbie Beckett, 1999
Joe Beckwith, 1977
Ollie Bejma, 1933–35, 1937
Bill Bell, 1958
Jerry Bell, 1975
Juan Bell, 1988
Bob Belloir, 1973–75
Adrian Beltre, 1998
Stan Benjamin, 1947
Johnny Berardino, 1938

Peter Bergeron, 1998
Richard Bertell, 1959–60
Larry Bettencourt, 1933–37
Tom Bianco, 1972
Dann Bilardello, 1981–82
Jim Bilbrey, 1946
Emil Bildilli, 1938–39
Harry Billiard, 1910
Babe Birrer, 1956
Frank Biscan, 1947, 1949, 1950
Bud Black, 1952
Henry Blanco, 1993–96
Nate Bland, 1997–98
Fred Blanding, 1910
Ted Blankenship, 1931
Clarence Blethen, 1924
Willie Bloomquist, 2001
Randy Bobb, 1968
Hiram Bocachica, 1999–2000
Ping Bodie, 1926
Bob Boken, 1942
Bill Bolden, 1922
Julio Bonetti, 1937
Everett Booe, 1917, 1919–25
Ike Boone, 1923
Rafael Bournigal, 1990–91
Pat Bourque, 1971
Chick Bowen, 1921
Bob Boyd, 1963
Don Bradey, 1963–64
Mark Bradley, 1978–81
Harvey Branch, 1960–62
Darrell Brandon, 1964
Sid Bream, 1982
Bill Brennan, 1986
Jim Brewer, 1959
Tony Brewer, 1982
Harry Bright, 1968
Greg Brock, 1981
Jerry Brooks, 1990
Alton Brown, 1956
Bobby Brown, 1977

Eddie Brown, 1919–20
Jophrey Brown, 1969
Walter Brown, 1950
Willard Brown, 1956
Frank Browning, 1912–13, 1915–16
Will Brunson, 1995–97
Ralph Bryant, 1984
Freddie Burdette, 1960–62
Tom Burgmeier, 1963
Leo Burke, 1957
Bill Burns, 1908
George Burns, 1930
John Burrows, 1937
Ed Busch, 1941–42
Mike Busch, 1992
Kid Butler, 1916
Jeff Byrd, 1976
Milt Byrnes, 1936–38
Wayne Cage, 1974–75
Miguel Cairo, 1995
Earl Caldwell, 1934–35
Dick Calmus, 1968
Kevin Campbell, 1989–90
Conrad Cardinal, 1963
Paul Casanova, 1962
Joe Casey, 1921
Braulio Castillo, 1990–91
Juan Castro, 1993–94
Wayne Causey, 1957
Roger Cedeno, 1993
Tiny Chaplin, 1929–30
John Chapman, 1928
Chin-Feng Chen, 2000
Larry Cheney, 1922
Len Church, 1968
Al Cihocki, 1953
Jim Clancy, 1976
Bill Clark, 1897
Danny Clark, 1925
Ed Clark, 1896
Jim Clark, 1912, 1914, 1916
Jim Clark, 1956

Harlond Clift, 1933

Gene Cocreham, 1911, 1917–18, 1920–21

Jim Colborn, 1968

Ed Cole, 1939–40, 1946–47

Bob Coleman, 1923–25

Percy Coleman, 1899

Ray Coleman, 1946

Edgar Collins, 1912–14

Bud Connolly, 1934

Joe Connolly, 1921, 1924

Merv Connors, 1935, 1940

Bill Conway, 1888

Dennis Cook, 1991

Bob Cooney, 1933

Wilbur Cooper, 1930

Alex Cora, 1997

Claude Corbitt, 1939

Dan Corder, 1971

Edwin Correa, 1993

Clint Courtney, 1963–64

Jack Coveney, 1908

Tex Covington, 1917

Bill Cox, 1939

George Crable, 1912, 1914–15

Steve Crawford, 1988

Anthony Criscola, 1936–39

Frank Croucher, 1946–47

Don Crow, 1979–80

Cal Crum, 1915

Bobby Cuellar, 1976

John Cummings, 1995

Jack Curtis, 1960

Omar Daal, 1992

Jay Dahl, 1963

Cliff Daringer, 1911

Claude Davenport, 1920–21

Dave Davenport, 1912–15

Brock Davis, 1963–64, 1969, 1975

Jacke Davis, 1964

Ron Davis, 1963–64

George Decker, 1970

Billy DeMars, 1951

John DeSilva, 1994

Mike Devereaux, 1986–87

Bernie DeViveiros, 1931

Juan Diaz, 1998–99

Johnny Dickshot, 1933

Bob Dillinger, 1941

Alec Distaso, 1969–70

John Dolan, 1907

Len Dondero, 1930

Brian Doyle, 1976

Sammy Drake, 1959–60

Darren Dreifort, 1994

Mariano Duncan, 1984

Bill Dunlap, 1932

Jim Dunnegan, 1970–71

Dan Duran, 1976

Ryne Duren, 1953–55

Joe Durham, 1954, 1957

Jim Dyck, 1950–51

Don Eaddy, 1960–62

Dennis Eckersley, 1974

George Edmondson, 1925

Red Ehret, 1888

George Elder, 1948

Harry Elliott, 1957

James Elliott, 1924

Rob Ellis, 1972

Kevin Elster, 1993

Charlie Engle, 1933–35

Jack Enright, 1914

Jewel Ens, 1908

Al Epperly, 1954

Frank Ernaga, 1959

Cecil Espy, 1983–85

Bobby Estalella, 1950

Homer Ezzell, 1922

Lenny Faedo, 1986

Pete Falcone, 1989

Cliff Fannin, 1952

Frank Fanovich, 1955

Jeff Farnsworth, 2001

John Felske, 1969

Terry Felton, 1984

Stan Ferens, 1947

Sid Fernandez, 1983

Don Ferrarese, 1955

Mike Figga, 2000

Dana Fillingim, 1927–28

Bill Fincher, 1919–21

Tommy Fine, 1949, 1951–52

Brian Fitzgerald, 2001

Howie Fitzgerald, 1932

Ray Flaskamper, 1926–28, 1931–32

Les Fleming, 1952

Darrin Fletcher, 1988

Kris Foster, 1999

Howie Fox, 1955

Ray Francis, 1917

John Franco, 1982

Tito Francona, 1954–55

Joe Frazier, 1948–51

Jim Fridley, 1953

Owen Friend, 1947

Oscar Fuhr, 1924

Frank Fuller, 1919–24

Eric Gagne, 1999

Stan Galle, 1946

Jim Galloway, 1923–24

Balvino Galvez, 1985, 1992

Oscar Gamble, 1969

Mike Garbark, 1948

Karim Garcia, 1996

Earl Gardner, 1905

Daniel Garibay, 1994

Debs Garms, 1935–36

Adrian Garrett, 1970

Clarence Garrett, 1915

Ned Garver, 1946–47

Dave Gerard, 1959–60

Al Gerheauser, 1949

Frank Gibson, 1917–20

Geronimo Gil, 1998–2000

Larry Gilbert, 1911

George Gillpatrick, 1897

Joe Girard, 1929

John Goetz, 1959–60, 1964

Walt Golvin, 1926

Jesse Gonder, 1958

Eusebio Gonzalez, 1925–26, 1928

Jose Gonzalez, 1985

Orlando Gonzalez, 1974–75

Charlie Gooch, 1932

Wilbur Good, 1926

Marv Goodwin, 1911–14

Tom Goodwin, 1990

Rick Gorecki, 1993, 1997

Gary Gray, 1976

Lenny Green, 1955

Tim Griesenbeck, 1927

Hank Griffin, 1910

Pug Griffin, 1928

Art Griggs, 1907–1908

Ray Grimes, 1928–29

Turkey Gross, 1920–24

Jerry Grote, 1963

Frank Grube, 1941

Sig Gryska, 1936–39

Wilton Guerrero, 1995

Chris Gwynn, 1986

Tom Hafey, 1942

John Hairston, 1968–69

Sam Hairston, 1958

Sammy Hale, 1917–18

Darrel Hall, 1998

Jeff Hamilton, 1985

Garvin Hamner, 1948–50

Fred Hancock, 1952

Mike Handiboe, 1915

Lee Handley, 1959

Gerald Hannahs, 1978

Loy Hanning, 1940–41, 1948

Greg Hansell, 1992

Dave Hansen, 1989

Charlie Harding, 1915–16

George Harper, 1932

Jack Harper, 1917–19

Bon Harrison, 1954–57

Chuck Harrison, 1963–64

Sam Harshaney, 1934–37, 1940, 1946

Mike Hartley, 1987–88

J.C. Hartman, 1960, 1963–64

Jeff Hartsock, 1990

Luther Harvel, 1930

Mickey Hatcher, 1978

Grady Hatton, 1958–60

Phil Haugstad, 1953

George Hausmann, 1940–42, 1951

Ray Hayworth, 1949

Tommy Heath, 1933–34

Danny Heep, 1987

Mel Held, 1950, 1953–55

Hank Helf, 1948

John Henry, 1923

Snake Henry, 1921

Ubaldo Heredia, 1980

Matt Herges, 1995–98

Babe Herman, 1924

Carlos Hernandez, 1989

Leo Hernandez, 1979–82

Procopio Herrera, 1947–51, 1954

Orel Hershiser, 1980–81, 1991

Gus Hetling, 1917

Jesse Hickman, 1963–64

Pinky Higgins, 1931

Shawn Hillegas, 1985–86

Hob Hiller, 1922

Joe Hoerner, 1963

Dutch Hoffman, 1933

Frank Hoffman, 1888

Tex Hoffman, 1917

John Hofford, 1888

Eddie Hohnhorst, 1910

Todd Hollandsworth, 1993

Stan Hollmig, 1954–56, 1958

Darren Holmes, 1989

Brian Holton, 1979–80

Joel Horlen, 1973

Gene Host, 1958

Ken Hottman, 1974

Matt Howard, 1992–93

Steve Howe, 1979

Ken Howell, 1983

Ken Hubbs, 1960

Clarence Huber, 1930

Ken Huckaby, 1993–94

Hal Hudson, 1948, 1950, 1955

Mike Huff, 1987–88

Ben Huffman, 1939–41

Terry Hughes, 1968–69

Tom Hughes, 1932

Bernie Hungling, 1927

Garey Ingram, 1991–94, 1997

Hooks Iott, 1941–42, 1946

Hank Izquierdo, 1956

George Jackson, 1919

Sonny Jackson, 1964

Pat Jacquez, 1968–70

Sig Jakucki, 1946–47

Lefty James, 1917

Mike James, 1990–92

Rick James, 1968, 1970

Garry Jestadt, 1968, 1970

Adam Johnson, 1920

Darrell Johnson, 1951–52

Dick Johnson, 1959–60

Elmer Johnson, 1920

Fred Johnson, 1922–23

Keith Johnson, 1996–98

Larry Johnson, 1973

Lou Johnson, 1959

Rett Johnson, 2003

Johnny Johnston, 1911

Jake Jones, 1949

Ross Jones, 1981

Bubber Jonnard, 1918

Jimmy Jordan, 1933

Rip Jordan, 1921

Tom Jordan, 1947–48

Pinky Jorgenson, 1940

Mike Judd, 1997

Ken Jungels, 1948

Ike Kahdot, 1925

Bob Kaiser, 1973

Eric Karros, 1990

George Keefe, 1896–97

Jim Keenan, 1924

Frank Kellert, 1954

Walt Kellner, 1958

Kenny Kelly, 2001

Ren Kelly, 1920, 1922

Jim Kern, 1973

Harry Kimberlin, 1937–38

Dennis Kinney, 1974–75

Mike Kinnunen, 1989

Wayne Kirby, 1987–89

Joe Kirrene, 1955

Hugo Klaerner, 1929

Tom Klawitter, 1982–83

Rudy Kneisch, 1929

Austin Knickerbocker, 1951

Pete Knisely, 1920

Kevin Kobel, 1972

Paul Konerko, 1996

Fabian Kowalik, 1931–33

Jack Kramer, 1938

John Kroner, 1933

Otto Krueger, 1898

Jeff Kubenka, 1997

Duane Kuiper, 1973

Jerry Kutzler, 1993

Pete LaCock, 1971

Al LaMacchia, 1942, 1946–47, 1949–50

Dick Lanahan, 1948

Pete Lapan, 1930

Sam LaRoque, 1907

Don Larsen, 1968

Chris Latham, 1995

Ron Law, 1968

Gene Layden, 1917

Pete Layden, 1948

Fred Lear, 1920

Bill Lee, 1922

Dave Lemonds, 1968–69

Don Lenhardt, 1948

Jeffrey Leonard, 1977

Roy Leslie, 1927

Sam Leslie, 1930

Ed Levy, 1949

Dennis Lewallyn, 1987

Francisco Libran, 1969

Glen Liebhart, 1937

Ted Lilly, 1998

Jim Lindsey, 1925–27

Ed Linke, 1939

Royce Lint, 1948

Charlie Locke, 1954–57

Paul LoDuca, 1995, 1997

Luis Lopez, 1988–89

Slim Love, 1928

Tom Lovelace, 1924–25

Vance Lovelace, 1984–85

Johnny Lucadello, 1939

Ray Lucas, 1930

Charles Lucas, 1923

Dick Luebke, 1956–58

Memo Luna, 1957

Tom Lundstedt, 1970

Tony Mack, 1988

Morris Madden, 1981–83

Scotti Madison, 1982

Sal Madrid, 1948

Bob Mahoney, 1952

Frank Mancuso, 1942

Gus Mancuso, 1948

Jim Mangon, 1958

Johnny Marcum, 1946–47

Joe Margoneri, 1959

Fred Marolewski, 1956–57

Isidro Marquez, 1989–91, 1993

Oreste Marrero, 1995

Fred Marsh, 1957

Mike Marshall, 1980

Rube Marshall, 1917

Jack Martin, 1919

Joe Martina, 1917

Marty Martinez, 1976

Pedro Martinez, 1991

Ramon Martinez, 1988, 1996

Onan Masaoka, 1998

Julio Mateo, 2002

Nelson Mathews, 1961–62

Ron Mathis, 1988

Scott May, 1985–87

Sam Mayer, 1924

Melvin Mazzera, 1933–36

Jamie McAndrew, 1990, 1992

Roger McCardell, 1962

Jerry McCarthy, 1949

Von McDaniel, 1964

Alex McFarlan, 1892

Dan McFarlan, 1892

Howard McGranor, 1912

Otto McIvor, 1909–10

Red McKee, 1922–23

Jim McKeever, 1896

Pat McLaughlin, 1941

Marty McManus, 1941

Jimmy McMath, 1968–69

Tom McMillan, 1973

Herb McQuaid, 1922

Glenn McQuillen, 1939

Gil Meche, 2002

Irv Medlinger, 1952–54

Heinie Meinke, 1923

Adam Melhuse, 2000

Bud Messenger, 1927–29

Mike Metcalfe, 1995, 1998–2000

Ed Mickelson, 1953

Ezra Midkiff, 1912

Ed Mierkowicz, 1957

Bill Miller, 1936–37

Lemmie Miller, 1981–82, 1989

Orlando Miller, 2000

Howard Mills, 1934–35

Mike Mimbs, 1992

Bobby Mitchell, 1978

Roy Mitchell, 1908

Willie Mitchell, 1909

Ron Moeller, 1957

Blas Monaco, 1938

Raul Mondesi, 1991–92

Rafael Montalvo, 1984

Manny Montejo, 1959

Al Montreuil, 1969

Euel Moore, 1931–32

JoJo Moore, 1930

Chet Morgan, 1934

Joe Morgan, 1964

Moe Morhardt, 1962

Walter Morris, 1903, 1905

Guy Morrison, 1923

Jose Mota, 1987–88

Greg Mulleavy, 1929

Bob Muncrief, 1935–38, 1940

Red Munger, 1958

Jose Munoz, 1991

Mike Munoz, 1988

Noe Munoz, 1994

Danny Murphy, 1960–61

Jim Murray, 1899

George Myatt, 1933

Rod Myers, 1999

Doc Nance, 1912

Bob Neighbors, 1938, 1940–41

Maury Newlin, 1940–41

Jeff Newman, 1973

Ray Newman, 1969–70

Pat Newnam, 1903, 1905, 1907–1908

Fred Nicholson, 1915

Chris Nichting, 1989, 1992

Tom Niedenfuer, 1981

Jim Norris, 1973–74

Billy North, 1970–71

Hub Northen, 1918–20, 1922

Don Nottebart, 1970

Charley O'Leary, 1917

Chuck Oertel, 1954–57

Jose Offerman, 1989

Ed Olivares, 1963

Dave Oliver, 1974–75

Jesse Orndorff, 1904

Eddie Oropesa, 1995

Ernie Orsatti, 1926

Hector Ortiz, 1992–94, 1999

Javier Ortiz, 1988

Antonio Osuna, 1994

Willis Otanez, 1995

Billy Ott, 1962

Joe Otten, 1896

Frankie Pack, 1949

Chan Ho Park, 1994

Jose Parra, 1992–93

Tacks Parrott, 1906

Dave Patterson, 1977–78

Pat Patterson, 1925

Tom Patton, 1957

Stu Pederson, 1983–84, 1987

Red Peery, 1930

Angel Pena, 1998

Jim Pendleton, 1963

Jack Perconte, 1978

Ron Perranoski, 1959

Pol Perritt, 1920

Clay Perry, 1917–18

Parson Perryman, 1924

Sid Peterson, 1942

Jesse Petty, 1916

Mike Piazza, 1992

Cy Pieh, 1917

Jim Pisoni, 1954–55

Aaron Pointer, 1963–64

John Poloni, 1976

Elmer Ponder, 1915

Jim Poole, 1990

Paul Popovich, 1960–61

Leo Posada, 1964

Dante Powell, 2000

Dennis Powell, 1984

Ted Power, 1977–79

Walt Preston, 1892

Don Prince, 1960–61

Luke Prokopec, 1998–2000

Pid Purdy, 1933–34

J.J. Putz, 2002

Jim Pyburn, 1957

Eddie Pye, 1990

Ewald Pyle, 1935, 1937–41

Jim Qualls, 1968

Eddie Quick, 1909

Joe Rabbitt, 1926

Eric Raich, 1973–74

Mike Ramsey, 1985–87

Gary Rath, 1995

Doug Rau, 1980

Jim Ray, 1964

Fred Raymer, 1905

Harry Raymond, 1888

Dick Reichle, 1924

Earl Reid, 1949

Paul Reuschel, 1970–71

Rick Reuschel, 1971

Dennys Reyes, 1997

Gilberto Reyes, 1983–84

Archie Reynolds, 1968

R.J. Reynolds, 1982–83

Charlie Rhodes, 1914

Dave Richards, 1979–80

Adam Riggs, 1996

Jim Riley, 1929–30

German Rivera, 1982–83

Tink Riviere, 1928

Dave Roberts, 1955–57

Jim Roberts, 1923

Daryl Robertson, 1961–62

Brooks Robinson, 1956–57

Rich Rodas, 1981

Emmett Rodgers, 1888

Felix Rodriguez, 1994

Henry Rodriguez, 1990

Ron Roenicke, 1978–79

Damian Rolls, 1998

Dave Rosello, 1970–71

Si Rosenthal, 1924–25

David Ross, 2000

Don Ross, 1949

Gary Ross, 1968

Ken Rudolph, 1968–70

Mickey Rutner, 1951

Dee Sanders, 1948

Fred Sanford, 1941

Jose Santiago, 1958–59

Ron Santo, 1959

Frank Saucier, 1950

Jack Savage, 1987

Rick Sawyer, 1973

Dave Sax, 1981

Steve Sax, 1981

Jeff Schaefer, 1987

Art Scharein, 1934–39

Carl Scheib, 1956–57

Red Schillings, 1924

Rudy Schlesinger, 1968

Norm Schlueter, 1941

Henry Schmidt, 1914

Johnny Schulte, 1923

Len Schulte, 1941–42

Art Schwind, 1913

Mike Scioscia, 1978

Tim Scott, 1987–90

Ken Sears, 1946–47

Larry See, 1983–85

Pat Seerey, 1949

Kal Segrist, 1955

Hank Severeid, 1933–35

Red Shea, 1929

Neil Sheridan, 1952

Pete Shields, 1922

Zak Shinall, 1990–91

Craig Shipley, 1987

Steve Shirley, 1977–80

Ray Shore, 1948–49

Ed Sicking, 1917–18

Roy Sievers, 1951

Paddy Siglin, 1926

Eddie Silber, 1938–41

Syl Simon, 1923

Ed Sixsmith, 1888

Roe Skidmore, 1970

Lou Sleater, 1950

Chris Snelling, 2002–2003

Marcelino Solis, 1960

Bill Sommers, 1948–49

Rafael Soriano, 2001–2002

Dennis Springer, 1989–92

Buck Stanton, 1934–39

Denny Stark, 2001

Dolly Stark, 1908–1909, 1916

Morrie Steevens, 1961–62

Justin Stein, 1940

Bryan Stephens, 1950

Vern Stephens, 1940

Earl Stephenson, 1970

Chuck Stevens, 1940

Dave Stewart, 1978

Ricky Stone, 1997–98

DaRond Stovall, 1999

Bill Strickland, 1938–39

Jim Strickland, 1974

Jamaal Strong, 2002

Marlin Stuart, 1947

Franklin Stubbs, 1983

Guy Sturdy, 1933

John Sullivan, 1950, 1952–53

Brian Sweeney, 2001

Bob Swift, 1938–39

Lou Sylvester, 1892

Willie Tasby, 1955–56

Fred Tauby, 1933

Alex Taveras, 1978, 1980, 1982

Aaron Taylor, 2002

Chuck Taylor, 1964

Ed Taylor, 1903

Harry Taylor, 1929

Tommy Taylor, 1928

Zack Taylor, 1937

Jeff Tesreau, 1909

Gorman Thomas, 1972

Bobby Thompson, 1976

Frank Thompson, 1908

Cotton Tierney, 1917

Les Tietje, 1937, 1939

Jim Todd, 1970–71

Phil Todt, 1923

Andy Tomasic, 1953

Leo Townsend, 1916, 1918

Bill Travers, 1972

Brian Traxler, 1989, 1991

Bill Trotter, 1938

Frank Truesdale, 1919

Bob Turley, 1950–51

Johnnie Tyler, 1941

Ismael Valdes, 1993–94

Fernando Valenzuela, 1980

Ben Van Ryn, 1993–94

Joe Vance, 1932–33

John Vergez, 1926

Ollie Voigt, 1921–22

Jake Volz, 1898–99, 1910

Howard Wakefield, 1911

Rube Walker, 1960

Jim E. Walkup, 1933

Jack Warner, 1960–62

Bill Warwick, 1924–25

Ron Washington, 1977

Frank Watt, 1925–26, 1928

Eric Weaver, 1995–97

Farmer Weaver, 1888

Charlie Weber, 1896–97, 1899

Neil Weber, 1999

Pete Weckbecker, 1899

Gary Weiss, 1979

Bon Welch, 1977

John Wetteland, 1988

Dutch Wetzel, 1929

Gary Wheelock, 1981

Lew Whistler, 1888

Charlie White, 1953

Elder White, 1961–62

Mike White, 1963

Myron White, 1978–79, 1981

John Whitehead, 1942, 1946

Nick Willhite, 1968

Billy Williams, 1959

Jeff Williams, 1997–98

Reggie Williams, 1985

Todd Williams, 1992

Chief Wilson, 1917

Roy Wilson, 1926

Tack Wilson, 1979

Hal Wiltse, 1933, 1936

Fred Winchell, 1907–1909

Fred Winchell, 1906

Ralph Winegarner, 1942

Clarence Winters, 1924–26

Kettle Wirts, 1925–27

George Wisterzil, 1908, 1916

Jerry Witte, 1941–42

Wally Wolf, 1963

Ken Wood, 1946, 1948

Tracy Woodson, 1986

Ricky Wright, 1980

Jimmy Wynn, 1963

George Yantz, 1910

Larry Yellen, 1963

Tony York, 1941

Eric Young, 1991

Ross Youngs, 1913

Chris Zachary, 1964

Al Zarilla, 1941–42

Chad Zerbe, 1996

Appendix 3

San Antonio Records

SINGLE SEASON

Hitting

Batting average: .402, Ike Boone, 1923
Games played: 166, John Baggan, 1917
At-bats: 656, Lee Stebbins, 1931
Runs scored: 144, Danny Clark, 1925
Hits: 241, Ike Boone, 1923
Hitting streak: 37 games, Ike Boone, 1923
Extra-base hits: 94, Ike Boone, 1923
Total bases: 391, Ike Boone, 1923
Singles: 161, Lee Stebbins, 1931
Doubles: 53, Ike Boone, 1923
Triples: 26, Ike Boone, 1923
Home runs: 41, Frank Kellert, 1954
Runs batted in: 146, Frank Kellert, 1954
Sacrifice bunts: 37, George "Cap" Leidy, 1908
Sacrifice flies: 14, Henry Rodriguez, 1990
Hit by pitch: 16, Jim Galloway, 1923
Walks: 115, Bob Caffery, 1956
Intentional walks: 9, Henry Rodriguez, 1990
Most strikeouts: 171, Gorman Thomas, 1972
Fewest strikeouts: 11, Lee Stebbins, 1934
Stolen bases: 70, Eric Young, 1991
Slugging percentage: .677, Danny Clark, 1925
On-base percentage: .482, Danny Clark, 1925
Most consecutive hits: 11, Si Rosenthal, 1924

Pitching

Wins: 25, Emmett Munsell, 1915
Losses: 23, Beans Parvin, 1896
Winning percentage: .824 (14-3), Dennis Eckersley, 1974
Earned-run average: 1.20, John Whitehead, 1942

Games: Freddie 65, Burdette, 1962
Games started: 36, Hobo Carson, 1931; Emil Bildilli, 1939
Complete games: 27, Hobo Carson, 1931
Games finished: 56, Matt Montgomery, 1999
Shutouts: 7, Marty Newlin, 1940
Innings pitched: 382, Emmett Munsell, 1915
Hits allowed: 335, Hobo Carson, 1931
Runs allowed: 198, Hobo Carson, 1929
Earned runs allowed: 162, Hobo Carson, 1929
Home runs allowed: 28, Charlie Locke, 1954
Hit batsmen: 31, George Crable, 1914
Walks: 159, Ryne Duren, 1953
Intentional walks: 14, Dean Burk, 1968
Strikeouts: 310, Harry Ables, 1910
Wild pitches: 22, Bob Grossman, 1974; John Wetteland, 1988
Balks: 9, Mike Schweighoffer, 1988; Phil Torres, 1988
Saves: 36, Jared Hoerman, 2003

TEAM SEASON RECORDS
Most games: 166, 1917
Fewest games: 128, 1977
Most wins: 95, 1908
Fewest wins: 46, 1914
Most losses: 106, 1929
Fewest losses: 48, 1908
Highest winning percentage: .664, 1908
Lowest winning percentage: .309, 1914
Highest attendance: 411,959, 1994
Lowest attendance: 31,761, 1932
Most runs scored: 1,036, 1925
Fewest runs scored: 466, 1919
Most hits: 1,586, 1923
Fewest hits: 980, 1972
Most home runs: 171, 1925
Fewest home runs: 19, 1932

Notes

CHAPTER 1

1. Dan Holmes, "Managerial Records," *BaseballLibrary.com,* (accessed Sept. 5, 2003), <http://www.baseballlibrary.com/stats/lists_managers/managers.htm>.

2. Bill O'Neal, *The Texas League, 1888–1987: A Century of Baseball* (Austin: Eakin, 1988), p. 3

3. William Ruggles, *The History of the Texas League of Professional Baseball Clubs, 1888–1951* (Dallas: Texas League of Professional Baseball Clubs, 1951), p. 25.

4. Ibid.

5. *San Antonio Express,* Jan. 18, 1888.

6. Ibid., Apr. 8, 1888.

7. *San Antonio Light,* Apr. 9, 1888; *San Antonio Express,* Apr. 9, 1888.

8. *San Antonio Express,* Apr. 14, 1888.

9. Ibid., Apr. 19, 1888.

10. *San Antonio Light,* May 8, 1888.

11. *San Antonio Express,* May 9, 1888.

12. *San Antonio Light,* May 24, 1888.

13. O'Neal, *Texas League.*

14. *San Antonio Express,* July 15, 1888.

15. Ibid., July 31, 1888.

16. *Louisville (Ky.) Courier-Journal,* Nov. 18, 1940.

17. *The Sporting News,* Dec. 5, 1940; Ruggles, *History of the Texas League,* p. 15.

18. O'Neal, *Texas League,* p. 296.

19. *San Antonio Light,* June 30, 1897.

20. *San Antonio Express,* June 30, 1897.

21. *San Antonio Light,* July 1, 1897.

22. *San Antonio Express,* July 2, 1897.

23. *San Antonio Light,* May 4, 1930; *San Antonio Express,* July 26, 1930.

24. Ruggles, *History of the Texas League,* p. 76.

CHAPTER 2

1. Ruggles, *History of the Texas League,* p. 81.

2. *San Antonio Light,* Apr., 1903.

3. Ibid., Apr. 25, 1903.

4. Ruggles, *History of the Texas League,* pp. 299–337.

5. *Houston Chronicle*, Aug. 8, 1903.

6. *San Antonio Light*, Aug. 26, 1903.

7. *San Antonio Daily Express*, Sept. 7, 1903.

8. *San Antonio Light*, Sept. 9, 1903.

9. Ruggles, *History of the Texas League*, p. 94.

10. Tom Kayers, "Archives of the Texas League of Baseball Clubs," unpublished notes, San Antonio.

11. Tom Kayser, "This Date in Texas League History," unpublished manuscript, 2003.

12. *San Antonio Light*, July 24, 1907.

13. Ibid.

14. Ibid.; *San Antonio Daily Express*, July 24, 1907.

15. Tom Kayser and Scott Hanzelka, eds., *2002 Texas League Official Media Guide and Record Book* (San Antonio: Texas League of Professional Baseball Clubs, 2002), p. 154; *San Antonio Daily Express*, July 24, 1907; Ruggles, *History of the Texas League*, p. 107.

16. *San Antonio Light*, July 25, 28, 1907.

17. *San Antonio Daily Express*, July 30, 1907.

18. *San Antonio Light*, July 30, 1907.

19. Ibid., Aug. 26, 1907.

20. Ibid., Aug. 31, Sept. 9, 1907.

21. *San Antonio Express*, Dec. 2, 1927.

22. *San Antonio Light*, Aug. 14, 1907.

23. "Joe Williams," *National Baseball Hall of Fame and Museum*, (accessed Sept. 5, 2003), <http://www.baseballhalloffame.org/hofers_and_honorees/hofer_bios/williams_joe.htm>.

24. *San Antonio Light*, Apr. 19, 1908; *San Antonio Express*, Apr. 19, 1908.

25. *San Antonio Light*, May 9, 1908.

26. Ibid., May 11, 1908.

27. Ibid., May 17, 1908; *San Antonio Express*, May 23, 1908.

28. *San Antonio Light*, June 21, 22, 1908; Kayser and Hanzelka, *Media Guide*, p. 146.

29. *San Antonio Light*, July 11, 1908; Kayser and Hanzelka, *Media Guide*, p. 161.

30. *San Antonio Express*, July 22, 1908.

31. *San Antonio Light*, Aug. 11, 1908.

32. Ibid., Aug. 19, 1908.

33. Ibid., Aug. 23, 1908.

34. Ibid., Aug. 19, 1908.

35. Ibid., Aug. 22, 1908.

36. Ibid.; James Riley, *The Biographical Encyclopedia of the Negro Leagues* (New York: Carroll and Graf, 1994).

37. *San Antonio Light*, Sept. 6, 1908.

38. O'Neal, *Texas League*, p. 37.

39. *San Antonio Light*, Sept. 8, 1908.

40. Kayser and Hanzelka, *Media Guide*, p. 161.

41. Riley, *Biographical Encyclopedia*.

CHAPTER 3

1. Neil J. Sullivan, *The Minors: The Struggles and the Triumph of Baseball's Poor Relations from 1876 to the Present* (New York: St. Martin's, 1990), chaps. 5, 11.

2. Kayser and Hanzelka, *Media Guide*, p. 161.

3. *San Antonio Light*, Feb. 8, 1951.

4. *San Antonio Daily Light and Gazette*, Apr. 28, 1910; *San Antonio Express*, Apr. 28, 1910.

5. *San Antonio Daily Light and Gazette*, June 14, 1910.

6. Ibid., July 6, 1910.

7. *San Antonio Express*, Aug. 9, 1910.

8. Ibid., Sept. 5, 1910.

9. Kayser and Hanzelka, *Media Guide*, p. 125.

10. Lloyd Johnson, *The Minor League Register* (Durham, N.C.: Baseball America, 1994).

11. *Shiner Gazette*, Oct., 1907.

12. *San Antonio Express*, ca. 1908.

13. Ibid., Aug. 27, 1913.

14. Kayser and Hanzelka, *Media Guide*, p. 149.

15. *San Antonio Evening News*, Sept. 12, 1919.

16. Ibid., June, 1919.

17. Ibid., July 6, 1919.

18. Riley, *Biographical Encyclopedia*, pp. 502–504; *San Antonio Evening News*, Sept. 12, 1919.

19. John B. Holway, *Voices from the Great Black Baseball Leagues* (New York: Da Capo, 1992), p. 291; Roy Campanella, *It's Good to be Alive* (New York: New American Library, 1959), p. 65.

20. *San Antonio Express*, Sept. 2, 1919; *San Antonio Evening News*, Sept. 9, 1919.

21. Ibid., Sept. 12, 1919.

22. Ibid., Sept. 29, 1919.

23. *San Antonio Daily Express*, Sept. 28, 1919.

24. John B. Holway, *Blackball Stars: Negro League Pioneers* (Westport, Conn.: Meckler, 1988), p. 220.

25. Ibid., pp. 224–25; Larry Lester, *Black Baseball's National Showcase: The East-West All-Star Game, 1933–1953* (Lincoln: University of Nebraska Press, 2001), p. 295.

26. Kayser, "This Date in Texas League History."

27. Ibid.

28. *San Antonio Light*, Nov. 10, 1922.

29. Johnson, *Minor League Register*.

30. *San Antonio Light*, June–July, 1923.

31. Kayser and Hanzelka, *Media Guide*, p. 157.

32. Robert Obojski, *Bush League: A Colorful, Factual Account of Minor League Baseball from 1877 to the Present* (New York: Macmillan, 1975), p. 298.

33. Kayser, "This Date in Texas League History."

CHAPTER 4

1. *San Antonio Light,* Dec. 2, 1927.

2. Ed Price, "Aggressive Play Defined Ty Cobb," *Augusta (Ga.) Chronicle,* June 21, 1996, <http://www.augustachronicle.com/history/cobb.html>.

3. *San Antonio Express,* Dec. 4, 1927.

4. Ruggles, *History of the Texas League,* pp. 319–20.

5. *San Antonio Express,* Dec. 4, 1927.

6. Rene Torres, e-mail interview with author, Feb. 15, 2003.

7. "Famous People: Leonardo 'Leo Najo' Alaniz (1889–1978)," *City of Mission (Tex.),* <http://www.missiontexas.us/lnajo.html>.

8. Torres interview.

9. *San Antonio Light,* Mar. 31, 1930.

10. Ibid., Apr. 1, 1930.

11. Harold Scherwitz, "Yank Visit Recalls That Ruth-Estill Incident," *San Antonio Light,* Apr. 3, 1939.

12. Clark Nealon, telephone interview with author, Aug. 14, 1991.

13. Robert Gregory, *Diz: The Story of Dizzy Dean and Baseball during the Great Depression* (New York: Viking, 1992), p. 32.

14. Vince Staten, *Ol' Diz: A Biography of Dizzy Dean* (New York: Harper-Collins, 1992), pp. 198–99.

15. Sam Harshaney, interview with the author, San Antonio, May 17, 2000.

CHAPTER 5

1. Kayser and Hanzelka, *Media Guide,* pp. 34–36.

2. *San Antonio Light,* June 19, 1932.

3. Ibid., June 20, 1932.

4. *San Antonio Express,* June 19, 1932.

5. O'Neal, *Texas League,* p. 304.

6. Ibid., p. 296.

7. Ibid., pp. 74–75.

8. *San Antonio Express,* Sept. 5, 1933.

9. *San Antonio Evening News,* Sept. 18, 1933.

10. *San Antonio Express,* Sept. 19, 1933.

11. Ibid., Sept. 26, 1933.

12. Harshaney interview; *San Antonio Light,* Apr. 2, 1934.

13. Harshaney interview.

14. Ibid.

15. Kayser, "This Date in Texas League History."

CHAPTER 6

1. *San Antonio Light,* Dec. 15, 1946.
2. Al LaMacchia, interview with the author, San Antonio, June 1, 2000.
3. *San Antonio Light,* Apr. 17, 1947.
4. Ibid.
5. Ibid., Sept. 11, 1946.
6. LaMacchia interview.
7. Daniel Herrera, interview with the author, San Antonio, May 22, 2000.
8. John A. Simpson, "Sulphur Dell," *The Tennessee Encyclopedia of History and Culture,* www.tennesseeencylopedia.net, (accessed Sept. 8, 2003), <http://160.36.208.47/FMPro?-db=tnencyc&-format=tdetail.htm&-lay=web&entryid=S113&-find=>.
9. Kayser, "This Date in Texas League History."
10. Ryne Duren, telephone interview with the author, May 18, 2000.
11. Patric J. Doyle, "Old-Time Data," unpublished manuscript, 2000.
12. Dick Clark and Larry Lester, eds., *The Negro Leagues Book* (Cleveland: Society for American Baseball Research), 1994.
13. Kayser, "This Date in Texas League History."
14. Duren interview; Herrera interview.
15. Kayser, "This Date in Texas League History."
16. O'Neal, *Texas League,* pp. 116–17.

CHAPTER 7

1. *San Antonio News,* Dec. 6, 1957.
2. *San Antonio Express,* Feb. 21, 1988.
3. J. C. Hartman, telephone interview with the author, May 23, 2000.
4. Billy Williams, telephone interview with the author, May 24, 2000.
5. Hartman interview; Williams interview.
6. Michael Gershman, exec. ed., "Billy Williams," *Microsoft Complete Baseball CD-ROM,* 1994.
7. Williams interview.
8. Ibid.
9. John Trowbridge, interview with the author, San Antonio, Apr. 20, 2000.
10. Johnny Janes, *San Antonio Express,* Apr. 14, 1961.
11. *San Antonio Express,* Apr. 16, 1961.
12. O'Neal, *Texas League,* p. 321.
13. Kayser, "This Date in Texas League History."
14. John Trowbridge, *San Antonio Light,* Sept. 10, 1961.
15. *San Antonio Light,* Sept. 11, 1961.
16. O'Neal, *Texas League,* p. 297.
17. Dave Adlesh, telephone interview with the author, Aug., 1997.
18. Don Bradey, telephone interview with the author, Aug., 1997.

19. Don Arlich, telephone interview with the author, Aug., 1997.

20. Lou Fitzgerald, telephone interview with the author, Aug., 1997.

21. Chris Zachary, telephone interview with the author, Aug., 1997.

22. Adlesh interview.

23. Fitzgerald interview.

24. Ibid.

25. *San Antonio Express,* Aug. 13, 1964.

CHAPTER 8

1. Kayser and Hanzelka, *Media Guide,* pp. 34–35.

2. Elmer Kosub, interview with the author, San Antonio, Apr. 20, 2000.

3. Henry Christopher, interview with the author, San Antonio, May 22, 2000.

4. Kosub interview.

5. Ibid.

6. John Trowbridge, *San Antonio Light,* Apr. 17, 1968.

7. Kosub interview.

8. John Trowbridge, *San Antonio Light,* Apr. 15, 1973.

9. Joel Horlen, interview with the author, June 22, 2000.

10. Galen Wellnicki, *San Antonio Light,* Sept. 13, 1973.

11. Horlen interview.

CHAPTER 9

1. Carmina Danini, *San Antonio Express-News,* Jan. 25, 2001.

2. Jerry Briggs, *San Antonio Light,* Aug. 12, 1990.

3. Don LeJohn, telephone interview with the author, June, 2002.

4. Steve Ford, telephone interview with the author, June, 2002.

5. Tom Beyers, telephone interview with the author, June, 2002.

6. Jerry Briggs, *San Antonio Light,* Aug. 12, 1990.

7. *San Antonio Light,* Sept. 10, 1980.

8. Kayser and Hanzelka, *Media Guide,* p. 154.

9. David Oldham, interview with the author, July 10, 1998.

10. Burl Yarbrough, interview with the author, July 10, 1998.

11. Brad Townsend, *San Antonio Light,* July 16, 1988.

12. Ibid.

13. *San Antonio News,* July 18, 1988.

CHAPTER 10

1. Tim Griffin, *San Antonio Express-News,* Nov. 15, 1989.

2. Tim Griffin, *San Antonio Express-News,* Jan. 22, 1991.

3. Burl Yarbrough, interview with the author, May, 2000.

4. Nelson Wolff, interview with the author, May, 2000.

5. Yarbrough interview.

6. Wolff interview; Kayser and Hanzelka, *Media Guide,* pp. 32–33.
7. Lance Parrish, interview with the author, Aug. 10, 1997.
8. Ron Roenicke, interview with the author, May, 2000.
9. David King, *San Antonio Express-News,* Apr. 11, 1997.
10. Kevin Gibbs, interview with the author, May, 2000.
11. Roenicke interview.

CHAPTER 11

1. Greg Dobbs, interview with the author, Jan. 11, 2003.
2. Dave Brundage, interview with the author, Jan. 10, 2003.
3. Dobbs interview.
4. Brian Anderson, interview with the author, Jan. 9, 2003.
5. Dobbs interview.
6. Ibid.
7. Ibid.
8. Brundage interview.

Bibliography

BOOKS

Adelson, Bruce. *Brushing Back Jim Crow: The Integration of Minor-League Baseball in the American South.* Charlottesville: University Press of Virginia, 1999.

Campanella, Roy. *It's Good to be Alive.* New York: New American Library, 1959.

Chadwick, Bruce. *Baseball's Hometown Teams: The Story of the Minor Leagues.* New York: Abbeville, 1994.

Clark, Dick, and Larry Lester, eds.. *The Negro Leagues Book.* Cleveland: Society for American Baseball Research, 1994.

Finch, Robert L.; L. H. Addington; and Ben M. Morgan, eds. *The Story of Minor League Baseball.* Cleveland: National Association of Professional Baseball Leagues, 1953.

Gregory, Robert. *Diz: The Story of Dizzy Dean and Baseball during the Great Depression.* New York: Viking, 1992.

Guinn, Jeff (with Bobby Bragan). *When Panthers Roared: The Fort Worth Cats and Minor League Baseball.* Fort Worth: Texas Christian University Press, 1999.

Holway, John B. *Blackball Stars: Negro League Pioneers.* Westport, Conn.: Meckler, 1988.

———. *Voices from the Great Black Baseball Leagues.* New York: Da Capo, 1992.

Ivor-Campbell, Frederick; Robert L. Tiemann; and Mark Rucker, eds. *Baseball's First Stars.* Cleveland: Society for American Baseball Research, 1996.

Johnson, Lloyd. *The Minor League Register.* Durham, N.C.: Baseball America, 1994.

Kayser, Tom, and Scott Hanzelka, eds. *2002 Texas League Official Media Guide and Record Book.* San Antonio: Texas League of Professional Baseball Clubs, 2002.

Lester, Larry. *Black Baseball's National Showcase: The East-West All-Star Game, 1933–1953.* Lincoln: University of Nebraska Press, 2001.

Obojski, Robert. *Bush League: A Colorful, Factual Account of Minor League Baseball from 1877 to the Present.* New York: Macmillan, 1975.

O'Neal, Bill. *The Pacific Coast League.* Austin: Eakin, 1990.

———. *The Texas League, 1888–1987: A Century of Baseball.* Austin: Eakin, 1988.

Riley, James. *The Biographical Encyclopedia of the Negro Leagues.* New York: Carroll and Graf, 1994.

Ruggles, William. *The History of the Texas League of Professional Baseball Clubs, 1888–1951.* Dallas: Texas League of Professional Baseball Clubs, 1951.

Staten, Vince. *Ol' Diz: A Biography of Dizzy Dean.* New York: Harper-Collins, 1992.

Sullivan, Neil J. *The Minors: The Struggles and the Triumph of Baseball's Poor Relations from 1876 to the Present.* New York: St. Martin's, 1990.

BIBLIOGRAPHY

Witt, Wayne, ed. *San Antonio Missions 1995 Media Guide.* San Antonio: San Antonio Missions, 1995.

Wolff, Rick, ed. *The Baseball Encyclopedia, Eighth Edition.* New York: Macmillan, 1990.

INTERNET SITES

Baseball-almanac.com

The baseball online library.com

Baseball-reference.com

Handbook of Texas Online

NegroLeagueBaseball.com

Minor League Baseball History

UNPUBLISHED MATERIALS

Foltz, Chris. "San Antonio Year-by-Year Results." In "San Antonio Club Records," by Scott Hanzelka.

Kayser, Tom. "This Date in the Texas League." 2003.

NEWSPAPERS

Louisville (Ky.) Courier-Journal

San Antonio Express

San Antonio Express-News

San Antonio Light

San Antonio News

Shiner Gazette

The Sporting News

Index